SPEECH

Content and Communication

SPEECH

Content and Communication

Fifth Edition

CHARLES S. MUDD
California State University, Northridge

MALCOLM O. SILLARS
University of Utah

1817

HARPER & ROW, PUBLISHERS, New York
Cambridge, Philadelphia, San Francisco,
London, Mexico City, São Paulo, Singapore, Sydney

Sponsoring Editor: Louise H. Waller
Project Coordination, Cover Design, Text Art: Caliber Design Planning, Inc.
Photo Research: Mira Schachne
Compositor: Kachina Typesetting, Inc.
Printer and Binder: R. R. Donnelley & Sons Company

Speech: Content and Communication, Fifth Edition

Library of Congress Cataloging-in-Publication Data

Mudd, Charles S.
  Speech : content and communication.

  Includes index.
  1. Public speaking. I. Sillars, Malcolm O.
(Malcolm Osgood), 1928–   II. Title.
PN4121.M695 1986   808.5'1   85–17536
ISBN 0–06–044661–7

85 86 87 88 9 8 7 6 5 4 3 2 1

Contents

MAR   1990

Preface

The importance of communication is so well recognized in the 1980s that there is no need to develop a case for people becoming more able public speakers. Although everyone learns something about communication merely by living in society, that fact does not guarantee anyone a high level of skill. Becoming a good speaker requires systematic study, competent instruction, and supervised experiences. It is very important to make what will be for most students their first *and* last experience with formal training in public speaking as profitable as possible. It is the purpose of the fifth edition of *Speech: Content and Communication* to make a useful contribution to that experience.

Because it is fundamentally sound, we have retained the same rhetorical theory in this text as that on which the first edition was based. Our perspective is evident and our biases clear:

1. The basic assumptions of the ancient tradition of rhetorical theory are still useful.
2. Clear thinking is essential to all public communication. Effective speaking is not the product of simplistic formulas but of hard mental activity, critical reading, and perceptive listening.

3. No matter what the purpose in speaking may be, the speaker must always meet the audience where it is. Thus, audience analysis and adaptation to the audience are essential to good communication.
4. Speakers are responsible for what they say. This implies not only that they be competent but that they be ethical as well.
5. Skill in speaking will not develop without knowledge and practice. One must *understand* the principles of good communication and must also *apply* them in actual speaking situations. Toward that end, we have incorporated into the classical doctrines the best results of appropriate modern research. And we have supplied a number of exercises and activities that give students occasions to apply these principles and to practice the techniques discussed in each chapter.
6. The principles we discuss and exemplify are not easy formulas or recipes to be applied mechanically. Good communication is the creative product of a speaker's understanding of the interaction of message and receiver.

The changes that appear are made for two principal reasons: to keep the materials as current as possible and, insofar as we can, to make the book interesting to students and comfortably teachable for instructors. Despite the fact that a truly apt example is often very difficult to find, in updating the material we have in the great majority of cases used selections from actual speeches. Whenever possible, we have resisted the temptation to make up an example to illustrate a rhetorical principle, even though this is usually *much* easier than finding a real example. We believe it is better for students to see how real speakers interact with real audiences.

Our students seem to have a greater interest in the speeches of other students than they have in the speeches of well-known people in the professions. For that reason, all of the "Speeches for Study" in Appendix B are by students. To make them easier to find and more convenient to use, we have grouped all of these sample speeches into a single appendix.

The organization of the book is similar in essential respects to the previous edition. It retains the flexibility that characterized earlier editions. *Speech: Content and Communication* can be adapted to a one- or two-term course. Yet no chapter has been left unchanged. Each has been closely examined and in most cases extensively rewritten. We have made a positive effort throughout to make the book as brief and clear as possible without watering down the theory. The following are among the more significant changes to be found in the new edition:

The chapter on ethical responsibility has been considerably shortened. It is also much less theoretical and more applied in its perspective.

We have developed an entirely new example to illustrate the analysis of issues in Chapter 6 and have reintroduced the very useful concept of stock issues, a subject omitted from the previous edition.

The discussion of supporting materials has been made more manageable by dividing it into two shorter chapters: one on the types of supporting material and another on how to find them.

To signal the inseparability of the rational and the motivational functions of arguments, we have combined argument and values into a single chapter.

In earlier editions speech organization was discussed in each of the chapters devoted to types of speaking situations. We have eliminated much unnecessary repetition in this area by considering general organizational principles in the chapter on outlining. Only those aspects of organization peculiar to a particular type of speech are discussed in the chapters devoted to different types of speaking situations.

A new chapter on introductions, conclusions, and transitions gives unified attention to those important elements.

Finally, the very brief discussion of visual aids found in the fourth edition has been significantly expanded and made into another new chapter.

We owe a large debt of gratitude (and are happy to pay it) to the several people who examined the manuscript. Their thorough and insightful reviews have made this a better book. We are indebted also to the many colleagues who have through the years given us generous amounts of comment and advice. Much of this is reflected in each succeeding edition and accounts for a large measure of any merit the book may have. Whatever shortcomings readers will find in this edition we do not hesitate to claim as our own. We particularly want to thank B. Aubrey Fisher, Paul Mogren, and George Nagel of the University of Utah; Sue Pendell, David Vancil, and Carl Burgchardt of Colorado State University; Bernard Coyle, William Freeman, and Leonard Wurthman of California State University, Northridge; John Lyne of the University of Iowa; Ellen Reid Gold of the University of Kansas, and John Louis Lucaites, University of Alabama. Charlane Sillars and Jennifer Duignan prepared the manuscript and kept us from numerous errors. The editorial staff of Harper & Row, especially Louise Waller, has been generously helpful. We are, of course, grateful that the number of both students and instructors who have found the book useful has been large enough to justify its presentation for the fifth time.

Charles S. Mudd
Malcolm O. Sillars

one

INTRODUCTION

The Competent Speaker

In November 1984 the American people went to the polls to choose a President of the United States, 33 Senators, 435 members of Congress, and thousands of state and local officials. Although major attention focused on the contest between Ronald Reagan and Walter Mondale for President, each of the other elections drew the attention of interested people.

While the major newspapers and television networks turned our attention to presidential speeches and debates, candidates for state legislatures and county offices made countless speeches and participated in many debates. Speech making has always played a vital role in political campaigns. Indeed, political campaigns are exercises in communication.

Political campaigns, however, are not the only situations that call for public speaking. Communication skills are essential in the work situation. Vast changes now underway will make communication even more important to your success. "Technological advances and expanded trade promise to transform work and the American economy in the late 20th and early 21st centuries at least as much as the industrial revolution did in the late 19th and early 20th centuries."[1] Robotization and computerization will eliminate many existing jobs and create millions of new ones. These new jobs will be in white-collar and service areas.[2] They will depend heavily on communication skills.

A change in the way companies are managed is also taking place. Workers are becoming more involved in decision making.[3] Business leaders and educators alike recognize that this new work situation means a greater need for skills in communication. "As our society becomes more complex it is evident that our survival and prosperity depend on a single word . . . communications. Communication is what makes us who we are. If we cannot communicate we cannot work, we cannot play, we cannot live productively."[4] The changes in the American way of working and managing will make communication skills more important than they have been. As participants in the political processes of a democracy, public speaking skills will be required of you; and the same skills will become increasingly important to your career.

In addition to business and politics, your personal life requires you to be a public speaker. A study of blue-collar workers showed that about half of them had given a public speech during the previous two years, and the more educated among them were called upon to speak more often.[5] These figures may very well be low because most people have a limited idea of what a public speech is. Have you thought about the fact that when you must return a pair of slacks to a department store because you do not like the fit, you sometimes plan and rehearse what you will say? If you have a job and decide to ask for a raise, you assemble your arguments and go tell your employer. Are these public speeches? If you want your club or fraternity to participate in homecoming, you tell the other members your reasons at the next meeting. Isn't that a public speech? If you are asked to explain the lesson at the church school weekly meeting, aren't you giving a public speech?

You may never be President or even a city council member, but you will be called upon to speak. When your employer says, "The board meeting is tomorrow morning at 10:00. Could you bring us up to date on the Amex contract negotiations?" you are going to give a speech.

So, you see, there are many occasions in your political, professional, and personal life when you are called upon to give a public speech. When you add to those occasions all the times that you are a receiver of public speeches, you will realize how important communication is to you.

THE PUBLIC SPEAKING SITUATION

In each of the hypothetical situations mentioned above you can see that a public speech is not just saying what you think. Each situation involves much more than just you.[6] How about the example of your being asked (told?) to explain the Amex contract negotiations? Many people and factors are involved: the members of the board, your employer, the negotiations, the objectives of the company, the beliefs of various participants about the contract and each other. The speech you give takes place at a particular time and place (the board meeting at 10:00). It has a purpose (to inform the board), and it takes place as part of an ongoing process of communication by which your company develops. Let's look at some of the factors that determine the nature of a public speaking situation.

Political speaking is an exercise in communication. (© Hine, The Picture Cube)

You Are Both Unique and Social

There is no other you; there is no one in the universe past, present, or future who was, is, or will be exactly like you. You, like everyone else, at least most of the time, think in language. You also use language to communicate what you think. The meanings you have for the words and other signs of the language you use are built, however, out of your experience. Because no one has had exactly the experiences you have had, no one else has precisely the same meanings for these words and signs. In a sense, therefore, language can be a stumbling block to communication. It is fortunate that this stumbling block is not insurmountable, because language of one kind or another is the only means you have to communicate with others.

Even though you are unique, you are like others in that you have intellect, you use language, you are aware of yourself and of your life-style. Certain aspects of your life-style might be very much like other members of whatever social groups you belong to. For example, if you are a Democrat, you will share many beliefs and values with other Democrats. But you will be different from many of them, too, for if you are a Baptist as well as a Democrat, you'll find a smaller number of others who share the whole set of your responses to both politics and religion. And again, politics and religion are only two of the limitless number of areas about which you have perceptions and judgments that, taken together, constitute your "image" of the world.

Skill in communication is necessary if you are to fit the unique person you are into the various social groups to which you belong. Skill in communication is one of the major ways you understand and influence your environment so that you can reap the greatest rewards from it and minimize its potential punishments. Communication is also essential to your personal adaptation. Through your ability to hear and understand others you are able to use information and to achieve your own personal goals. Your control over the speaking situation can never be perfect, of course. Communication is never perfect, because those who listen to you are as unique and social as you are. It is human to want to communicate. Yet it is the very humanness that makes communication the most difficult yet most essential of all human activity.

Communication Acts Are Transactions

When you discuss some plans for the weekend with a friend, what each of you says and does affects the other. When you hear a professor lecture in a biology class, there is interaction that changes both of you. Even when you don't speak but only listen, you influence the speaker in at least two ways. One, your interpretation of what is said is the only way you have of determining what the speaker means. Two, the feedback you give through your attentiveness and physical action will influence what the speaker says. When you watch the President of the United States on television explaining the state of the economy, he affects you; and because he knows that your reactions are important to his programs (and even his political life), you, although he doesn't know you personally, also affect him. Consequently, the full meaning of a message is not in the dictionary definition of the words; it is in the mutually affective transaction that takes place among unique yet social people.

Decisions About Speaking Are Influenced by Time and Place

What kind of speaking is called for is determined, in part, by the occasion. Before you decide to speak up in favor of a project to raise funds for handicapped children at your club meeting, you consider the occasion. Is this the appropriate time to bring up the subject? It may not be, in the midst of a lengthy and heated debate about the sorry financial situation of the club. On the other hand, such a proposal might be exactly the right subject to bring into the middle of a debate (no matter how heated) about how to improve the club's image. A tragic earthquake somewhere may be exactly the occasion for a speech on "How to Protect Yourself in an Earthquake." Thus, the events that influence people's thoughts create occasions for speeches.

Some occasions virtually dictate the kinds of responses that are called for because they have a long tradition built around them. These are known as special occasions (see Chapter 20). Birthdays, holidays, award ceremonies, funerals, and roasts require that you respond in a particular way. You can be creative in what you say and how you say it, but always within the limits that tradition has prescribed for the occasion.

Communication Is Purposive

There is no such thing as serious communication among human beings that is not done to achieve some purpose or goal. Of course, if you hit your thumb with a hammer, you're likely to mutter some expletive you wouldn't normally expect to hear in church. If anyone hears you, you will certainly have communicated something even though you had no intention of doing so. The same is true when you sing in the shower. But all examples of this kind aside, most of your talk will be because you have a goal in mind and you feel that communication is the best way to achieve it.

It isn't true that the failure of the members of a group to achieve consensus or that the failure of a speaker to get a desired response from an audience is the result of a "communication breakdown." This notion presupposes that there are such things as communication gaps or breakdowns, but there aren't. When the minimal conditions for communication are present, it cannot fail to occur.[7] A term more accurate than "communication breakdown" would be "failure of purpose." The significant question, then, is not whether you will communicate, but *what* you will communicate.

The speech situation to which you choose to respond is a combination of elements: you, the audience, the occasion, the thing "waiting to be done" that governs the purpose of your speech. But as you may have guessed from what we have said so far, these are not static elements. They are constantly changing and interacting with one another in ways we need to examine now.

Communication Is a Process

When you flip a switch, the light goes on. If you cross your knees and tap your leg just below the kneecap, your leg will jerk. There has been for a very long time the mistaken notion that communication occurs in pretty much the same way as turning on a light or getting a knee-jerk reflex. Not at all so. It is impossible to get a correct image of communication by likening it in any way to a static series of discrete occurrences. Instead, communication is much more correctly viewed as a number of variables, always in some relationship with each other and constantly in a state of change.

Imagine a conversation. The number of people in the conversation is not important. In a lively conversational situation everyone is actively participating, sometimes as listener—giving and getting responses; thinking, speaking, and listening; and shifting and causing shifts in beliefs and values. Conversation is continuous, flowing, continually changing. It does not start and stop, nor is it static. Everyone is actively engaged in it all the time.

What is clearly discernable in conversation is characteristic of public speaking as well. Public speaking does not begin when you stand before an audience to speak, or when you sit down to listen. All that the participants have ever been, done, read, or seen is a part of the process. The effects of a particular transaction will continue to other persons and other times.

If you consider your speaking experiences as a part of a larger process in which human beings communicate with one another, you can make a more realistic evaluation of your own efforts. One speech does not reveal all truth, revolutionize behavior, or make major changes in beliefs. The process of communication has been going on for a long time before you and will go on for a long time after you. Do not make the achievement of major changes a criterion of a successful speech.

BECOMING A COMPETENT PUBLIC SPEAKER

When you choose to respond to a speaking situation, and the evidence is clear that you will many times in your lifetime, how will you respond? That is the single question this book tries to answer: How should you go about becoming a competent public speaker? The answer? By learning and practicing the principles that competent public speakers have followed for centuries. The competent public speaker does at least these things:

1. Recognizes a situation that requires speech
2. Is willing to prepare a response to the situation
3. Understands and adapts to the situation
4. Has an adequate understanding of the elements of the situation: self, audience, occasion
5. Recognizes how the speech can be organized and supported to meet the situation
6. Utilizes the physical and vocal aspects of delivery and the quality of language required to meet the situation

The principles of public speaking are not new, and much that you will be learning is part of an ancient tradition. Let's look first at the tradition, and then see what your study of public speaking will involve.

The Tradition of Public Speaking

Public speaking was seen by early civilizations as a necessary and practical art. The Romans learned rhetoric from the Greeks, and the subject was carried over into the Latin language. In a typically Roman manner they systematized rhetoric just as they systematized everything they put their minds to. Thus, without making significant contributions to basic theory, they introduced the useful practice of looking at rhetoric through what has come to be called the five classical "canons." The word *canon*, derived from the Greek, is used in the sense of a body of laws. In the case of rhetoric, of course, the laws are rules or principles for the composition and transmission of successful, effective messages.

The first canon is called in English *invention*. It is concerned with the discovery of the subject matter of the speech. When you talk, presumably you have something to say. Any considerations that help you to determine what you will say are part of the canon of invention.

This book is probably most concerned with the canon of invention, the discovery and analysis of appropriate purposes and claims for communication. Such analysis requires that you examine the beliefs and values of an audience to find out what arguments, what values, what means of enhancing your personal credibility will be most effective, and what kinds of supporting material will best support the claim being made.

The second canon is *disposition*. It is concerned with organization, the structure of the message. Every message must have some arrangement or another so that any decisions you make about how to put a message together—how to organize it—are guided by the principles of the canon of disposition.

The third canon is *elocution*. This canon is concerned with the style of the message. Every message, of course, must be transmitted in some language and must have some kind of style. Discussions of the nature and use of language are part of the canon of elocution.

The fourth canon is *memory*. It has often been called the "lost" canon because nowadays speeches are not memorized and data can be easily recovered from libraries and the memory banks of computers. Elaborate mnemonic systems for aiding a speaker's memory are no longer needed. Therefore, memory no longer has any great significance in the theory of rhetoric. But careful note taking and outlining do.

Finally, the fifth canon of rhetoric is *delivery*. A speaker's judgments about how to transmit a message most effectively are guided by the principles of this canon.

Although the term "communication" has widely replaced the term "rhetoric" in our literature, the impact of the rhetorical tradition is great and the term rhetoric is still appropriate for the kind of public, purposive communication discussed in this book. The debt this book owes to the rhetorical tradition is great. Where possible we have supported our suggestions to you with modern research findings, but for much of the theory we owe a debt to the rhetorical tradition.

Your Study of Public Speaking

This book is organized into six parts: Introduction, Analyzing the Speaking Situation, Preparing Speeches, Communicating Speeches, Types of Speaking Situations, and Evaluating Speeches. Your instructor will probably not ask you to read the chapters in the order they are printed here. You may read one of the chapters in Part Five early in the course, depending on whether your first speaking assignment is an informative, persuasive, special occasion or a small-group speaking experience. Nonetheless the chapters are organized according to a plan.

The introductory part, in addition to this chapter, prepares you to give short speeches and discusses the subjects of listening and ethical responsibility. These will help you to be a better participant in the speaking situation, both as a speaker and as a member of the audience. Part Two deals with the development of purpose for your speech, finding its major issues and seeing its relation to your audience. Part Three is intended to help you to organize and support the purpose to make what you say more believable and interesting. Part Four develops your understanding of how to deal with anxiety, and how to use language, visual aids, voice, and physical activity to help get your ideas across to the audience. In Part Five the principles of good public speaking are applied to different situations that call for public speaking: informative, persuasive, special occasions, and small groups. Part Six is concerned with evaluating the speaking of others.

However your instructor chooses to organize the course, your objectives are clear: to learn how to respond to public speaking situations with speeches that have a clear and appropriate purpose, that are well organized, that are supported with clear and interesting materials, that have language and delivery which help to make your purpose effective with an audience. As a member of an audience you will need to listen and evaluate the speeches of others carefully.

Millions of public speaking students before you, using this and other texts, have discovered the rewards that come from a careful study of the principles, ancient and modern, of effective public speaking. We hope that you will find your study equally rewarding.

SUMMARY

In your role as citizen in a democracy you will be involved in many public speaking situations. In addition, economic changes and a greater emphasis on technology are making communication increasingly important to a successful career. Even in your social associations outside of politics and work you will be called upon to speak.

The public speaking situation involves more than you as a unique and social person. It is a transaction between you and an audience. Your speech is adapted to the time and place it is given. The speech needs to have a purpose that is clear to you and that you make clear to your listeners. Your speech is a part of the ongoing communication of your society—it does not stand alone. It is part of the communication process.

To be a competent public speaker, therefore, you must: (1) recognize the situation; (2) be willing to respond; (3) adapt to the situation; (4) understand yourself, your audience, and the occasion; (5) recognize how to organize and support the speech; and (6) use language and delivery to meet the situation.

The long tradition of rhetoric dating back to ancient Greece provides a basis for understanding how to be a competent public speaker. *Speech: Content and Communication* is organized around this tradition in a way that it may be adapted by your instructor to your particular needs.

NOTES

1. "The Work Force of the Future," *Nation's Business,* **70** (Nov. 1982), p. 58.
2. Max L. Carely, "Occupational Employment Growth Through 1990," *Monthly Labor Review,* **104** (Aug. 8, 1981), p. 43.
3. "A Work Revolution in U.S. Industry," *Business Week* (May 16, 1983), pp. 50–51.
4. Robert G. Scanlon, "The Year 2000: The Challenge to Education Today," *Vital Speeches of the Day,* **46** (Sept. 15, 1980), p. 729.
5. Kathleen Kendall, "Do Real People Ever Give Speeches?" *Central States Speech Journal,* **25** (Fall 1974), pp. 233–235.
6. See Lloyd F. Bitzer, "The Rhetorical Situation," *Philosophy and Rhetoric,* **1** (Jan. 1968), pp. 5–6.
7. Dennis R. Smith, "The Fallacy of the Communication Breakdown," *Quarterly Journal of Speech,* **56** (Dec. 1970), pp. 343–346.

EXERCISES

1. Keep track for one day of the speaking situations in which you find yourself. How many different kinds of situations can you identify? How were you involved? In what sense were they transactions? Compare your findings with others in the class.
2. Observe a public speaking situation (on campus, in class, on TV, etc.). How well did it reflect the public speaking situation defined in this chapter? Does the definition need to be revised?
3. Write a one-page paper analyzing how an audience you know well might respond to a public speaking situation with you as a speaker.
4. Are the five canons of public speaking from ancient times still appropriate today? Discuss your answer to this question with the other students in your class.

chapter 2

The First Speeches

To be a competent public speaker is a goal that virtually anyone, given adequate knowledge, experience, and industry, can very reasonably hope to attain. Both theory and practice are needed. But which should come first? If you wait until you have a good background in theory before you begin to make speeches, you suffer from a lack of practice; if you make speeches from the beginning, you lack the guidance of theoretical knowledge.

To begin speaking at the outset seems to us the better choice. The theoretical basis of your speaking will admittedly need development, but the value of practice is great and your understanding of the theory will grow as you examine the principles of speaking in greater detail. Our purpose in this chapter, therefore, is to give you an introduction to the theory of public speaking so that you can practice the skills right away. As the course goes on you will go deeper into theory and continue to practice on your way to becoming a competent speaker.

A competent speaker is someone an audience considers worth listening to because that person knows, at least, how to select a subject and purpose, organize a speech, support it, and deliver it.

SELECTING A SUBJECT AND PURPOSE

The first step in preparing a speech is deciding what to talk about. This means selecting a subject and a purpose. The number of different purposes or goals a speaker may have is quite limited. Occasionally, a speech is intended to amuse the audience, but by far the greatest majority of speeches are meant to inform or to persuade. There is no need to say more about speech purposes now, because Chapter 5 discusses them in some detail.

Despite a limited number of purposes, however, the number of potential subjects for a particular speech is unlimited. Making a choice among them is the first important step in preparing a speech. We also explain the criteria for choosing a topic in Chapter 5, so we will mention them only briefly here.

The first consideration in selecting a subject is simple: It ought to be worth talking about. This is important not only because no one likes to waste time on insignificant matters, but also because of the problem of interest. You know from your own experience that if students aren't interested in a subject, they simply don't listen. That applies to any audience, but it does not mean that a speaker should tell an audience only what it wants to hear. Rather, the task is to decide what the audience *ought* to hear and then find ways of making the subject interesting.

Second, the subject must be one the speaker is competent to discuss. No audience is willing to waste time with someone not worth listening to.

Finally, the subject must be appropriate to the listeners. It would make no sense to ask an audience to listen to something it cannot understand or do something it cannot do.

Once the purpose is decided (to entertain, inform, or persuade) and the subject is identified, the next consideration is time. Fidel Castro talks to Cuban audiences for several hours at a stretch. You and your potential audiences are doubtless happy to know that you don't have that luxury. Because time is limited, the subject must be narrowed in scope in order to develop it adequately in the time allowed. The narrowed subject is then further specified in a *statement of specific purpose,* which indicates what the speech is going to be about.

GENERAL SUBJECT: Transistors
NARROWED SUBJECT: How transistors work
SPECIFIC PURPOSE: To explain to the audience how the phenomenon of electron borrowing makes transistor radios possible

GENERAL SUBJECT: Skin diving
NARROWED SUBJECT: Skin-diving equipment
SPECIFIC PURPOSE: To inform the audience about the minimum equipment necessary for the beginning skin diver

GENERAL SUBJECT: Capital punishment
NARROWED SUBJECT: The effect of capital punishment on crime
SPECIFIC PURPOSE: To persuade the audience that capital punishment is a deterrent to crime

Notice how concrete these statements of specific purpose are. Each points to one clear-cut effort and excludes any others. Compare them with the following statements of purpose, which are alleged to be specific but instead are multiple, diffuse, and therefore badly drawn:

SPECIFIC PURPOSE: To inform the audience of the popularity of the transistor radio and how it works, especially how it uses electron borrowing
SPECIFIC PURPOSE: To inform the audience of the equipment needed for skin diving and how skin diving is not only safe but fun
SPECIFIC PURPOSE: To persuade the audience that capital punishment deters crime and, as a matter of fact, that severe punishment is effective, even with children in the home

All three of these statements of purpose are poor. They show that the speaker does not have a clear, unified subject in mind. Instead, the statements give only vague notions about what the subject will be.

Once a statement of specific purpose has been carefully drawn, it becomes a guide to test the materials and organization of the speech. Every statement and every piece of supporting material should relate directly to accomplishing that purpose. If any piece of material does not help to achieve the purpose of the speech, it cannot be justified and should be excluded.

ORGANIZING THE SPEECH

Speeches are organized into three parts: an *introduction,* the *body,* and a *conclusion.* The body is organized first because it is primarily responsible for accomplishing the purpose of the speech. The introduction and the conclusion are developed after the body of the speech has been prepared.

Organizing the Body of the Speech

Think of the subject of your speech as a jigsaw puzzle you have made. If you give it to your listeners as a jumble of pieces in a bag, they will have to put the pieces together themselves to make an intelligible picture. But if you hand them the pieces one at a time and in such an orderly sequence that they can easily fit them together, then the picture you have made grows before their eyes. Organizing a speech is very much like that. You find the right way to put together the ideas and supporting materials so that you can see the whole picture yourself, and you decide in what order you will hand the pieces to your audience.

To make sure that your listeners see the same picture you do, divide the subject of your speech into a series of main points and organize them in a clear and orderly pattern. These main points, along with their supporting material, constitute the body of your speech. We will mention four such patterns here. These, and others, will be discussed in somewhat greater detail in Chapters 18 and 19.

Chronological Order　The main points in the body of the speech may be arranged in the order of their occurrence in time.

SPECIFIC PURPOSE:　To inform the audience about Germany's submarine warfare policy in World War I
  I. February 1915, the British Isles were declared a war zone
  II. May 1916, Germany pledged not to sink ships without warning
  III. January 1917, Germany commenced unrestricted submarine attacks on shipping

Geographical or Spatial Order　The main points occur in the speech in the same order in which the listeners might visualize themselves moving physically from one to another.

SPECIFIC PURPOSE:　To inform the audience about the major dialects of English spoken in the British Isles
  I. Ireland
  II. Scotland
  III. Northern England
  IV. Southern England
  V. Wales

Topical Order　The subject is broken down into its main elements, and these are discussed in the body of the speech. Added together these elements, or *topics,* make up the whole idea.

SPECIFIC PURPOSE: To inform the audience about the operation of the speech
                     mechanism
     I. Respiration
    II. Phonation
   III. Resonation
   IV. Articulation

Argumentative Order   The body of a speech to persuade is organized in what may
be thought of as a form of topical order. The main points are arguments, and they give
the audience reasons for believing what the speaker is trying to prove.

SPECIFIC PURPOSE: To persuade the audience that the prices at the college
                     bookstore are too high
     I. The store has increased its prices every year for the
        past three years
    II. The bookstore made an excessive profit last year
   III. The same books cost less at neighboring colleges

Organizing the Conclusion

After you have organized the body of the speech, you plan a *conclusion* to pull
together the main ideas. One effective way to end a speech is with a brief summary
that reminds the audience of your specific purpose and the main points that develop it.
A summary conclusion is particularly valuable because a listener cannot rehear what
has gone before, the way a reader can reread. Not all conclusions are summaries, but
you will find them useful in your first speeches. More sophisticated kinds of conclusions will be discussed in Chapter 13. Use them when experience has developed
your skill.

Organizing the Introduction

The last section you develop is the *introduction*, even though it is delivered first. The
introduction is prepared last because, until you have developed the body and the
conclusion, you don't know what you are going to say. Once you know that, you will
be able to prepare an introduction that is related to the subject and purpose of the
speech.

An introduction has two essential parts. First, there is an interest factor: a story,
incident, description, startling statement, or quotation that will catch the attention of
the audience. This interest factor should be immediately pertinent to the subject of the
speech, because its primary function is to arouse interest in what you are going to say
and direct that interest toward the purpose of the speech.

The second major part of the introduction is the subject sentence. In informative speeches, this is a statement that expresses the specific purpose of the speech in an informal oral style.

SPECIFIC PURPOSE: To explain how the process of electron borrowing makes transistor radios possible
SUBJECT SENTENCE: Transistor radios are made possible by the phenomenon of electron borrowing

The subject sentence of a persuasive speech says what you want the audience to understand, believe, or do. In some situations—for example, when the audience has strong negative attitudes toward your proposal—the subject sentence will be less direct. We will have considerably more to say about that circumstance in Chapter 19. For now, however, you will do no harm by telling your listeners openly what you want them to accept. You will learn how to use more sophisticated argumentative patterns later.

SPECIFIC PURPOSE: To persuade the audience that capital punishment is a deterrent to crime
SUBJECT SENTENCE: The best evidence available indicates that capital punishment is a deterrent to crime

SUPPORTING THE IDEAS IN THE SPEECH

Examples, statistics, quotations, and arguments all help to make your ideas more interesting, believable, and clear. Always use *at least* one item of specific material in support of each important point in the body of the speech. (Usually two or more pieces are necessary and desirable.) This specific material will make the ideas more precise and vivid, clarify the subject, add interest, and establish belief.

The best way to put the content and the organization of the speech on paper is in the form of an outline. The outline will also serve as speaking notes. Here is a sample outline suitable for organizing either an informative or a persuasive speech.

Introduction
  I. Interest factor
  II. Subject sentence
Body
  I. First main point of the speech
    A. Supporting material
    B. Supporting material
  II. Second main point of the speech
    A. Supporting material
    B. Supporting material
    [and so on]

An outline displays the contents and organization of a speech. (Siteman, The Picture Cube)

Conclusion
    I. Summary statement including subject and purpose
        A. First main point
        B. Second main point
           [and so on]

DELIVERING THE SPEECH

The ideas, organization, and supporting details in any communication can be the same whether the message is written or spoken. Except for some differences in style, what most distinguishes writing from speaking is that a speech must be delivered. Indeed, it doesn't become a speech until it is delivered. Consequently, good delivery makes a significant contribution to the effectiveness of a speech. It is the vital, physical means by which ideas are transmitted to an audience. Good delivery is direct and spontaneous, shows your involvement in the subject, and makes it intelligible to the audience.

When you have what you think will be the final draft of your outline, practice speaking from it several times to fix the ideas in your mind. If you can find an audience to practice on, so much the better. Don't write the speech out or try to memorize it. Use the words that come to mind at the time. And you don't have to wait until you have the final draft of the outline to begin working on delivery. The more often you practice during the preparation period, the easier it will be to find the right words to get the reaction you want from the audience.

SUMMARY

It seems better to begin speaking early in the course, even though you lack theoretical background, than to wait until you know the theory better. That is because of the benefits you get from practicing the essential skills of organization and delivery. In preparing your first speeches, remember these four basic steps:

1. Choose a subject that is interesting to you, that you think you can make interesting for the audience, and that you can handle adequately in the allotted time. Formulate a specific statement of purpose.
2. Organize the speech by considering the possible ways of dividing the subject into its main points and choosing the one you think will make it most effective. Depending on your purpose, the organizational pattern you use can be chronological, geographical, topical, or argumentative. An outline is a very great help in organizing. Organize a conclusion that summarizes the body and an introduction that arouses the interest of the audience and provides a subject sentence.
3. Search for supporting materials that will make your ideas clear, interesting, and acceptable to your audience.
4. Practice delivering the speech. Think in terms of *oral* delivery from the moment you begin to prepare, and practice enough to get the ideas and supporting materials firmly in mind. Don't write out the speech, and don't try to memorize it. If you know the subject, the words will come to mind when you speak.

EXERCISES

1. Organize and deliver a three-minute informative speech explaining some local historical place, person, or thing.
2. Listen carefully to a lecture by one of your instructors. Come to class prepared to explain briefly what you noted about the strong points and weak points of the organization, supporting material, and delivery of the lecture.
3. Organize and deliver a three-minute persuasive speech that proposes a change in some university policy.
4. Organize and deliver a three-minute speech in which you introduce yourself or a classmate to the class.

chapter 3

Listening Effectively

No one can be a competent communicator without the ability to use four essential skills: writing, reading, speaking, and listening. We list them in that order because universities and colleges stress their importance in that order. But notice two interesting facts: (1) this is precisely the reverse of the order in which people learn these skills in childhood,[1] and (2) it is probably the reverse of the frequency with which adults use them. Although estimates vary, it is generally agreed that listening occupies by far the greatest amount of your time.[2] Despite this, few people listen well. Tests done at a number of universities show that immediately after listening to a ten-minute talk, the average person remembers only half of what was said and within two weeks loses another 25 percent. In other words, people listen at 25 percent efficiency.[3]

The fact that listening occupies so much time does not mean that it is more important than reading or writing, but it does suggest the importance of giving it some consideration here.

THE IMPORTANCE OF LISTENING

The development of printing and an increased interest in universal education gave great importance to reading. Even so, in this electronic age of radio, television, and stereo systems, for the great majority listening is still the primary means of receiving messages.

Poor listening is a frequent cause of problems in social, personal, and business relationships. Good listening, on the other hand, fosters these relationships in a number of ways.

At the present time, perhaps the most obvious importance of listening is in the classroom. Students spend several hours a week listening to lectures and discussions. There is little chance of success for anyone who doesn't listen at better than the 25 percent level of efficiency we mentioned. In a public speaking class, listening is a courtesy you owe to your classmates. Active participation in the communication process not only sharpens the listening skills of the audience but enables listeners to give honest reactions and advice to speakers.

The ability to listen well is also an important social asset. In *The Devil's Dictionary,* humorist Ambrose Bierce defines a bore as someone who talks when we want him to listen. But listening is more than just the courtesy of letting someone else talk. Communication is the exchange of understood messages and, because good listeners are willing to work at understanding a message, they are likely, at least in that respect, to make more friends.

In a business environment and in political situations, active and efficient listening is a defense against speakers who try to manipulate others by using language and appeals that trigger unthinking responses.

THE NATURE OF LISTENING

Too often people take the skill of listening for granted. The general attitude seems to be that listening is a simple skill and that everyone develops it naturally. The truth is quite to the contrary.

Listening Is More Than Hearing

Although the hearing mechanism is quite complicated, it is completely automatic. A normal, healthy hearing mechanism never shuts off and is ready to work 24 hours a day. When sound waves stimulate it, you hear. Otherwise, you don't.

Listening, however, is a complex activity that goes far beyond the mere reception of sound. It involves intellectual, emotional, and social factors: who is talking; what is said; when, where, and why one listens.[4] Listening, then, is not only hearing; it is an active intellectual process of decoding, interpreting, understanding, and evaluating messages.

Kinds of Listening

There are several different ways of listening to messages. That is, poems, music, arguments, explanations, or conversations with friends all call for different kinds of listening. Every message gives an audience a reason for listening with some particular purpose in view. Let's examine briefly some of these different kinds of listening.[5]

Comprehension   No matter what the circumstances or the context of communication, the *primary* goal of listening is always the same: correct understanding of the message. Because language of some kind (words, gestures, numbers, signs) is necessary to convey any message, the primary need of a listener is to understand the language used. In oral communication, adequate mastery of the grammar, vocabulary, and syntax of the language supplies at least the basic tools for understanding. But words don't automatically mean something. Instead, the meaning of a communication grows out of the context in which the words are used and out of the relationship the participants have to each other and to the context.[6] That is, a listener "participates in the development of understanding as he or she encounters the discourse."[7] Thus, to make sense of a message requires a conscious listening effort.

Criticism   People often feel they can't depend on what they hear. They have heard so much about false advertising and the empty promises of campaigning politicians that they begin to look for hidden meanings in messages and hidden motives in speakers. That's unfortunate, because it becomes an obstacle to communication. It is better to recognize that there are both good and evil conditions in the world and people can have either good or evil intentions.

But no matter how obvious the purpose of a speech may seem, it is impossible to know with certainty what is in the mind of another human being. Luckily, it isn't necessary to know. No matter what a speaker has in mind, the audience's *perception* of the speech is the deciding factor. If a speech seems informative, it is informative. If it seems persuasive, it is persuasive. More important than judging the purpose of a speech is to sort out the good from the bad in what a speaker says, to make sound judgments about what to accept and what to reject.

When the subject of a speech is in any degree controversial, the first reaction of the audience should be to listen with a critical ear. Critical listening goes beyond the basic goal of comprehension. Its purpose is to identify the rhetorical devices and appeals in the message, to distinguish fact from opinion, to understand and evaluate the speaker's reasoning, and to guard against prejudice and propaganda.

Empathy   Empathy is the ability of one person to feel the emotions of another. A familiar example of empathic response is what happens in the theater. The members of an audience can actually feel within themselves all the emotions of joy, sorrow, pain, triumph, or terror portrayed by the actors.

Empathic listening takes place easily and often among friends. Suppose, for example, that your brother told you about going to class unprepared for a test because he had forgotten about it. Hearing and understanding him and sharing his feeling of embarrassment would be an example of empathic listening. It's the way a friend will act. Empathy is not the same thing as sympathy, because emotions like pity or compassion are not necessarily involved. You might think your brother was pretty dumb to forget the test and that he deserved the bad grade he got, but that shouldn't keep you from sharing his feeling of chagrin.

One reason for doing this kind of listening is that more often than not it has therapeutic value for the speaker. People usually feel better when they share their joys and sorrows with someone they trust.

Appreciation   The goal in listening to a concert or a play, to poetry or a stand-up comedian, is the pleasure it gives. It is true, of course, that those who know and understand the music, literature, or whatever are best equipped to listen appreciative-ly. And when the purpose of listening goes beyond the esthetic pleasure of the experience, as it does, for example, in the case of a music critic, expertise is required. But when listening is appreciative, the goal is enjoyment and professional levels of expertise are not needed.

Two writers on listening have noted the following ways in which appreciative listening can enhance the quality of life:

1. It can increase the enjoyment of life.
2. It can enlarge one's experience.
3. It can improve one's use of language.
4. It can expand the range of what one enjoys.
5. It can decrease the tension of daily living.[8]

It would be a mistake to think that any speaking occasion calls for a single kind of listening. There will be elements of all kinds of listening in every situation. Suppose, for example, that you're listening to a debate in the student senate over a proposal to ban certain magazines from the campus bookstore. Even though you are listening for comprehension, you will also give critical attention to the arguments. At the same time, there is nothing to keep you from appreciating the flashes of wit and empathizing with the concerns of the senators.

There is also a temptation to think of one kind of listening as "better" than another. For example, you might be told, "Don't be critical. Try to be supportive."

Careful listening leads to better understanding. (© Goell, The Picture Cube)

This says that empathic listening is better than evaluating what you hear. In some situations it is. But even though it might be appropriate on occasion to emphasize one kind of listening rather than another, no one of them is always best.

A change in the context of communication will often call for a different kind of listening. For example, suppose that someone who has spent a lot of time in foreign countries is telling you about personal experiences with terrorists. As the conversation progresses, it develops into a debate over whether the United States should use military force against foreign governments that export terrorism. You began by listening for comprehension, but when arguments came into the conversation, the new context required critical listening.

OBSTACLES TO EFFECTIVE LISTENING

Unfortunately, a course in public speaking can be a hinderance rather than a help in developing listening skills. That is because almost the entire burden of the communication is put on the speaker. Speakers are expected to be interesting and clear, to command attention, and to use language, materials, organization, and delivery so well that it is virtually impossible for an audience not to listen. That is a worthwhile objective for speakers, but it does not mean that listening should be passive. Listening is not merely a courtesy given because someone needs to practice on an audience. The audience has a greater share than this in the communication act, and a greater responsibility than passive listening implies. A little later in this chapter we will offer some advice about how to refine and sharpen listening skill. Perhaps the best way to set about this is to look at some of the factors that stand in the way of efficient listening.

Physical Factors

As we have said, listening is more than merely hearing, but the ability to hear a message is a necessary part of listening. The most basic obstacle to listening, therefore, is not being able to hear. One reason for this is an uncorrected hearing loss. That kind of problem requires professional help that is not available in a speech class. Many other times, however, auditory acuity has nothing to do with difficulty in hearing a message. In these cases, poor audibility is either the fault of the speaker or the result of external distractions. Among all of the factors that can cause distraction, inattention is probably the most common. The many causes of inattention are not only physical (for example, fatigue); they can be intellectual or emotional as well.

Intellectual Factors

Contrary to much common-sense popular reasoning, listening skill is not a simple matter of intelligence,[9] although, of course, there is some connection between the two.[10] A listener must be intelligent enough to see the connections among the speaker's ideas and to see the reasoning behind them. But an even more basic source of difficulty for a listener has to do with the language of the speech. Someone who doesn't understand English very well will obviously have trouble listening to a speech in that language. Even native speakers of the language can have trouble if the speaker uses it at too esoteric or technical a level. Conversely, subject matter or language at too low a level leads to boredom. The point is that any language difficulty is an obstacle to effective listening.

Emotional Factors

Audiences have a hard time paying attention even when neither audibility nor intelligence stands in the way of easy reception and clear understanding of a speech. Perhaps the worst obstacle to effective listening is the personal baggage that listeners bring with them: a recent conversation, last night's bowling, tomorrow's test. Emotional factors such as egocentricity, narrow-mindedness, impatience, and prejudice make the listener tune a speaker out and miss what is said. The task you must set yourself is to recognize these when they happen to you and work to overcome them. As one writer has said, "Anything that impairs an individual's ability to perceive through listening impairs that individual's ability to function well in society."[11]

IMPROVING LISTENING SKILLS

Except for a hearing loss that can't be remedied, none of these obstacles is inescapable. Rather, the most important factor in becoming a good listener is the development of specific skills such as the following.

Overcome Distractions

No matter how perfect the speaking situation, there will always be distractions: Someone coughing, a restless child, an airplane flying by, a thunderstorm, or workers down the hall can take attention away from the speaker. Concentration will force many of these distractions into the background, but if there is likely to be external noise, sitting up closer will help. Sometimes it is necessary to let the speaker know that he or she needs to speak louder. Focus attention on the speaker. Everything we say in Chapter 17 about the importance of eye contact to the speaker applies to the listener as well. Looking directly at the speaker develops an immediate sense of interaction and makes a listener more attentive.

Take some time to prepare for what the speaker will discuss. You have probably run from one activity or class to another and sat down wondering where you were and why. "If it's eleven o'clock, this must be sociology." It's a common practice among college students to read the campus newspaper or chat among themselves while waiting for a class to begin. This can make listening less effective. Even if you have only a minute, remind yourself of what went on the last time the class met. Prepare to listen.

Don't Judge Too Quickly

What often passes for inability to listen is merely unwillingness. People miss a great deal if they are willing to listen only to the subjects they already care about. If they literally limit themselves to that degree, they will never learn anything. Of course, it helps to have a real interest in a subject, but the topic may be important even if you don't. Be selfish about listening. Develop the attitude, "What's in it for me?" It's advantageous to listen attentively until you can make a reasonable decision about what is significant. In short, you should earn the right to be bored by initially giving the speaker the benefit of the doubt. Be open-minded and flexible enough to give the speaker a fair hearing.

Judge the importance of the data as you go along. No one listens without bias or waits until the end to judge. Retain or discard what you hear on the basis of what you already know. But resist the temptation to evaluate too soon. It's perfectly natural to have preferences, but that doesn't justify turning people off on a whim. "I can't stand that Reagan." "I'm just not interested in religion." "Health food addicts give me a pain." When you disagree with someone or think a subject will be uninteresting, there is a tendency to establish a mind-set more negative than the situation calls for.

Don't Short-Circuit Your Critical Faculties

Another kind of listener tends to go along with the views of others in the audience. Many people in a group, because they want to be socially acceptable, are more easily polarized to one view than they would be as individuals.[12] Attentive listening will not stop this tendency but will help to control it.

Among all the elements of a speaking situation, the one most likely to dull critical faculties is delivery. The less training one has in public speaking, the greater the significance of delivery seems. But even the most experienced speakers see its importance. The great Greek statesman and orator, Demosthenes, is said to have claimed that the three most important elements of speaking are "Delivery, delivery, delivery."

Delivery can nonetheless be quite beguiling and lure a listener away from the substance of a speech. The story is told of a Southern politician who wrote in the margin of a speech, "Argument weak here. Yell like hell." A listener has to get at the speaker's meaning and not be fooled by delivery. Substance is the only essential element. There's a piece of doggerel that makes the point nicely:

> As you wander on through life, friends,
> Let this be your goal:
> Keep your eye upon the doughnut,
> Not upon the hole.

Listen for Main Ideas

Only about 25 percent of an audience understands the central idea.[13] Many people do not know how to listen for main ideas. They treat each sentence as if it were as significant as every other. That is one reason listeners can often repeat a story they heard in a speech but cannot say what the central point was. When one part of a speech seems to be no more or less important than another, the stories will command attention because they entertain the most.

Look specifically for the central idea of the speech and the main points that support it. The central idea may not be completely clear until the end of the speech, so you should keep reevaluating the relative importance of individual points. The aim at the end of a speech is to be able to say, "The proposal was that we ought to convert industry to coal because it is cheaper, more abundant in the United States, and a benefit to the economy." If you can remember some of the evidence that supported the points, so much the better.

Listen for the Full Meaning

Good listeners do more than simply recall what a speaker says; they try to discover its full implication. What makes this speaker's ideas unique? To what extent are they objective observations? To what extent are they biased conclusions intended to persuade? To what extent is emotional language used?

Some subject matter seems ordinary on the surface, but full understanding brings new insights into the ideas. A speaker may support legalized abortion on a number of bases: to control overpopulation, to give freedom to women, to avoid dooming unwanted children to poor living conditions, and so on. Opponents will use a variety of arguments as well: Abortion is murder, it is selfish, it violates the standards of Western culture. Recognizing the values on which either side bases its position—social well-being, freedom, the quality and sanctity of life, and so forth—helps to clarify any controversy. When listeners find the values behind the ideas, they can see how the ideas relate to their own beliefs and values.

Listen Actively

A classroom speaker talks at about 100 words per minute. In general conversation, about 125 words per minute is the average. But one can understand speech as fast as 400 words per minute. Given these conditions, and the additional fact that some sections of a speech do not demand as much attention as others, it is clear that a listener has more time than necessary to follow a speaker. This time can be used effectively or ineffectively. There is danger, for example, of daydreaming passively. But good listening is not a passive process. It requires a listener to cooperate with a speaker by participating actively in the communication transaction.

The kneeling benches in old churches were unpadded, and the hard wood was often slanted a bit. Kneeling was not unbearable, but it was not overly comfortable either. The thinking was that being too much at ease while praying would lead to drowsing and distraction. The same holds true for listening. Listeners shouldn't be so relaxed that they can't stay alert. Hearing is passive and automatic, but listening always involves tension. Here are some ways to listen actively.

Summarize   From time to time, summarize what has been said. "Now, let's see. The point is that we ought to convert industry to coal and the reason given so far is that coal is cheaper than oil or gas." Summaries like this help to keep the material in mind and make it more comprehensible.

Anticipate   Try to anticipate what will come next. Anticipation can be a great help in critical listening. Even if the predictions are inaccurate, they are an aid to concentration.

Question   Although an audience doesn't usually ask questions until after a speech, bringing them to mind while listening can be an important aid to critical listening because it avoids the danger of blindly accepting the speaker's point of view. The questions can be about such matters as the reasonableness of an idea, its practicality, its possible consequences, or the arguments the speaker uses to support it. But be patient. Don't spend time preparing to attack what you hear until you're sure you understand it.

William Work makes an important point when he says:

Nutritionists tell us that we—quite literally—*are* what we eat (and drink and breathe). In terms of our physical being, this is true. In terms of our psychic selves, we—quite literally—*are* what we hear and read and view. As our social systems and structures become more complex, each individual becomes more dependent on the ability to process information effectively. Competence in speaking and listening is central to the achievement of that end. Being a good listener will not guarantee "success" or happiness or the securing of one's life goals, but, for most, poor listening will stand in the way of their achievement.[14]

SUMMARY

Although listening is no more essential than reading, writing, or speaking, it commands by far the largest amount of the time spent in communication. The fundamental reason for listening to anything is to understand the message. Comprehension is the primary goal, but listening can also be critical, in order to evaluate; appreciative, in order to enjoy; or empathic, in order to give solace.

Physical factors such as a hearing loss, distracting elements in the environment, or a speaker who doesn't talk loud enough are obstacles to efficient listening. Intellectual and emotional factors can also interfere. Recognizing these impediments helps one to overcome them.

Effective listening is active, not passive. Here are some ways to make it active and effective:

1. Overcome distractions by concentrating on the speaker.
2. Give a fair hearing. Don't judge the significance or interest value of a subject too quickly.
3. Don't let the herd instincts of the audience, the mood of the setting, or the effectiveness of the speaker's delivery dull the critical function of listening.
4. Listen for main ideas rather than trying to retain all the details.
5. Listen for the full meaning the speaker is trying to convey, principally the values underlying the ideas.
6. Make periodic summaries of what is said, try to predict what is coming, and make a continuing critical analysis of the message.

NOTES

1. Andrew D. Wolvin and Carolyn Gwynn Coakley, *Listening Instruction* (Falls Church, Va: SCA and ERIC Clearinghouse on Radio and Communication Skills, 1979), p. 5.
2. William Work, "Listen, My Children . . ." *Communication Education*, **27** (Mar. 1978), p. 146.
3. Ralph G. Nichols, "Do We Know How to Listen? Practical Helps in a Modern Age," *The Speech Teacher*, **10** (Mar. 1961), p. 118.
4. Paul Bakan, "Some Reflections on Listening Behavior," *The Journal of Communication*, **6** (Autumn 1956), p. 108.

5. For a more detailed discussion of the question, "Why Do We Listen?," see Wolvin and Coakley, op. cit., pp. 7–13.

6. Ronald C. Arnett and Gordon Nakagawa, "The Assumptive Roots of Empathic Listening," *Communication Education,* **32** (Oct. 1983), pp. 374–375.

7. John Stewart, "Interpretive Listening: An Alternative to Empathy," *Communication Education,* **32** (Oct. 1983), p. 383.

8. Ralph G. Nichols and Thomas R. Lewis, *Listening and Speaking* (Dubuque, Iowa: Wm. C. Brown, 1954), pp. 68–69.

9. Ibid., p. 8.

10. Ibid. See also Ralph G. Nichols, "Factors in Listening Comprehension," *Speech Monographs,* **15** (1948, no. 2), p. 8.

11. Work, op. cit., p. 147.

12. Walter W. Stevens, "Polarization, Social Facilitation, and Listening," *Western Speech,* **25** (Summer 1961), pp. 170–174.

13. Nichols, op. cit., p. 158.

14. Work, op. cit., p. 152.

EXERCISES

1. When a speaker is first introduced in class, write down what you think the main idea of the speech will be. As the speech goes on, each time you change you mind about what the central idea is, write down your new statement of it. At the end of the speech, compare your various versions with what the speaker intended to communicate. Were any differences caused by the speaker? If your listening was at fault, where did it go wrong? How might it have been improved?

2. Listen to two speakers speak to the class on the same day. Afterwards, engage in a class discussion on how successful you were in retaining what each said. If you listened to one more than the other or understood one better than the other, speculate on why that happened.

3. Listen carefully to a speaker and try to duplicate the speaker's outline. After the speech, compare your outline with the speaker's.

4. For one week, consciously take five to ten minutes before each of your classes to review what was discussed at the last meeting of the class and speculate on what is to be covered that day. Do you see an improvement in the comprehension you have of the class subject matter?

chapter *4*

Ethical Responsibility

I. Defining the morally good speaker
   A. Impartial
   B. Knowledgeable
   C. Deliberate
   D. Rational
   E. Humane
II. Playing by the rules
   A. Free choices benefit speaker and society
   B. Informed choices benefit speaker and society
   C. Strike a fair bargain with your audience

With very rare exceptions, rather than living apart from others, people form societies in and through which they conduct their lives—educational, professional, political, recreational, and so on. These societies wouldn't function, or even exist, if people couldn't communicate. When you talk to someone, it's never in a vacuum. Your purpose invariably is to influence the way people behave or how they view the world. Obviously, therefore, communication has an important bearing on the well-being of society. It is a tremendous force for either good or ill. You know that there is more to responsible communication than speaking skills. There is an element not measured by immediate effectiveness. That element is the ethical responsibility you have to yourself and to society.

Ethics is the theory of the good and the right. It defines the standards for making moral judgments and establishes moral codes. There are, of course, many ethical systems and almost as many answers to moral questions as there are thinkers who address them. Our purpose in this chapter, then, is not to campaign for any one of these positions. Instead, we want you to understand some of the moral obligations you accept when you speak.

DEFINING THE MORALLY GOOD SPEAKER

Here is a reasonable definition of a morally good speaker: *one whose judgments about the proper use of the skills of communication are impartially, knowledgeably, and deliberately compatible with a rational, humane ethical code*. Let's look briefly at the key terms of the definition.

Impartial

Every day you make judgments about the moral rightness or wrongness of what you and other people do. But these judgments ought to be impartial. One requirement of impartiality is consistency. That is, there should be no double standards for moral judgments. Ask yourself, therefore, "In similar circumstances, would I impose the same requirements on myself?" Another element of impartiality is constancy. That is, you should be guided by your ethical principles on all occasions, not just when it suits a particular situation.

Knowledgeable

It's easy enough, really too easy, to make moral judgments that can't be better than half-baked because they are based on ignorance. It is a necessary condition of sound moral judgments that they be informed. Before you argue that capital punishment is moral because society should be protected from repeated murders by paroled killers, you should at least know whether paroled killers do, in fact, commit further murders. Being knowledgeable also requires you to have a clear conception of what you're talking about. How, for example, can you speak for or against euthanasia unless you know whether in this particular case euthanasia is letting someone die or causing someone to die?

Deliberate

You are much more likely to make sound moral judgments when you have a cool head. Under the stress of any emotion, you can be misled. There is enough sad experience to make the point clear: unhappy teen-agers who commit suicide, angry adults who dissolve marriages, ambitious politicians, greedy businessmen, all make what often prove to be disastrous decisions. But even more important than this, to be sound, a moral judgment must be free. In fact, a coerced decision can't be called a moral judgment at all. If you are working in a grocery store and an armed robber forces you to give up all of your employer's money, the robber won't be called persuasive and you certainly won't be accused of an immoral act.

Rational

Ideally, the ethical code that guides your actions will not only require certain acts to be done and certain others to be avoided, but it will also give you good reason for doing what is right. It is quite possible that no one will ever construct the ideal ethical system. Therefore, all you can do is to make sure your decisions are not logically contradictory to your personal code. It simply would not compute, at least not in any logical sense, to say, for example, "Euthanasia is all wrong, but my grandmother has suffered enough."

Humane

A humane speaker acts toward an audience with kindness, sympathy, benevolence, and compassion. This requires most of all that you respect your listeners as human beings. They are not things for you to use; they are persons with intelligence and dignity. To subvert that intelligence or to diminish that dignity may very well be the ultimate immorality in communication. You have the power to ennoble or to corrupt. If your speaking is marked by nobility of thought and purpose, you will be a true participant in the cooperative enterprise of seeking societal wisdom. An ethical code that does not require this of you cannot reasonably be called humane.

PLAYING BY THE RULES

There wouldn't be much point in playing any kind of game if you didn't want to win. Wanting to win is a perfectly natural desire. It's the way you go about winning that sometimes causes problems. In a casual game among friends it usually doesn't matter a lot who does win. Then it's easy and comfortable to say it matters "not that you won or lost—but how you played the game." But if winning becomes so important that the rules of the game are ignored, there is an ethical problem.

As a speaker, you have an obligation both to society and to yourself. This obligation grows out of the fact that Americans in general consider democracy the ideal form of government. By putting their faith in democracy, the audiences you address have made themselves vulnerable because they trust you to tell them the truth and to give them honest advice. They face the danger that there are always charlatans more concerned with prestige, power, and wealth than with truth or giving honest advice.

Democracy fails if it does not create an atmosphere in which the self-realization of individuals and the benefit of society as a whole can be achieved. It is impossible to attain these goals unless the vast majority (ideally, all) participate significantly and fruitfully in the process of making *free, informed* choices.

Free Choices Benefit Speaker and Society

No one has exclusive knowledge of the best thing to do in any particular case. In matters of public policy, therefore, judgments are likely to be better if they are the result of free and open discussion. Thus, speaking that prevents or inhibits free choice by an audience is a matter of grave concern. It amounts to unethical manipulation of much the same sort that so-called subliminal advertising is said to be. It inhibits the rational ability of people to make intelligent decisions.

Practices that inflame the emotions of an audience to the point of irrational behavior or introduce emotional appeals irrelevant to the case at hand may help you win, but you will still lose because you demean not only your audience but yourself as well. No ethical code permits you to have a selfish, arrogant contempt for the dignity and worth of the persons you address.

Be sure to interpret correctly what we are saying. One conclusion easily drawn from an insistence on rational discourse is that other kinds of appeals are somehow wrong. This is definitely not the case. Human beings are considerably more than logic machines. People are much more complex than that. You are a whole person speaking to whole persons. Audiences are not influenced by reason alone. They have emotions and values and emotional attachments to their values, and these are all part of what it is to be a human being. There is no intrinsic evil in using arguments that appeal to what is quite natural and universal in human nature.

Nor is there anything wrong with taking a strong stand. Because you believe in your position, present the arguments that support it with vigor, even passion. Because you believe the opposition to be wrong, denounce it with vigor, even passion. When you speak in this fashion, no one can fairly cry foul.

The morality of arguments is determined by how they are used. Appeals to emotions and values become morally objectionable when they aim at making a listener more beastlike and less human, when they play on the emotions in order to still the critical voice of the intellect.

Informed Choices Benefit Speaker and Society

Freedom from overwhelming and irrelevant emotion is not the only necessary condition for making good choices. Good choices are also informed choices. In spite of its flaws, democracy works as well as it does because information is, in large measure, freely available in the decision-making process. There is much good sense, then, in the zealous guardianship of First Amendment freedoms so often mentioned in the news. The First Amendment is designed to ensure that people can make informed decisions. This is why democracy protects the rights of the media to provide the public with both facts and opinions. You have a similar obligation to be sure your listeners have the information vital to their decision making.

In the preceding section we said that the principal cause of interference with *free* choice is manipulation. Similarly, we say here that when choices are *uninformed*, the primary ethical problem is misrepresentation.

Probably the most obvious example of misrepresentation is when a speaker advocates one position but actually holds the opposing point of view. Lawyers on occasion find themselves required by the duties of their office as counsel to do this. University debaters are required to support an affirmative or negative position, and their own beliefs about the case are irrelevant. In times of war, hot or cold, governments will go to great lengths to misinform hostile forces. Special cases of this kind put aside, however, when you argue in support of a claim you don't believe, you are engaged in an outright lie.

To speak honestly, you must avoid misrepresentation. You owe your audience honest advice. However, to tell the truth does not mean that you have to be absolutely

Legislators have to make many ethical judgments. (Forsyth, Monkmeyer)

literal in every respect. That is, in order to enhance the stylistic quality of a speech, it is quite legitimate to use all of the figures of speech discussed in Chapter 15 as long as you don't make your audience misinterpret the truth of what you say. Nobody has to tell you when you intend to cross the line between dramatizing a point and mis-representing it. You know.

Even though every issue has two sides and both sides have a right to the strongest legitimate defense possible, you are not required, in order to be ethical, to present the opposition case. A prosecutor does not argue for the defense. The defense doesn't give evidence for the prosecution. But you are expected to be honest about the arguments you make for your claim.

You can make bad decisions anywhere along the line in speech preparation. One very sensitive area is in the use of evidence. Questions about manufacturing phony statistics, or taking quotations out of context, are not difficult to answer. Even the speaker who deliberately does these things knows they are wrong. But what about withholding information? That can be a more delicate matter. If you think the blind date your roommate set up for you is a self-centered bore, unless your opinion is vital to someone, no one will blame you for keeping it to yourself. But you ought to be concerned when you sell your car if you try to hide the fact that the transmission is shot. The significant criterion here again is the audience's need to know. Sound judgments can't be based on ignorance or misunderstanding. You have to give your audience the facts it needs in order to make an informed judgment.

Since an audience has a right to be told the truth, a speaker has an obligation to be informed. Surely, no one can know everything about anything, but when you deliver a speech it's your responsibility to know what you're talking about. If you don't, you can't possibly give your audience the grounds for making informed judgments. It happens, then, that audiences are vulnerable not only to charlatans but to ignoramuses as well. People deserve better than that.

Strike a Fair Bargain with Your Audience

Think of a speaking situation as one in which you make a bargain with your audience. You make an unspoken agreement with an audience that is intended to be to the mutual benefit of all concerned. In striking such a bargain, you say in effect, "If you will give critical and thoughtful consideration to what I am going to tell you, I promise in return to do my best to make it worth your while." Your bargain with the audience promises that you will be worth listening to, that your advocacy will be reasoned, that your counsel will be honest.

Our discussion of your ethical responsibility as a speaker is admittedly brief, overly simplified, and incomplete. It should be clear, however, that unscrupulous folk can abuse the faculty of speech so that it becomes a weapon to victimize people. This fact makes it important to recognize your responsibility, understand it, and accept it. For accept it you must. The best way to go about it is to ask, "What is the right thing to do?" When your decision is justified by an impartial, rational, humane ethical code, you have made a sound moral judgment. If your use of the skills of communication is knowledgeably and deliberately compatible with that code, you have accepted your ethical responsibility as a speaker.

SUMMARY

The societies in and through which people live their lives cannot exist without human communication. Because communication has tremendous influence on society for good or ill, it is necessary to make moral judgments about it. These judgments should be made in the light of a defensible ethical code.

A morally good speaker is one whose judgments about use of the skills of communication is impartially, knowledgeably, and deliberately compatible with a rational, humane ethical code. Impartiality requires that justified norms be applied to all persons equally and on all occasions. To be knowledgeable, judgments should be based on the facts of a case and on a clear, correct understanding of the ideas involved. To be deliberate, judgments must be free from the stress of emotion and free from coercion. A rational ethical code is ideally one that not only requires certain actions but also supplies the correct reasons for the actions. Even though your ethical code, like any other, is debatable, the judgments you make ought to be logically compatible with it. To be humane, your code must require choices characterized by kindness, sympathy, benevolence, and compassion. It requires you to respect your listeners as persons, not things. To subvert their intelligence or to diminish their dignity demeans both you and them.

Our society considers democracy to be the best form of government. But democracy fails if the desire to achieve individual goals, such as power, status, money, and the like, motivates a kind of speaking that prevents the legitimate self-realization of individuals or the well-being of society as a whole. To avoid these problems, demand of yourself that you decide what is the morally right thing to do and then do it.

EXERCISES

1. Write a short paper explaining and justifying the ethical responsibilities you impose on yourself as a communicator.

2. Discuss with others in class what you consider to be your moral responsibility in one of the following, or some other, situation of moral conflict:

   a. In a class discussion, someone supports your proposal and convinces others that you are right by presenting evidence you know to be incorrect. What should you do? Why?

   b. A good friend of yours is selling a car in order to buy a newer one. A possible buyer comes to look at it while you are there, and your friend says the car has good brakes. Just last week you heard your friend say that one of the reasons for getting rid of the car was that the brakes were bad. What should you do? Why?

   c. No speaker can say everything there is to say on a subject. The speaker must select. Therefore, no matter how hard you try, you cannot give all the "facts" on a subject. What principles do you think should guide you in deciding what facts you should exclude if time is short? For instance, do you have an obligation to explain the arguments against your idea? Should you cut your evidence short to be sure you make all your arguments, or should you cut the number of points you make and develop them more fully?

d. A friend of yours believes that God is the supreme ruler of the universe and that God has decreed that abortion is immoral. In an argument with someone else who favors abortion, but does not believe in God, your friend does not admit to believing in God. Is such an act ethical?

two

ANALYZING THE SPEAKING SITUATION

chapter 5

The Subject and Purpose of the Speech

No matter what the context, every communication, either written or oral, must have a subject. It is impossible to imagine a speech that does not talk about *something*. The notion makes no sense at all. And no matter how admirable a speech may be for cogency of argument, clarity of structure, brilliance of style, and elegance of delivery, these questions will always arise: Arguments in support of what *claim?* Structure of what *substance?* Style for communicating what *ideas?* Delivery that says *what?*

In addition to a subject, every communication has a second significant feature: Even when people are just gabbing, they do it because they enjoy it and the talking has a purpose.

Every speech, then, must have a subject and a purpose. The subject of the speech is the theme that is dealt with in the message. The purpose of the speech is the goal it is intended to achieve, the specific response the speaker wants from the audience. In this chapter, we will examine these two elements of communication.

SOURCES OF SPEECH SUBJECTS

Although the speaker makes the final decision as to what the subject of a speech will be, the audience strongly influences the choice. Let's look first at the matter of choosing a subject from the speaker's point of view, and then see what part the audience plays.

Personal Interests

It's a lot easier to make a speech on an interesting subject than one that seems dull. For example, any area of study that you like well enough to make it your academic major will supply a large number of interesting subjects. But beyond that specific field is a whole world of fascinating people, places, and ideas, including hobbies, sports, cultural events, a variety of social, political, and religious activities, and perhaps a job.

Many other experiences are also potentially good sources of speech subjects. What you learned on a trip to Mexico could become a good speech on the language, culture, architecture, or art of the country. And it is also possible that having the stereo stolen from your car could motivate you to investigate the problem of crime and use that as a speech subject.

Reading, talking to people, getting involved in school and community affairs, developing an interest in national and international politics and economics are all instructive activities. Wide interests and experience will supply any number of subjects quite suitable for speeches. Appendix A contains a list of subjects that may give you some ideas for a speech. Remember, however, that in the end you and your audience are the best sources of speech subjects.

Audience Needs

There are people who prepare speeches and then search for audiences to deliver them to. Newspapers carry advertisements for public lectures of every sort. Look at the religion page next Saturday. Or look at the financial page any day for advertised investment seminars. The subjects of such speeches are chosen because they will appeal to certain people. They are chosen to attract an audience.

On occasion, however, the audience comes to seek the speaker. A congress-woman, well known as a fighter against waste in government, might be asked to speak to the Rotary Club because they want to hear what she has to say about the cost of junkets that government officials take at the taxpayers' expense. In a case like this, the speaker has little or no choice because she is assigned a subject that meets a specific audience need.

Suppose, on the other hand, that a scientist is asked to speak at a church men's group breakfast. Even though the invitation seems to give complete freedom, the subject must be adapted to the given audience. In this case the factor that brings the men together is their religion. The occasion is not as formally religious as a church service, but it still has religious overtones. Thus, the scientist would be wise to consider the moral implications of the subject. Different as these two situations may seem, they show that the choice of a speech subject is never the speaker's alone. Audience needs must play a part in subject selection.

CHOOSING THE RIGHT SUBJECT

There is no such thing as an inherently good subject, nor is there any such thing as a bad one. Rather than good or bad subjects, there are only good or bad speeches on any subject whatsoever. A subject is right when it is one on which you are *competent* to speak, when an audience will judge it to be *significant,* and when it is *appropriate,* both to the audience and to the response you want from the audience.

Speaker Competence

The assumption that a good speaker can talk well on any subject is wrong. Good speakers are avid readers and investigators. They pursue all kinds of knowledge, but they cannot be expert on everything. They must, therefore, speak on subjects chosen from areas of their greatest competence.

But a subject need not be in an area of your greatest competence *before you choose it*. When you choose a subject, you may know very little about it. If you are interested in it and you think it is worth talking about, then you can add to your knowledge through study. Your initial knowledge and your research can make you competent. The important requirement is to be competent *when you make the speech*.

Significance

For an art major, the fact that the cost per tube of watercolors has almost doubled is apt to be of considerably greater interest than it would be to an English major whose creativity takes forms other than painting. A lecture on the Hopi Indians that an anthropology major might go out of the way to hear would not necessarily interest an astronomy student. Many students of political science would gladly spend time tabulating returns of a campus election in which other students had not taken the time to vote. But all of these students would respond sharply to news that their tuition had been increased 25 percent. In each instance, the events they considered significant would get their attention.

The factor of significance also influences the choice of a subject. It will be of interest to an audience if it seems significant to the audience. The greater the significance, the greater the interest. If listeners are not aware of how much the topic affects them, they may not have any feeling at all in the matter. Indifference of this kind does not mean that the subject is necessarily a poor choice. Rather, it means that you must stimulate interest in the subject by helping your listeners see how important the topic is. Unless they understand the significance of the subject for them, they won't know why they should be interested and they will have no reason to listen.

Appropriateness

Usually, it is a specific occasion that draws people together as an audience. In choosing a subject, then, the occasion is an important factor. A speech delivered on Lincoln's birthday should indicate at least an awareness of the great President's philosophy and deeds, and on the Fourth of July some aspect of patriotism is traditionally in order.

Choosing a subject that is inappropriate for the occasion is much less likely to be a problem in a speech class than it is elsewhere, simply because the classroom is a laboratory for experimenting with different kinds of speeches and speaking techniques. The choice of subject in relation to the occasion is therefore not so critical.

It is quite important, however, that in all instances the subject be appropriate to the *audience*. A young woman made a very good speech in class on the need for automobile insurance. At first glance it might appear that the subject was inappropriate because any listener who owned a car probably had insurance already. Knowing this, she made it quite clear that the subject was appropriate by saying, "Even if you are not among the 40 percent of all drivers who don't have insurance, the chances are very good that you have friends who are. And you can help them."

In every case, the subject reflects not only what you want to give to the audience, but also what you want the audience to give to you. To the audience, you give ideas, organized and supported. From the audience, you want a response. The subject of the speech and the response desired from the audience are closely related and determine the purpose of the speech. Selecting a subject requires an awareness of the different speech goals. We will call these different goals *the general purposes of speaking*.

THE GENERAL PURPOSES OF SPEAKING

For more than 2000 years, the sole concern of people interested in public speaking was with speeches intended to *persuade*. Slightly more than 200 years ago, other goals, so-called general ends, were recognized and, depending on who was writing about them, they varied in name and number. Even today, there is not complete agreement on just what or how many of these goals there are. We think it makes the most sense to identify three general purposes of speaking: to *entertain*, to *inform*, and to *persuade*.

Speaking to Entertain—To Give Amusement

On many occasions, both formal and informal, a speaker will have the sole purpose of entertaining an audience. Ordinarily, humor will be the means. For example, in Appendix B is a speech that was given at an annual awards banquet of a communication department, as a part of the entertainment. A member of the forensics team gave the after-dinner speech that had been successful in competition. It gives a humorous view of being a college student. Many comedians use satire as a stock-in-trade. Although they draw much of their humor from the foibles and incongruities they see in society, with a consequent strong undertone of social criticism, the goal they seek is the amusement of their audiences.

An audience will respond well to a speaker with an interesting subject. (© Herwig, The Picture Cube)

There is an important distinction between the use of ideas to create humor and the use of humor to support ideas. A speech to entertain should not be confused with an informative or persuasive speech that uses humor for interest or argument. The use of humor will be discussed at some length in Chapter 20.

Speaking to Inform—To Bring About Understanding

Making something known to an audience, clarifying ideas, giving facts or information, is speaking to inform. The primary response desired from the audience is understanding of something such as an object, an operation, a condition, or an idea. To fulfill a requirement in a course on international relations, you might give a report on the organization and function of the Presidium of the Supreme Soviet of the USSR. In a report of this kind, you have no immediate concern for the attitude the audience might take toward the Presidium or toward the Soviet Union; nor are you concerned directly with what your listeners might do with the information they get from you. Your goal is that they understand and remember what you say. Your purpose is to give information. Understanding and retention by the audience are the criteria of a successful speech to inform. Chapter 18 discusses techniques that will help you meet these criteria.

Speaking to Persuade—To Influence Belief or Action

A speech to persuade gives listeners reasons for changing their behavior in some way. This becomes necessary when the speaker and the audience hold different opinions or similar opinions but at a different level of intensity. Consider the following instance:

Irritated by the fact that you can't find a clean table in the student union because students don't remove their dirty dishes, you decide to embark on a clean-up campaign on the campus. You would need to persuade your friends to give active support to the campaign.

But even if your friends agree that the cafeteria ought to be clean, they may not care about it as much as you do because they have concerns that are more important to them. Therefore, your specific problem in persuasion depends on how involved your friends are with the situation (how much it bothers them).

Distinguishing Between Informative and Persuasive Purposes

Many communication theorists say that because every speech causes some kind of change, all messages are, for that reason, persuasive. Nevertheless, it is useful to make a distinction between informative and persuasive speeches. The desired response to an informative speech is understanding. It doesn't support a controversial position. Persuasive speeches do. And that's the way to tell them apart. The subject of a persuasive speech is a matter in debate and demands proof. True, persuasive speaking will give the audience information, but in almost every case, more than information is needed to persuade.

It will be no problem to decide whether any speech of *yours* is informative or persuasive. You know what you have in mind. But unless your listeners are clairvoyant, *they* have no way of knowing for sure what's going on inside your head. Audiences make their own interpretations of what they know, and subjects have an irritating way of being ambiguous.

For example, think of some of the different speeches that can be made on the subject of abstract art. One student left an audience quite unsure of just what she had in mind when she spoke on the subject, "Abstract Art Is Fun!" Her listeners couldn't decide whether she meant to persuade them to take advice: "Try it. You'll like it." Or to persuade them to a higher appreciation of its value: "It has greater merit than people realize." Or to inform them of what it is: "Abstract expressionism is an interesting school of art."

Even telling your audience quite explicitly that a speech is intended to inform or persuade won't always make an audience interpret the speech that way. These questions help to predict how an audience will interpret a speech:

Does the Audience Consider Me a Credible Source?   If so, it is more likely to accept what you say as informative. If not, you will more likely be perceived as trying to persuade.

Does the Audience Consider My Subject to Be Controversial?   If so, the audience will almost certainly interpret what you say as persuasive in intent. If not, it is very likely to accept what you say as informative. The audience's knowledge of the subject is often a significant deciding factor. Debates over whether there is life elsewhere in the universe, or the theory of continental drift, or the existence of UFOs are familiar examples. Someone may one day find proof for one position or another on these issues. Once that happens, a speech on the subject would clearly be perceived as informative.

Does the Audience Agree with My Stand on a Controversial Matter?   If so, it may very well consider your speech informative. If not, it will unquestionably judge it to be persuasive. Earlier, we mentioned a student who argued in favor of having automobile insurance. Many of the people in the audience agreed with her. They realized that, like it or not, insurance is a necessity. Because they already believed it, they nodded and agreed and considered the speech to be informative. Even though they weren't aware of it, the speech did have the persuasive effect of reinforcing their belief.

Does the Audience View the Occasion as Requiring Informative or Persuasive Discourse?   Instructors talking to students in the classroom are usually viewed as speaking informatively even when the point under discussion is debatable. At political rallies, on the other hand, speakers will appear to audiences as trying to persuade.

DEVELOPING A SPECIFIC PURPOSE

In Chapter 1 we spoke of communication acts as transactions between speakers and audiences. That is, the speaker and the audience become in a sense a single entity while they cooperate with each other in creating a mutually understood meaning for the speech. The way this union between the personal interests of the speaker and the needs of the audience comes about can be understood quite easily if you think of speeches as devices people use in order to solve problems. All speeches have in common the fact that their ultimate purpose is to solve a problem of some kind. Let's look at a few examples.

For years there has been growing concern in California over the inevitability of a major earthquake. It is generally acknowledged that the question is not whether but when. Yet people go about their business without much visible concern. If you were trying to arouse people to the danger, one factor you would have to deal with is a widespread lack of understanding of just what an earthquake is. If you want an audience to know how earthquakes happen, an obstacle to that goal might be, "They don't understand how complicated the process is." Thus the goal of the speech is understanding, and its purpose would be to inform. If the speech is successful, you and the audience have cooperated in a communication transaction and the problem is solved. The same is true of any informative speech. In every case, the goal is to solve a problem—the need for understanding.

Persuasive speeches are also means of solving problems. For instance, your purpose might be, "Elect Shannon to the state assembly." Here you will have a different kind of problem, and merely giving information is not likely to solve it. A speech on this subject obviously needs to be persuasive. Again, if the speech gets the desired response, the transaction between you and the audience has solved the problem of what decision to make about the election.

Speeches to entertain work the same way. They are aimed at problems of the sort that say, "My audience doesn't see the humor in. . . ."

The way to identify the subject and purpose of a speech, therefore, is to get a clear understanding of precisely what problem needs to be solved in the communication transaction. The proposed solution is expressed as a statement called the *speech claim*. This claim clearly specifies what you want the audience to understand, to believe, to find humorous, or to do. There are three kinds of speech claims: *fact, value,* and *policy*.

Speech Claims

Every claim makes one or the other of two kinds of assertions. It says either that something *is* or that something *ought to be*. The kind of claim which says that something *is* appears in two forms: fact and value.

Factual Claims   A factual claim is *an assertion that in the real world certain specified conditions could be observed*. That is, the specified conditions don't exist only as opinions in somebody's mind. Instead they are activities that can be experienced in the physical world. For example:

1. There is a wide disparity among the divorce laws of the several states.
2. Before the year 2000, a woman will be elected President of the United States.

Notice that the first example talks about conditions that can be observed here and now. But in the second example, no amount of investigation *at the present time* will justify the claim. It is a prediction about the future. But it is still a factual claim because it says that a specified condition some day could (at least theoretically) be observed. And this kind of claim can be a legitimate speech subject.

Value Claims   Because of its form, a value claim can easily be mistaken for a factual claim. Yet the two are different in a very significant respect, and it is important to distinguish between them. A factual claim says that something in the physical world could (given the right conditions) be observed. In other words, it says something about the object referred to, and it is either true or false. That is, U.S. divorce laws either are or are not uniform; in the year 2001, there will either be a woman President or there will not. A value claim, however, expresses a state of mind. It cannot be shown to be either true or false through observation.

A value claim is *a statement expressing a judgment about the goodness, rightness, quality, or merit of something*. For example:

1. Professional boxing is a brutal sport.
2. The American educational system is superior to the educational systems of Europe.
3. Women are equal to men.

Policy Claims   You make decisions every day about how to conduct your life. Moreover, it is often useful to ask others to do something or in some way to change their lives. When you tell people what you want them to believe or to do, the expression you use is called a policy claim and it says something about how you think the world ought to be.

A policy claim is *a statement that identifies a course of action (a policy) and calls for its adoption*. For example:

1. The university should decrease student admission prices for athletic events.
2. The several states should adopt uniform divorce laws.
3. A woman should be elected President.

It is not always easy to know what kind of claim a statement expresses. We have already said that it is sometimes difficult to tell a factual claim from a value claim because the two look as if they make the same kind of statement. On the other hand, it should be easy to recognize policy claims even though they can be phrased in a wide variety of ways. For example, there are several ways of saying that the states should adopt uniform divorce laws:

> The states ought to. . . .
>
> It would be the best course of action (or the best policy) for the states to. . . .
>
> The states have to. . . .
>
> What we need are. . . .

And so on. But no matter how the claim is worded, it always implies the notion of "should" or "ought." Despite the clear-cut criteria for distinguishing one kind of claim from another, it is easy to confuse them if you classify them according to whether you believe them or not. The imaginary conversation that follows shows the kind of trouble this can cause.

"What kind of claim is this? Everyone should give good value for money received."

"That must be a factual claim because it's true."

"No, it's a policy claim because of the kind of proposal it makes. It identifies a policy, that is, a course of action, or a mode of conduct, and calls for its adoption. And policy claims cannot be either true or false because (like value claims) they express a state of mind. They aren't true or false, they simply exist."

"What kind of claim is this? There's no life anywhere in the universe except on Earth."

"That must be a value claim because it's only your opinion."

No, *all* claims are expressions of opinion. This claim identifies a condition that could, at least theoretically, be observed in the physical world. For that reason it must be either true or false. Therefore, it is a factual claim.

We have stressed the importance of identifying each kind of claim correctly because the differences among them are significant, and not to identify each one correctly makes for fuzzy thinking and blurred notions of what you want to say. It is particularly important in preparing a persuasive speech to know whether you are supporting a claim of fact, value, or policy. The significance of this will be clarified in Chapter 6.

Stating the Specific Purpose

Before you can organize a speech, or even begin to gather materials, you must develop a clear statement of precisely what response you want from the audience. A common procedure is to formulate an infinitive phrase that specifies the subject of the speech. This is called a *statement of specific purpose*. For example:

> To entertain the audience with a description of my first experience with college registration (a factual claim)
>
> To inform the audience about the mechanics of earthquakes (a factual claim)

To persuade the audience that there is extraterrestrial life (a factual claim)

To persuade the audience that the attitudes of the general public toward Vietnam veterans are grossly unfair (a value claim)

To persuade the audience that they should support my campaign to clean up the cafeteria (a policy claim)

The statement of purpose is used as a guide in speech preparation. It helps to determine what material belongs in the speech and what does not. There are always interesting ideas and tempting pieces of material to put into a speech. The problem is one of selection: to use the items that are essential and reject those that are not. Sometimes even the most interesting material must be omitted in order to preserve the unity of the speech. Once formed, the statement of purpose should be a rigorous standard to judge what materials to use.

Formulating a Subject Sentence

A statement of purpose is an admirable guide in speech preparation, but its style is not suited to good *oral* communication. Therefore you won't use it in the speech. Instead, you will use a *subject sentence*. This, in effect, is the statement of purpose cast into the sort of sentence you might use in conversation. It says briefly, clearly, and gracefully what the speech is going to be about. In Chapter 13 we will discuss the subject sentence in more detail.

SUMMARY

Every speech has a *subject* (the topic under discussion) and a *purpose* (the reason for which it is given). The subject of the speech grows out of the personal interests and experiences of the speaker, but it must be adapted to the needs of the audience and the requirements of the speaking occasion. An audience may choose the subject by asking a speaker to talk on a specific topic. But even when the speaker has the freedom to choose, the choice of subject is a joint venture between the speaker and the audience.

There are no such things as good or bad subjects, but only good or bad speeches on any subject whatsoever. Therefore, it is better to look for the *right* subject, that is, one that meets three criteria: It is a subject on which the speaker is (or can become) competent. It is appropriate to the audience and the occasion. It is significant to the interest and well-being of the audience.

The purpose of a speech is best thought of in terms of the kind of response the speaker wants from the audience. There are three kinds of response and these are called the general purposes of speaking: to entertain—to give amusement; to inform—to bring about understanding; to persuade—to influence belief or action.

Sometimes it's not easy to know whether an audience will interpret a speech as being meant to inform or to persuade. Its judgment is influenced by such factors as these: When the speaker is a credible source, when the subject is considered noncontroversial, or when the audience agrees with the speaker's position on a controversial subject, the audience is likely to consider the speech informative. The contrary of any of these conditions tends to make the speech seem persuasive. Moreover, the tradition of giving one kind of speech or another on certain occasions influences the audience's expectations and, therefore, its perceptions.

A speaking situation is a transaction in which the speaker and the audience work toward the solution of some problem: the need for amusement, or understanding, or advice. The speaker's proposed solution to the problem is called the speech *claim*. There are three kinds of speech claims:

A *factual* claim says that certain specified conditions can (at least theoretically) be observed in the real world. It is either true or false. A *value* claim makes known the speaker's attitude toward something. It is neither true nor false. A *policy* claim identifies a course of action and calls for its adoption. Like the value claim, it is neither true nor false. It is important to be able to distinguish among these three types of claims, because confusing one with another seriously blurs the speaker's understanding of what the needs of the audience and the occasion are.

The statement of specific purpose of a speech is an infinitive phrase that identifies precisely which general purpose the speaker wants to achieve (to entertain, inform, or persuade) and makes clear exactly what the speaker wants the audience to understand, believe, do, or laugh about. The statement of purpose is an invaluable aid in deciding what materials belong in the speech and what do not. To tell the audience what the subject and purpose of the speech are, the speaker casts the statement of purpose into a sentence in good oral style.

EXERCISES

1. Phrase a factual claim and a value claim from the same general subject. Explain, by using them as examples, the difference between claims of fact and value. What policy claim might be related to these factual and value claims?
2. Select one of the audiences below or one assigned by your instructor and make a list of five speech subjects you believe would interest that audience:
   a. A church group to which you belong
   b. An assembly of the high school from which you graduated
   c. An organization to which your parents belong
   d. A meeting of the students in your major department
3. Make a list of five general subjects on which you believe you are qualified to speak. Form a specific purpose for an informative and a persuasive speech from each general subject.
4. Discuss, in a group of three or four students, the categories in Appendix A in order to decide which category is likely to generate specific purposes interesting to the group and the class as a whole.

chapter *6*

Analyzing Issues

Every speech makes a claim of fact, value, or policy that is intended to influence the way its audience views the world. But all speech claims need support, and different kinds of claims need different kinds of support. In speeches to entertain, for instance, humor is the principal means of supporting the claim. Informative speeches use supporting materials solely for the purpose of clarifying the subject of the speech and holding the interest of the audience. A persuasive speech, on the other hand, must not only accomplish these tasks, it must *justify* its claim as well.

The only way to justify the claim of a persuasive speech is to find arguments (proofs) that will make the audience *believe* it. But many arguments are ineffective. When they are, a listener's response will be either, "Oh, no. That's got to be wrong," or "Yeah, that's right, *but* . . . !" The first response says that the listener sees an error in the reasoning or the evidence or both. In the second case, the response says that the proof is poor because the argument misses the point. We'll have more to say about avoiding errors of reasoning in Chapter 10, but in this chapter we show you how to find arguments that get to the point. To do this you have to understand *issues*.

ISSUES DEFINED

A dozen-and-a-half states and the District of Columbia operate lotteries to increase their revenues. The bulk of the money they bring in is usually used to support the educational budget of the state. Suppose that your state has no lottery and you want to support a proposal to have one. You might argue that the state's budget cannot adequately support education, and that increased taxes are undesirable. Moreover, you might be able to show that there are effective means of keeping organized crime out of the lottery, and that the poor who can least afford to buy lottery tickets would not play with disproportionate frequency.

Even though your case seems reasonable, many of the very people who cry the loudest about the educational needs of the state might vote against you. Why? Ask them. They might tell you, "As far as I'm concerned, a lottery is a form of gambling, and I have serious moral concerns about gambling." This is a serious objection to your plan, but none of your arguments responds to it.

Two claims are made: A lottery is gambling, and gambling is immoral. If you want to persuade these people, you will have to make them believe *either* that a lottery is not a form of gambling *or* that gambling is not immoral. Two questions, then, are of vital importance to your success: Is a lottery a form of gambling? Is gambling immoral? These questions are precisely what we mean by issues. Issues are *yes-or-no questions that identify the point over which opposing arguments clash*. In this case,

Claim	Counterclaim
A lottery is a form of gambling.	A lottery is not a form of gambling.

The issue
Is a lottery a form of gambling?

And again,

Claim	Counterclaim
Gambling is immoral.	Gambling is not immoral.

The issue
Is gambling immoral?

ANALYSIS—THE METHOD FOR FINDING ISSUES

Unless you know what specific issues stand between you and the audience, your arguments will be aimed randomly at an obscure target. Only by sheer luck will they answer the audience's objections. But because lucky accidents are not a dependable basis for effective persuasion, it is much better to have a sound method for finding the issues in a debatable claim.

Analyzing Policy Claims

Policy claims are more complicated to analyze than are claims of fact and value, and they are analyzed by a different method.

Finding the Issues More than 20 years ago, a Supreme Court decision outlawed the practice of saying any form of prayer in the public schools of the United States. However, in the minds of many people the matter is not yet settled, and the subject has been debated time and again in Congress.

On May 17, 1982, President Ronald Reagan proposed a constitutional amendment allowing voluntary school prayer, but no action was taken on the matter during the 97th Congress (1981–1982). In the next Congress, however, the subject came up again, and after two weeks of debate, on March 20, 1984, the Senate defeated President Reagan's proposal.[1] An attempt to force the matter onto the floor of the House of Representatives failed. The question of organized, voluntary prayer in public schools will, nonetheless, be debated for some time to come. No matter which side you take, here is how you might analyze the policy claim: "The Constitution of the United States should be amended to permit voluntary prayer in the public schools."[2]

First, draw a line down the center of a sheet of paper. On the left side of the line, list all the arguments you can find that support the proposal. On the right side of the page, list the arguments that oppose it. Match the arguments by pairing them against each other:

For the amendment	Against the amendment
This debate is of vital importance to the nation.	We face many problems of much greater importance. This debate is a waste of time.

Sometimes the same claim can be made by both sides:

For the amendment	Against the amendment
There are more than 80 separate religions with at least 50,000 members.	There are more than 80 separate religions with at least 50,000 members.

On the surface, there appears to be no disagreement in this instance and therefore no issue. The assertions accepted by both parties in a conflict constitute what is called *waived matter*. Anyone debating this subject would accept as waived matter statements such as, "Many religious people don't want the amendment," or "The government appoints and supports chaplains in the military services."

When both parties make the same statement, however, it is unwise to assume automatically that this means there is no issue. In the case at hand, the fact that in the United States there are more than 80 large religious groups can be used by one side as grounds to support the claim, "Many people would approve the amendment." But the other side, using the same grounds, could say, "That shows how impossible it would be to find a prayer formula that would satisfy everyone."

Sometimes you will find an argument that has no apparent opposition, at least not any that you have found:

For the amendment	Against the amendment
It is inconsistent to ban school prayer when the House and Senate pray, every Supreme Court session is begun with the cry, "God save the United States and this Honorable Court!," and our coins say, "In God We Trust."	No apparent counterargument

These unopposed arguments do not automatically constitute waived matter. The very fact that the argument is offered suggests the existence of an issue. To make the analysis complete, construct an argument that will clarify the dispute. For example:

For the amendment	Against the amendment
It is inconsistent to ban school prayer when the House and Senate pray, every Supreme Court session is begun with the cry, "God save the United States and this Honorable Court!," and our coins say, "In God We Trust."	That is true, and these practices should be stopped too. *or* These are purely voluntary, they are not protected by the Constitution, and they have nothing to do with institutionalized religion.

When you have eliminated waived matters and have set the opposing arguments up against each other, your analysis sheet will look somewhat like this:

For the amendment	Against the amendment
This debate is of vital importance to the nation.	We face many problems of much greater magnitude. This debate is a waste of time.
The First Amendment is intended to guarantee freedom of religion.	The First Amendment is intended to ensure complete separation of church and state. It is not being misinterpreted.
The proposed amendment would restore the religious freedom the courts have taken away.	The proposed amendment would diminish religious freedom by setting government in support of institutionalized religion.
It is inconsistent to ban school prayer when the House and Senate pray, every Supreme Court session begins with the cry, "God save the United States and this Honorable Court!," and our coins say, "In God We Trust."	That is true and these practices should be stopped too.
	or
	These are purely voluntary, they are not protected by the Constitution, and they have nothing to do with institutionalized religion.
A prayer that is general enough and nondenominational enough to satisfy everyone can be composed.	It is impossible to construct a prayer that will not offend some persons or some religion.
Participation in the prayer will be totally voluntary.	Peer pressure and the fear of embarrassment will force many students to join in prayers they do not believe.

Phrasing the Issues   After the analysis sheet is prepared, it is much easier to see where the arguments clash. The next step is to phrase *as a yes-or-no question* the clash implied in each pair of opposing arguments. This is done in the same way the clash was phrased in the example of the state lottery. The questions that result are issues.

Argument for	Argument against
This debate is of vital importance to the nation.	We face many problems of much greater magnitude. This debate is a waste of time.

Issue: Does the significance of this controversy warrant lengthy debate?

But examine each of the issues to see that all are clearly and properly stated. The following question is not phrased as an issue. "How serious is the threat to freedom of religion in this nation today?" Because it is not a yes-or-no question, it presents no issue between clearly opposed points of view. Moreover, it assumes that there is a threat to religious freedom when in fact that very point is widely contested.

Reducing the Number of Issues   Some issues need not be argued because the audience would consider them *trivial:*

For the amendment	Against the amendment
Justice Black said, "We are a religious people whose institutions presuppose a Supreme Being.	It was Justice Douglas who said it, but why argue over a minor point like that?

Some issues need not be argued because they are *irrelevant:*

For the amendment	Against the amendment
The large majority of European countries permit prayers in the classrooms of public schools.	That's not true, and even if it were, it has no bearing on what we do in the United States.

Whenever possible, combine issues that overlap. Even though the following issues involve different points, they address only one area of conflict.

ISSUE: Is it consistent to ban school prayer when the House and Senate pray?

ISSUE: Is it consistent to ban school prayer when every session of the Supreme Court opens with the petition, "God save the United States and this Honorable Court"?

ISSUE: Is it consistent to ban school prayer when our coins say, "In God We Trust"?

When the job of analyzing the claim is done, you will have a list of issues somewhat like the following:

ISSUE 1: Does the significance of this controversy warrant lengthy debate?

ISSUE 2: Is the First Amendment being misinterpreted?

ISSUE 3: Would the proposed amendment diminish freedom of religion?

ISSUE 4: Is it consistent to ban school prayer when other religious practices have the sanction of long tradition?

or, if it is not,

Are the other practices untenable also?

ISSUE 5: Can a satisfactory formula for prayer be found?

ISSUE 6: Could the wishes of those who do not want to participate in a school prayer be accommodated?

Using "Stock Issues" to Identify Crucial Specific Issues   Some issues, as we have shown, are irrelevant or trivial. Instead of arguing these insignificant points, It is more important to identify the *crucial* issues, those that will actually decide the case in a listener's mind. The so-called stock issues are helpful in this process. Here's the way they work.

To prove any policy claim whatever, the arguments must persuade the audience to answer "yes" to three questions that are inherent in every policy dispute. These questions identify the general areas where the crucial *specific* issues will be found.

1. *Is there a need for a change?* When you propose a course of action, you are asking your listeners to change their lives. But people are not easily motivated to change unless they are dissatisfied with the way their lives are now. If things are all right the way they are, why rock the boat? No new policy will be attractive unless it is presented as the solution to a felt need.

2. *Is the proposed new policy desirable?* Even if the audience is dissatisfied with the status quo, a proposal will not be appealing unless it is an overall improvement on the present situation. A plan may not be perfect, but whatever flaws it has must not make things worse than they are now.

3. *Is the proposed new policy feasible?* Many factors can stand in the way of putting an apparently desirable plan into operation. For example, if the cost is prohibitive, or the political climate makes it impossible, the plan is unworkable and an audience won't accept it.

Although stock issues identify the *general areas* where disputes may arise, they do not bring to light the *specific issues* that must be resolved in order to prove a claim. In the lottery case, for example, arguments don't clash over the question, "Is a state lottery desirable?" Instead, people ask, "Is a lottery a form of gambling?" Or, "Is gambling immoral?" But even though arguments are directed at specific issues, a speech that fails to satisfy an audience on any of the stock issues will probably fail. In fact, unless an issue in a policy dispute is essential in deciding one of the stock issue questions, it should be considered irrelevant or trivial. Later in the chapter we will show that the stock issues have an organizational value: They can be a basis for grouping the arguments in a speech.

Analyzing Claims of Fact and Value

The issues we have used as examples in this chapter illustrate the fact that in every case, the question that states an issue must be answered with a claim of fact or value. That is because policy decisions are made on the basis of fact and value judgments. But whether a speaker argues claims of fact and value for their own sakes or because they help to prove a policy claim, they have issues of their own. Even though these claims express two very different kinds of judgments, the same method is used to find the issues in both of them.

A claim of fact or value has two elements: first, *a subject term,* which refers to something or someone; and second, a *judgment term,* which in a word, phrase, or clause says something about the subject term. Any such claim asserts that the judgment term can properly be ascribed to the subject term. For example, the factual claim, "Flying saucers are real," says that the quality of reality can correctly be attributed to the objects—that they actually exist. The claim, of course, is debatable. Analyzing it will bring to light the issues that make it controversial.

The first step in analyzing a claim of fact or value is to *define the judgment term*. Analyze, for example, one of the claims in the controversy over school prayer: "Participation in the prayer will be totally voluntary." Here the subject term is "participation in the prayer" and the judgment term is "totally voluntary." A voluntary act can be defined as something done by one's own free choice—freely undertaken without force or threat. The act is totally voluntary if outside pressures are completely absent.

If this definition of the judgment term is acceptable, it will serve as a criterion for evaluating the evidence used support the claim. That is, to prove the claim, the evidence must show that participation in the prayer will have the characteristics described in the definition (in other words, will meet the criterion of free choice without pressure). If an audience is persuaded that no threats or pressure will be exerted to force students to participate, it will accept the claim.

Finding issues is not nearly as complicated as it may sound. It is made quite manageable by the fact that any issue whatever will arise from one or another of five potential sources.

THE FIVE POTENTIAL SOURCES OF ISSUES

We have called these the "potential" sources of issues because not every one of them will necessarily give rise to an issue in any particular dispute. However, whenever there is an issue, it will invariably arise from one of these five sources. Understanding the source of an issue is enormously useful in persuasion, because it makes instantly clear what kind of argument is needed to resolve the issue.

Consider an example. Many people are concerned about the amount of violence depicted on television programs. Suppose that someone were concerned enough to claim that the federal government should enact legislation requiring all television

Controversy over the effects of television violence on children has produced complex issues.   (O'Neil, Stock, Boston)

programs to be approved by a board of censors prior to broadcast. This hypothetical example will help us to explain the five sources of issues and why it is useful to understand them.

Issues over the Need for a Change

The most basic question in a policy controversy is the first stock issue: Are the problems of the status quo severe enough to warrant a change in policy? There is no sense in arguing either for or against a new course of action if people are satisfied with things as they are.

A large number of people would surely think that a plan to censor television programs prior to broadcast is a terrible idea, but before it would be evaluated in any way, a number of prior questions would arise: Do television programs portray graphic violence to a serious degree? Does television violence have a bad effect on viewers? And so on. These questions are issues, and they are relevant to this controversy. They are also related to the general question: "Is there a need for a change from present policy?" To make any progress, a speaker must find arguments and evidence that will make the audience answer "yes" to all these issues.

Issues over the Criteria

The second point at which an issue might arise is over the criteria to be used in choosing a new policy. Given a choice, no one will make a policy decision without some assurance that it is the most desirable course of action available. That applies to electing the best President, choosing the best classes, or buying the best pair of shoes.

The only way to know what is best is to have a set of *criteria* for evaluating the options. The criteria, as we have said, are found by defining the judgment term (what is meant by "the best" President, classes, shoes?). But for two reasons issues very often arise over the criteria.

The first reason is that there can be disagreement over how the judgment term of a claim is defined. No one would accept the argument that Abraham Lincoln was a great President because he (1) was more than 6 feet 3 inches tall, (2) wore a stovepipe hat, and (3) was in office during a war. Lincoln met all of these criteria, but they are a silly way to define a great President. In the case for TV censorship, it might be generally agreed that any plan that violated the First Amendment should be rejected. In other words, freedom of the press is an undebated criterion. But to say that the First Amendment doesn't protect TV stations would instantly raise the issue, "Is it reasonable to define freedom of the press in such a way that TV broadcasters are not protected under the First Amendment?"

Second, even when a criterion has been defined acceptably, it may generate an issue. For example, economy is often a factor in decisions. One can make an argument against TV censorship on the grounds that it would cost both the government and the television stations more than the respected benefits are worth. But many people would argue that in this case cost should not be a criterion. "Sure, it will take a lot of money to make this plan work, but when it comes to protecting our children, money is no object." The issue is then a disagreement over whether a particular criterion should be used at all. Issues over the criteria must be resolved by arguments that will justify the controversial criteria or the debated definitions.

Issues over the Relative Importance of the Criteria

Even when there is agreement on what criteria should be used in making a judgment, and even when the criteria are defined acceptably, an issue may arise over the relative significance of the criteria—that is, what rank order of importance they should be assigned.

An issue of this kind could easily arise in the debate over how to control TV violence. Both economy and freedom of the press might be accepted by everyone as reasonable criteria, that is, desirable goals that any approved plan would have to achieve. And yet, an issue might well spring up over which of them is the more important. Is it better to adopt a plan that costs more to operate but gives wider freedom to broadcasters, or should a plan be chosen that costs significantly less even though it limits to a degree the broadcasters' control over the materials they present? The question is clearly one of relative values and can be resolved only by value appeals. These are a central concern of Chapter 10.

Issues over Whether the Criteria Have Been Met

A fourth potential source of issues can be found in arguments over the application of the criteria to the evidence. The question then becomes, "Does the evidence show that the subject term meets all the criteria?"

Look again at the question of how to reduce the amount of violence shown on TV. Someone might argue that even though a board of censors large enough to preview all of the television programs that habitually contain violence would cost $10 million a year, it would be well worth the price. The claim would be, in other words, that the cost did meet the criterion of economy. If opponents argued that a cost of $10 million could in no way be called economical, there would be a clear issue: "Does a price tag of $10 million meet our criterion of economy?"

Issues over the Evidence

Although it is true that every argument must be based on some kind of evidence, it is also true that disagreements over the evidence can give rise to important issues. For example, an opponent of the plan to censor programs could argue, "I would agree that a price tag of $10 million would not be unreasonable given the ambitious nature of this plan and the cost of any government operation today. But I have made a careful cost analysis of the proposal, and I'm convinced that it would cost not less than $100 million a year—10 times what you claim." The issue is, "Is the evidence correct?"

Issues, then, can arise from five sources. Knowing the source of an issue is an important prelude to effective argument because it tells you what your arguments need to do. If you don't know what the source of the issue is, you can't know what kind of argument is needed. For example, an issue over criteria is obviously an issue over values and must be answered by the development of acceptable goals for a proposed policy. It won't do you a bit of good to prove that your plan is the most economical way to control TV violence if your audience believes that freedom is the most relevant value criterion.

In the same sense, issues over evidence can be answered only by showing the accuracy of your evidence. Suppose you argue that the cost of your proposed censorship program would be $10 million. Even if the audience agreed in principle to all that you said about the benefits of censorship, they might still reject your claim if they thought your evidence was wrong and that the true cost would be substantially greater than you said.

HOW ISSUES ARE USED

By the time you complete your analysis, you will have made several long strides toward successful persuasion: You will know what the issues are and what their sources are, and you will know what you need to argue and what you don't. The issues are then helpful in several different ways in organizing the speech.

To Indicate Lines of Argument

Finding the issues in a claim lays the groundwork for argumentation and shows the direction the line of argument must follow. To resolve doubt and opposition in an audience, the arguments that are most developed and best supported must be the ones that deal with the issues. A candidate for student council treasurer may be an honest, intelligent, and trusted member of the college community. But if the other students doubt her ability to keep good records, that doubt is the issue she needs to attack.

Stressing the importance of issues to this degree raises some questions: Do you always talk about issues? Do you ever use ideas that aren't disputed? In one sense you do always talk about issues, but in doing so you can use noncontroversial ideas in a very helpful way: Analyzing a claim identifies waived matter (areas of agreement) as well as points in dispute. Audience analysis discloses the beliefs and values of the listeners. The waived matter, along with any shared beliefs and values (see Chapter 10), serve as a common ground between you and the audience. They are the basis for justifying your position on the issues.

When you support a candidate for student council treasurer, the other students share your values for trustworthiness and honesty. They also believe that the person elected should have good ideas about student government. If, during the campaign, your candidate is acknowledged to be this sort of person, that is waived matter. Her supporters can use it to balance against her lack of training in accounting, which many students believe a treasurer needs.

But waived matter should not be used to hide or avoid an issue. The issue is, "Is it important that the student council treasurer have training in accounting?" And it must be resolved. But by giving a more complete picture of the contest, arguments built on waived matter help to establish the probability that as treasurer she would do the best job, *even though her opponent is an accounting major*. In this sense, even noncontroversial waived matter is used *to support the issues*.

To Determine Emphasis

Speaking time is always limited. You can use it more efficiently if you know what you need to emphasize in order to achieve the greatest effect.

Look back at the list of issues in the controversy over the school prayer amendment. Some of them would be more important to one audience than to another. For instance, some people are likely to be more sharply divided over the matter of peer pressure than over constitutional arguments about the interpretation of the First Amendment; others would be more concerned with freedom of religion than with a satisfactory prayer formula. The final decision about which issues to emphasize will be determined by analyzing the audience. But audience analysis will be most helpful if the issues have been clearly identified and related to one another.

To Group the Arguments

Issue analysis is an aid to organization because it shows how to group the arguments in some reasonable manner. Earlier in the chapter we said that stock issues can be used in a policy speech as a basis for grouping related arguments. Every argument is intended to resolve some specific issue. But if an issue is important (that is, neither trivial nor irrelevant), it will be related to one of the three stock issues. Arguments that show the severity of a problem, or the inadequacy of the present system to cope with it, all support the need for a change. They should be grouped together. Arguments related to the other two stock issues are grouped in the same way. Grouping the arguments this way offers a number of valuable benefits:

1. It gives your speaking a quality of thoroughness.
2. It avoids giving the impression that you have a loose collection of scattered arguments.
3. It creates the impression that you have blocks of arguments and evidence, first in one area and then in another.
4. It makes transitions easier, because arguments addressed to similar issues are presented near one another.
5. It adds to your credibility as a person with a clear understanding of the subject.

SUMMARY

Analyzing a claim brings to light the issues—the potential points of disagreement between speaker and audience. The issues are phrased as yes-or-no questions that identify the point over which opposing arguments clash.

Issues in policy claims are drawn from directly opposed arguments. The number of issues to be argued is reduced by eliminating waived matter, combining issues that overlap, and eliminating those that seem trivial or irrelevant.

Three "stock" issues are inherent in every disputed policy claim: (1) Is there a need for a change? (2) Is the proposed change desirable? (3) Is the proposed change feasible? The stock issues do not disclose the specific issues in any particular case, but they are valuable in two ways: They help to classify the specific issues, and they are an aid in organizing a persuasive speech.

To find the issues in claims of fact or value, define the judgment term in the claim. This definition is used as a criterion for determining whether the available evidence will justify the claim.

Every issue arises from one or another of five potential sources: (1) a dispute over the need for a change, (2) a dispute over what criteria are relevant, (3) a dispute over the relative importance of criteria, (4) a dispute over whether the criteria have been met, and (5) a dispute over the evidence. Knowing the source of an issue helps to clarify what an argument must do in order to resolve the issue.

Issues help to identify the lines of argument that will be needed to justify a claim. The relative importance of the issues suggests the most efficient way to use speaking time.

NOTES

1. A transcript of the debate on the floor of the Senate may be found in the *Congressional Record,* March 5–20, 1984. The May 1984 issue of the *Congressional Digest* contains a very useful and informative discussion of the controversy, its history, the relevant court decisions, and congressional actions on the matter.
2. In developing this example, we are not trying to make a complete analysis of all the arguments and all the issues in the debate. Our only purpose is to make the method of analysis clear.

EXERCISES

In 1984 the voters of California were asked to determine whether the state constitution should be amended to permit a state lottery which would provide "that 50% [of the profit] be returned for prizes, no more than 16% be used for expenses, and at least 34% be used for public education." Following are the statements made for and against Proposition 37 in the *California Ballot Pamphlet: 1984 General Election,* compiled by March Fong Eu, Secretary of State.

1. Identify the major arguments on each side.
2. Identify the issues they make.
3. Identify the most important stock issues.
4. Identify the most important source(s) of issues.

Argument in Favor of Proposition 37

The California State Lottery will provide hundreds of millions of additional dollars for public education without raising taxes a penny!

Proposition 37 guarantees by law that lottery revenue must supplement regular educational funding.

Local control is assured. No state bureaucrat can tell local school boards how to spend the money, except that it must be spent for educational purposes—not for real estate, building construction or research.

Lottery revenue goes directly into a special fund to benefit education, bypassing the legislature, Governor and bureaucracy.

The State Controller sends lottery revenue directly to local school boards and the governing boards of community colleges, the California State University system and the University of California.

First-year ticket sales are estimated at $1.7 billion, divided as follows:

A total of 680 million—40 percent—could go to public education. Education receives a minimum of 34 percent, plus all unredeemed prize money and anticipated operating savings.

$850 million—50 percent—will go for prizes that will be divided among millions of winners. And all those prizewinners will spend millions in California, meaning additional jobs for our residents and business for our employers.

$85 million will be paid to retailers as commissions for the sale of lottery tickets, also benefiting California's economy.

Proposition 37 guarantees the lottery will be run honestly and controlled tightly. All money received and prizes paid will be carefully accounted for on a daily basis, checked and rechecked by the most modern methods, and be subject to strict state and outside audits.

Anyone employed by the lottery, supplying goods or services or selling tickets will be thoroughly investigated after mandatory full disclosure.

Coupled with other requirements that are tougher than any in the nation, Proposition 37 assures that the California Lottery will continue the perfect record established by the other 17 state lotteries, of total freedom from organized crime infiltration. It also adds a new constitutional prohibition against casino gambling.

Lotteries are fun—and voluntary. There are many lottery games; some have instant winners, others have periodic drawings. The Lottery Commission has the flexibility to conduct a variety of lottery games using any technology, including traditional tickets, on-line computers, and instant game video terminals (which can't dispense cash or have fruit symbols like a slot machine).

In typical games, there can be several million winners—with prizes ranging from $2 upward to many million.

The games will be operated only through established retail outlets, such as supermarkets, convenience stores and liquor stores.

Lotteries are played predominantly by middle-income people. Numerous studies disprove claims that the poor buy more than their proportion of tickets; actually, they buy less! And no tickets may be sold, or prizes awarded, to anyone under 18.

State lotteries have been in existence for over 20 years. They now operate in 17 states (including Washington, Colorado and Arizona) which comprise nearly half of the country's population. Their unparalleled success dispels the unsupported criticisms which may occasionally appear.

The lottery won't solve all of education's financial problems. But it will be a big help!

Argument Against Proposition 37

Proposition 37 will open up California to a statewide lottery scheme.

All Californians who want the best for our state should vote no.

"You're seven times more likely to be killed by lightning than to win a million in the state lottery," according to a *Harper's* magazine article last year. Proposition 37 provides that only 50 cents for every dollar bet will return to the few lucky bettors in winnings.

It is a new and expensive tax. It will cost more than ten times what other taxes cost to collect. For every dollar in state revenue that Proposition 37 would raise, nearly 50 cents would end up in the hands of its promoters.

Who are its promoters?

The lottery's chief financial backer has been Scientific Games, a subsidiary of the East Coast-based Bally Corporation, the nation's leading slot machine manufacturer. For the lottery's campaign purposes, its backers and promoters are masking themselves as "Californians for Better Education." They want you to believe that Proposition 37's dedication of receipts to education will be a major boost for schools.

You should know that, assuming the rosiest predictions of its promoters, the lottery will add no more than around 5 percent for the present educational budget in the entire state in its first year. In successive years, just as now, increased educational funding will continue to be the responsibility of the Legislature and the Governor.

Other states have found that lotteries are not a stable, long-term funding source for education. This is why leading groups who care about education, like the PTA, oppose this measure.

Here are other reasons why you should vote No on Proposition 37:

Experience in other states shows that lotteries breed more crime problems for communities. Illegal numbers operations piggyback on state lotteries because these illegal operations can offer credit, tax secrecy and better odds.

A lottery has been described as a regressive tax. Studies indicate that, while lottery betting is not limited to any economic class, there is no structure to achieve equity between different levels of income as there is with the progressive income tax.

Lottery sales outlets will be located at thousands of bars, convenience stores and locations around the state. Anyone 18 years of age or older will be allowed to purchase tickets. Such activity can hardly benefit our communities.

Proposition 37 is not the solution to education funding. Neither schools nor the public will get rich from this scheme. Its promoters are the only ones who have a sure thing. They'll be enriched and the public will pay.

Republicans, Democrats, civic leaders and responsible community leaders: Appeal to your common sense and urge a no vote on Proposition 37.

7

Analyzing the Audience

I. The nature of audiences
  A. Audiences are complex
  B. Audiences vary in knowledge
  C. Audiences vary in cohesiveness
    1. Interests
    2. Central tendency
    3. Salience
  D. Audiences vary in degree of adherence to claims
    1. Favorable audiences
    2. Opposed audiences
    3. Undecided audiences
    4. Uninterested audiences
II. Beliefs and values influencing audience response
  A. Defining beliefs and values
  B. Beliefs and values about the subject
  C. Beliefs about the speaker
  D. Beliefs about the occasion
  E. Beliefs about itself
III. The composition of audiences
  A. Sex
  B. Age
  C. Economic position
  D. Social background
  E. Group membership
IV. Applying audience analysis
  A. Audience analysis in speech preparation
    1. Amount of material

2. Kind of material
3. Claims you need to prove
4. Speech organization
5. Selecting appropriate beliefs and values
6. Credibility
7. Language
8. Delivery
   B. Audience analysis during the speech
   C. Audience analysis after the speech

The communication transaction we call a speech is a shared venture between you and your audience. When you prepare for the cooperative give and take entailed in such an undertaking, you meet with this kind of problem: "I have a proposal to present and this audience has needs. How can I align these two facts in such a way as to maximize the outcome for them and for me?" The first step in solving the problem is to focus on your listeners. A number of factors will affect how they are likely to respond to the subject of the speech and to your purpose in giving it. In this chapter we will examine these factors.

THE NATURE OF AUDIENCES

In the broadest sense, an audience is any collection of people in a communication situation. But a communication situation can be anything from a Solemn Mass at the Vatican to a living room conversation after dinner or a group of people listening to a street-corner evangelist.

In a more precise sense, however, an audience is not just any collection of people. The fact that they have met suggests that they have something in common. As an audience, they interact with and influence one another and the speaker. The best way to understand this interaction is to examine four factors that help to determine how an audience will respond to a subject: complexity, knowledge, cohesiveness, and adherence.

Audiences Are Complex

Suppose a friend invites you to see a travel film being shown by a youth group at his church and then you discover that the film is intended to proselytize for the religion. Your reaction will be influenced not only by the "truth" or "usefulness" of what you hear, but also by your perception of your role on that occasion.

But you are only one member of the group. In an audience, the added presence of every other person increases the degree of complexity. Each one may have a different reaction to the information, a different judgment about the claims and merits of the film, and different interpretations about what role to play in the situation.

Audiences Vary in Knowledge

An audience's knowledge of the subject will influence its reception of a speech. Audiences with limited knowledge of a complex subject will quickly become irritated by too many words they don't know and concepts they are mistakenly assumed to understand. Equally disturbing is a speaker who assumes that the audience doesn't understand concepts or processes when indeed it does.

The problem is compounded by the fact that not only do audiences differ from one another in their knowledge of subjects, but individuals within any given audience will differ as well. In your classroom audience there are skiers and nonskiers, tennis players and non-tennis players, the mathematically sophisticated and the mathematically naive, those who have been to Europe and those who have not. The clear implication is that an audience either cannot or will not give you the response you want unless you adapt your speech to the level of its knowledge of the subject.

Audiences Vary in Cohesiveness

Some groups have very specific reasons for meeting, and the members share very definite beliefs and values. Other groups are not significantly united. Consider the difference between a church congregation and the crowd at a shopping center. Both groups have reasons for being where they are, but the former is truly an audience because its members have something in common that makes it cohesive.

However, degrees of cohesiveness differ. The congregation may be quite cohesive in church but a lot less so when they invite two candidates for mayor to debate the issues of the campaign at an open forum. People who join the Kiwanis, Rotary, or Lions clubs solely for business reasons or who go to church "for the children" don't add to the cohesiveness of the group. Some people are even hostile to a group in which they find themselves. Perhaps you have been disgruntled at having to sit through a required course that you would have been happy to forego.

One way you can get an idea of the degree of cohesiveness in an audience is to put it somewhere along a continuum between homogeniety (similarity of individuals) and heterogeneity (dissimilarity of individuals). Ask yourself, for example, where on the continuum you would put a typical college speech class. Here is a group of people who come from a variety of social and ethnic backgrounds and different economic levels. They represent a number of religions, have different academic majors, and cover a broad spectrum of political preferences. There may be little agreement among them on how to handle crime, whether abortion should be subsidized for the poor, whether tighter restrictions should be placed on strip mining, or whether the President of the United States is doing a good job.

The members of this group, no matter how diverse they may be, also have much in common. By and large they are young, have similar kinds of ambitions, have had many comparable experiences, have taken several subjects in common, and have either elected or been required to take the class they are in.

You can make a very good estimate of the degree of cohesiveness in an audience by examining its interests, its central tendency, and the particular beliefs that are salient for it.

Interests   Some groups have obvious interests. People join the Ski Club because they like skiing, the Photography Club because they are interested in photography, a church because of a preference for that religion. All audiences have interests, even though they may not be specific: the PTA has education, the Chamber of Commerce has business, university students have parking problems. When the subject of your speech appeals to some strong interest of the audience, you greatly improve the likelihood that it will respond favorably to what you say.

Central Tendency   The very fact that people meet as an audience shows that they have (even if it is only on that occasion) some mutual interest or some common problem to solve: a lack of information, a desire to be amused, a need for advice. Whatever the interest is, it identifies a central tendency. Think of this as any set of common denominators that gives the audience a collective "momentum" toward some goal. The goal is unspecified until your speech puts it into focus.

But this momentum doesn't automatically move everyone in the audience in the direction you want because, no matter how carefully you tailor a speech to fit your analysis of the audience, you can expect that someone will disagree with you. What you seek, therefore, is maximum approval and minimum disapproval. You cannot, in one speech, respond to all the possible attitudes an audience may have. Design your speech to appeal to the majority of the group. What Abraham Lincoln said about fooling all of the people all of the time can be applied to pleasing them just as well.

Salience   The central tendency of the audience gives you a *general* target at which to aim. But even more important are its salient beliefs—those *specific* beliefs that are most immediately relevant for the audience. If you want to convince your listeners that a certain candidate should be elected but they believe he is corrupt, that belief will carry more weight than the hard work you can show he does.

No matter how strongly a belief is held, if it does not apply at the moment, it will have no effect. Religious beliefs, for example, are not always salient in discussions of politics, music, or sports. To be salient, a belief must not only be important to the listener, it must also be considered relevant in the immediate communication situation.

Audiences Vary in Degree of Adherence to Claims

Just as you can place the cohesiveness of an audience along a continuum between homogeneity and heterogeneity, you can also put it on a continuum between the acceptance and the rejection of a proposal. Between these extremes, audiences tend to fall into four general classes: favorable, opposed, undecided, and uninterested.

Favorable Audiences   Favorable audiences are probably the most prevalent. It is ironic that when you set out to persuade someone to your point of view or to give information about some idea or process, you are most likely to find a group of people who know what you're talking about and agree with you. People don't usually go to hear someone with whom they disagree. They also tend to read authors, watch TV programs, and see films with which they already identify. Even so, when you speak to a favorable audience, you can reinforce their beliefs, give them new arguments they can use in talking to others, and inoculate them against counterpersuasion.

Opposed Audiences   It is difficult to deal with an opposed audience, because people who disagree with you listen selectively. They will "not hear" some things you say, and they will distort others. Some audiences will see your proposal to regulate natural gas rates as socialistic or communistic. Some will see your appeal for tolerance of your religion as a bigoted rejection of other points of view. Some will see your support for an end to government subsidies for agriculture as an attempt to destroy farmers. The strength or severity of opposition in the audience is also important for you to know. "How involved are these people? How vital is the subject to them? How vigorous and active is their opposition?"

Undecided Audiences   An undecided audience is frequently an uninterested audience. Most people make up their minds on subjects of even small concern. Their support or opposition may be bland, but they have made a decision. The idealized "independent" who makes no decision until all the arguments and evidence have been examined and who is open to arguments from both sides is exactly that: idealized. This is a rare breed of cat, simply because people don't like to live with indecision. It can be quite discomforting. When people are truly undecided about a subject of concern, they are most susceptible to change and are, therefore, the most likely candidates for persuasion. With undecided audiences, therefore, you have a good chance of immediate success.

Uninterested Audiences   Uninterested audiences are perhaps the most frustrating, and the difficulties of dealing with them are great enough that you will want to know your problem in advance rather than stumbling on it unaware. The solution lies in selecting interesting supporting materials and language, and in finding areas of audience interest that can be identified with your proposal.

BELIEFS AND VALUES INFLUENCING AUDIENCE RESPONSE

What we have said so far about the ways in which both audiences and individual listeners vary has to do mainly with the levels of audience *interest* in the subject. Now we want to examine more specifically the beliefs and values that influence audience *decisions* about speech claims.

Defining Beliefs and Values

Human behavior is determined largely by the beliefs and values that people hold. It is important, therefore, to understand what they are, how they influence an audience's views of the world, and how you can use them to make you and your speech claims believable.

A *belief* can be understood as "any simple proposition, conscious or unconscious, inferred from what a person says or does, capable of being preceded by the phrase, 'I believe. . . .' "[1] What follows the phrase, "I believe," is a claim of fact, value, or policy.

Beliefs are virtually infinite in number. You believe that the world is round, the Rockies are high, it is a mile from home to the city hall, candy is made with sugar, and so forth. You may also believe that the St. Louis Cardinals are the best baseball team, America is a great country, swimming is fun, and the Toyota is the most economical car. Likewise, you might believe that we should ban arms sales to foreign countries, join a church, buy a Buick, and so forth.

Values, on the other hand, are "abstract ideals, positive or negative, not tied to any specific attitude, object, or situation, representing a person's beliefs about ideal modes of conduct and ideal terminal goals."[2] Your values constitute broad bases for your behavior; you may value hard work, truthfulness, cleanliness, love, strength, or all of them. Values are general conceptions of what individuals and a society or culture regards as good or bad.

Beliefs and values function together in value systems. People do not live their lives by a single value or a single set of beliefs. Someone may judge freedom to be the most important value. But it is unlikely to be his or her *only* value. Others, such as

SOCIAL VALUES CONSIDERED VERY IMPORTANT IN A NATIONAL SURVEY[5]

Good family life	82%
Good physical health	81
Self-respect	79
Happiness-satisfaction	77
Freedom of choice	73
Living up to potential	71
Interesting job	69
Sense of accomplishment	63
Following God's will	61
Having many friends	54
Helping needy people	54
Helping better America	51
Exciting, stimulating life	51
Follow strict moral code	47
Active in church or synagogue	40
Nice home, car, etc.	39
High income	37
Enough leisure time	36
Social recognition	22

family, financial security, health, and self-respect, are sure to be important as well, and associated with these values are countless beliefs consistent with them.[3] You can identify your claim with these other beliefs and values of your listeners as well as with those that are most salient.

In any value system there are far more beliefs than there are values. "An adult," says Milton Rokeach, "probably has tens or hundreds of thousands of beliefs . . ., but only dozens of values."[4] Thus it is most practical for you to base your discussion on audience values. It would be impossible to catalog all the beliefs of even one individual, and yet you can discover the most salient beliefs and the few relevant values of an entire audience in the particular speaking situation. Your speech should utilize the most relevant value-belief system.

A Gallup poll taken in 1982 investigated the relative importance of a number of social values. (See the table on page 74.) Although the list does not constitute a complete catalog, it does give you an indication of the kinds of values that are important in contemporary American society.

Four areas of analysis will help you to assess an audience. You want to know what beliefs and values they have about your subject, about you the speaker, about the occasion, and about themselves.

Beliefs and Values About the Subject

Generally, you have considerable leeway in deciding what to say. If you want to tell your classmates how an internal combustion engine works or why a President should be elected for a single six-year term, most people will listen even though they aren't much interested in engines or they disagree with you about the Presidency. The internal combustion engine may be boring to them. "I'm no engineer," someone will think. "Why should I care?" But the same person may take pride in his or her car. To take advantage of that fact you might say, "Knowing how the engine works will help you to enjoy your car better, know when it has problems, and how to save money on repairs."

The subject, however, is yours. It's what you want to talk about, and you shouldn't reject it because of an audience attitude. You don't have to find a subject your audience is vitally interested in or agrees with. Instead, knowing what beliefs and values the audience is likely to associate with the subject can help you adapt your speech to the audience for greater interest and effect.

Beliefs About the Speaker

Sometimes it's really tough to make an adequate analysis of the beliefs an audience has about you. Scottish poet Robert Burns put it neatly:

> O wad some Pow'r the giftee gie us
> to see oursels as others see us!
> It wad frae monie a blunder free us
> And foolish notion. . . .

One natural but erroneous assumption is that others see you as you see yourself. The fact is that audiences use pretty much the same stereotype system to classify speakers as speakers use to sort out audiences. To an audience, speakers are engineering majors, football players, professors, or what have you. Nonetheless, you want to know as much as you can about what an audience thinks of you, no matter how erroneous its view may be.

An important element of what makes you believable is your reputation with the audience. You can better enhance your credibility during the speech (see Chapter 11) if you know the audience's opinion of you before you begin.

Beliefs About the Occasion

The way you handle a speech subject is strongly influenced by the way the audience perceives the speech occasion. If the occasion has some special meaning for the listeners, you can build interest by identifying your subject with it. Holiday speeches invariably do this. The speaker at a Labor Day meeting may talk about world affairs, but she will link the subject to the aspirations of workers. At religious meetings, people expect certain values to emerge; even if you don't share those values, you still have to recognize that they are important to the audience. Other occasions may not demand the same degree of adaptation. For instance, a sermon requires more adaptation than a speech at a church picnic.

Beliefs About Itself

What listeners think about themselves affects how they respond to a speech, because their conception of their role in the situation helps to polarize the group. Consider two men sitting side by side at a lodge meeting. Although one is a Democrat and the other a Republican, on this occasion they think of themselves as lodge members. For the present, they submerge their political differences and think of themselves as "brothers." Although their religious convictions, political loyalties, and economic stations are dormant for the time, they are still factors. You can arouse these associations to your own advantage or disadvantage.

Beliefs about self will also be related directly to beliefs about a message and about the speaker. A political science professor stops on campus to chat with the lead cellist of the university symphony; they discuss music. What the student believes and values about himself on this occasion is considerably different from his attitude toward self when comparative government is being discussed in the classroom.

Speakers who offer affront to the views of others do so at their own risk. An extraordinary instance of insensitivity was very much in the news in 1983. It was a part of what cost Secretary of Interior James Watt his job. In a misguided effort to show how free of bias he was, the Secretary seemed to forget that minority-group members, women, and the handicapped resent being identified by their group status rather than their qualifications for the job. He gave this description of a committee he had appointed: "We have every kind of mix you can have. I have a black, I have a woman, two Jews and a cripple."[6]

THE COMPOSITION OF AUDIENCES

The complexity of audiences can make analysis seem a discouraging task. The job will be easier if you understand five demographic factors that serve as primary indicators of how an audience is likely to respond to a particular claim: sex, age, economic position, social background, and group membership.

Sex

Recent years have seen great changes in our assumptions about the differences in values between men and women. The feminist movement has made us aware that men and women, particularly of the educated, upper middle class, are much more similar than we previously thought in their beliefs and values respecting professions, political activities, social action, and the like. Any male student speaker today who characterizes his women classmates as husband-hunters and sees their potential essentially as housewives is bound to get a real argument. Yet most middle-class, middle-aged men and women still see real differences between the sexes in self-image and in role.

In any event, as we have said, the self-image of an audience is salient. If you are addressing a group of women who consider themselves liberated, the beliefs and values salient for them will differ from those of the average male and from those of many other women. By the same token, anyone who wants to convince others of the values of liberation would best consider the sex of the audience and its self-image.

Age

Young people, it is said, tend to be flexible in their political and religious affiliations and are, perhaps, more idealistic. As they grow older, they tend to become concerned about the practical operation of ideas and to develop more fixed attitudes toward religious and political affiliations. Although these generalizations do not apply to everyone, they do provide a starting point for more specific analysis.

In the late 1960s and early 1970s, young people seemed to be more socially concerned than their parents, even radical. Some observers predicted a broad change in the nation's values because of the controversy over racism and the war in Vietnam. The college students of the 1980s seem to be oriented more toward practical success and financial security.[7] Traditional interests in athletics and in the "Greeks" have revived. But a quiet kind of activism can still be found in the disarmament movement, rape crisis centers, peer counseling, and opposition to nuclear power. In addition, active concern for religion has increased among young people in the last 15 years. The students in your audience may be more conservative than they used to be, but they can still be motivated by idealism.

Some claims will quickly trigger responses based on age. College men have loudly denounced a proposal to deny federal grants to students who have not registered for the draft. Older groups seem generally more supportive of the plan. Why? Because the proposal affects the younger people directly and inconveniently. The response of the older people reflects the changing perceptions of responsibility that normally come with age. This is not to say that either group is right or wrong. It says that they are different. And the differences are important to speakers.

Economic Position

It will come as no surprise that the greater one's wealth, the more conservative one's economic doctrine tends to be. Proposals that invoke an increase in taxes (larger welfare payments, more parks, better pay for teachers) are generally less acceptable to those who pay the largest share of the taxes.

Statistically, more well-to-do people are Republicans and fewer affluent people are Democrats. But don't push the generalization too far, because there are, of course, poor Republicans and wealthy Democrats. Jewish voters are cited as an obvious

Knowing the affiliation of an audience allows a speaker a clear indication of how the audience will probably respond. (Mercado, Jeroboam)

exception to rules of thumb about economic factors. Despite their higher average income among ethnic groups, they tend to support the Democratic party and high-tax social programs.

Past economic experience is often more important than present economic position. People who grew up in poverty, in the ghetto, the barrio, or a poor white neighborhood, often respond as if they were still poor even though they are now in a higher economic class.

Yet it is easy to give too much significance to economic position. "Economic determinists" consider all reactions to be economically motivated, but this is only one of a number of influential factors.

Social Background

The past conditions of people's lives—the way they grew up and the kinds of beliefs and values their parents had—make up the social background of an audience and have a significant effect on how it will react to your ideas. You can easily imagine that the views of one group might differ from the views of any other. Does an audience meet as a group of Polish-Americans? Of Nisei? Of blacks? Of Southerners? Of Methodists? Of Sons or Daughters of the American Revolution? Most people find it impossible to escape their background completely. Thus it may be more important that a listener is a Chicano, a white Anglo-Saxon Protestant, or a Jew than that this one is a woman or that one is 20 years old.

Group Membership

The sex, age, and economic-social background of an audience tells you much about it, but knowing the affiliations of its members will pinpoint your analysis more sharply. The fact that an audience has a substantial percentage of Democrats, American Legionnaires, or members of the National Organization of Women gives you a clear indication of a number of probable responses.

People usually join groups with ideas and goals similar to their own. The group further reinforces them. The American Farm Bureau, Chambers of Commerce, or Communication Workers of America represent recognizable social and economic positions. Service clubs, such as Rotary, Kiwanis, and Lions, all have projects that are important to them. Religious organizations—B'nai B'rith, the Knights of Columbus, the Women's Club of the First Baptist Church—have distinctive approaches not only to questions of faith and morals but to many other subjects as well. Political clubs have their obvious partisan views.

Many groups compose "mission statements" that specify their ideals and goals, and these are not difficult to find. Therefore, if you can identify the group memberships of an audience, you can tell much about its beliefs and values and associate your subject with them.

APPLYING AUDIENCE ANALYSIS

It is impossible for you to say all there is to say on any subject. What you do say will be determined by your audience analysis. It influences the way you adapt to the audience not only in preparing the speech but during and after the speech as well.

Audience Analysis in Speech Preparation

The use you make of your audience analysis in preparing a speech is its most important application. During this period you have time to adapt your speech in all the facets of preparation: selecting appropriate values and methods of building credibility, and choosing the language and the style of delivery.

Amount of Material   The amount of material needed to clarify or prove a specific point varies in relation to audience need. In a speech to inform, for example, you will need few specific details if you think the audience will quickly understand a given point. In persuasion, the keynote speaker at a political convention judges the amount of evidence needed to support arguments from knowing that the members of the convention will already agree with virtually all of the points to be made. When student body funds are allocated to various campus activities, a lack of student interest in music may motivate the members of the student council to cut the budget for the opera program. A speaker who is asking for more money for the opera program may need to give a great deal of evidence to the group.

Kind of Material   When you collect material for a speech, you will find more than you can use. Your selection from the pool of information you have gathered is made in light of your audience analysis. You will choose quotations not only because they say exactly what you want to say but also because the authorities you quote are respected by your audience. You will draw illustrations from the experiences that will make the most sense to your immediate audience. In a talk on the peaceful uses of atomic energy, you will need a different and simpler kind of material for students who have never had a physics course than would be the case if they had some knowledge of the subject.

Claims You Need to Prove   Not all of the claims you make will have to be proved, because the audience will accept some of them without question. Others are at issue. If you argue that federal licensing of all firearms should be required, among your subclaims you would probably include these two: "Gun-related crimes are a serious problem," and "Federal licensing of guns is constitutional." The first of these two claims is widely accepted and need not be argued at length. The constitutional claim is clearly controversial and needs support.

It is also true that controversial claims need different amounts of proof. For instance, some listeners may have little interest in technical arguments about constitutionality but may be quite concerned about losing the protection they feel they get from a gun. Your analysis of the audience helps you decide what claims are controversial and what levels of proof are required.

Speech Organization   Of the many methods of organizing a speech, the one that is best suited to a particular subject and occasion depends on such factors as the audience's knowledge of the subject and the extent to which it accepts or rejects your claim. Suggestions for making the decision are discussed in more detail in Chapters 18, 19, and 20.

Selecting Appropriate Beliefs and Values   Probably the greatest utility of audience analysis is the help it gives you in deciding what beliefs and values are most likely to be salient for the audience in relation to your subject. For example, suppose you are talking to your sister about the rehabilitation and punishment of criminals. She has high humanitarian values and assumes that people are essentially good. She might very likely believe that capital punishment is unacceptable. These are the salient beliefs and values for her in this situation. If they are appropriate to what you want to say, well and good. But if they are not, you will have to bring to bear other beliefs and values that she has in order to help her see the situation as you do and to motivate her to awareness and action. Chapter 10 discusses the use of beliefs and values.

Credibility   Credibility is the degree to which an audience has confidence that you know what you are talking about and can be trusted to tell the truth. It is not something that is inherent in you; rather it is a quality ascribed to you by your listeners. Chapter 11 offers suggestions about how to increase your credibility.

Language   The kind of language you would use in speaking to a labor union local might be quite unsuited to a board meeting of corporate directors, even though the subject matter could be substantially the same. The principal difference between the two groups—as far as language is concerned, at any rate—is in the differing levels of education you would expect to find among the listeners. What we said earlier in this chapter about the differences among audiences with regard to levels of knowledge is relevant here. In Chapter 15 you will find suggestions for adapting language to various audiences.

Delivery   Like language, delivery can be too complex for an audience. Queen Victoria said of her prime minister, "Mr. Gladstone always addresses me as if I were a public meeting." The level of intensity in voice and physical action appropriate to an occasion is dependent on the audience. Your audience analysis will suggest whether to use a vigorous delivery or to be calm and relaxed. Chapter 17 offers advice on delivery.

Audience Analysis During the Speech

While you may do a lot of careful audience analysis before the speech, there are several additional steps you can try as the actual communication situation is met. When you are invited to speak at a meeting of a group you do not know, be sure to go a little early. Talk to the leader of the meeting and, if possible, some of the members. Ask them about themselves and others in the group. Check out your predictions about their beliefs and values. Look for specific references you can make to identify with this audience.

While you are giving the speech, be alert to the reactions you get. If the audience responds quickly to a claim, you will know the claim doesn't need much support. If the audience seems to be knowledgeable, you can give more complex explanations than you had planned.

To be useful, audience feedback must not be unduly colored by what you *want* it to be. That is, make sure that you don't attribute your own attitudes and feelings to the audience. It can be disastrous to assume that others understand or believe things in the same way that you do.

Audience Analysis After the Speech

Learning to be an effective speaker is not a one-time experience, it is an ongoing process. So, when you make mistakes in a speech, you can avoid them in the future. Take a few moments after a speech to remind yourself what your assumptions were about the audience. Even make a list of the main ones. Then check them against the responses you got during the speech and afterwards. In cases where you were in error, think how the error came about and decide how best to avoid it in the future.

SUMMARY

A speech is a transaction between you and your audience. For it to be successful you have to think carefully about your listeners. While an audience is a collection of people, it is also more than that. Each audience is different, and you need to consider its nature carefully. Audiences are complex. Individual members will have different interpretations of a speaking situation and their role in it. Audiences vary in knowledge, and their knowledge must be adapted to. They vary in cohesiveness depending on their interests, central tendency, and salience.

Audiences can also be differentiated by the degree of adherence they give to claims. You need to consider whether your audience is favorable, opposed, undecided, or uninterested. Each will require a different approach.

The beliefs and values of an audience are probably most important in influencing audience responses. Beliefs are simple propositions that are virtually infinite in number. Values are abstract ideas about what a person thinks is the ideal mode of behavior or terminal goal. Beliefs and values function together in systems and influence responses to speeches. It is useful to know the kinds of beliefs and values an audience has about your subject, you as a speaker, the occasion, and about itself.

It is easier to understand an audience if you look at five demographic factors: sex, age, economic position, social background, and group membership. These won't tell you everything and sometimes you can be fooled, but they will help to give you a general understanding of the group.

Your audience analysis can help you to determine the amount and kind of material you need, which claims you need to prove, your speech organization, audience values, how to enhance your credibility, what language and delivery will be appropriate. Just before the speech you can check your analysis in discussions with your hosts, and during the speech you can test your analysis by the reactions you get. Afterwards it is wise to check out your analysis to avoid future errors.

NOTES

1. Milton Rokeach, *Beliefs, Attitudes and Values* (San Francisco: Jossey Boss, 1968), p. 113.
2. Ibid., p. 124.
3. Richard D. Rieke and Malcolm O. Sillars, *Argumentation and the Decision Making Process* (Chicago: Scott Foresman, 1984), pp. 109–110.
4. Rokeach, op. cit., p. 124.
5. George Gallup, "Americans Believe Personal Goals More Vital Than Material Gain," *Salt Lake Tribune*, Jan. 28, 1982, p. A3.
6. "James Watt Strikes Again," *U.S. News and World Report*, **95** (Oct. 3, 1983), p. 10.
7. "Why It's All Quiet on the Campus Front," *U.S. News and World Report*, **94** (Jan. 31, 1984), pp. 44–47.

EXERCISES

1. Write a brief paper (no more than three double-spaced, typewritten pages) in which you explain what you need to know about one of your parents or a brother or sister before you ask a favor. You will probably find it easier to write this paper if you select a specific favor to ask. Your purpose in this paper is to make an "audience" analysis of that one person, so do not write about the techniques you would use to get the favor. For instance, what do you need to know about your father's ideas and attitudes in order to successfully ask him to let you use his car for the weekend?

2. Select any one of the five demographic factors. Also select for consideration some specific question of current news interest. How do you think the attitudes of any two groups of people within the classification (for example, men and women, teen-agers and middle-aged people, well-to-do people and poor people, blacks and Caucasians) would differ *generally* on the question? What limitations do you see in this generalization? If you believe that there are no differences on the question you have chosen, explain why you believe so.

3. Make a careful and honest assessment of yourself as an "audience" for a speaker. What do people who wish to communicate with you have to know about you?

4. Think for a moment about the following subjects and audiences. Which demographic factors are most important, and what beliefs and values will come into play in each of the nine possible combinations?

Subject	Audience
1. To inform the audience about the training of a fashion model.	A. Young black women college students from urban areas.
2. To persuade the audience to support the university football team.	B. White Protestant businessmen at least 40 years of age.
3. To persuade the audience to support an immediate reduction in federal taxes.	C. Mostly white students of both sexes at a Roman Catholic college.

Do certain factors seem less important than others? Do some factors immediately give you some clues as to how you ought to prepare your speech for maximum effectiveness? What is the audience's attitude likely to be toward you?

5. With four or five classmates, develop an analysis of the class as an audience for a speech on a specific subject selected by your instructor. Share your findings with the class. Do they agree with you? What factors did you analyze correctly? On which did you miss?

6. For one of your classroom speeches assigned by your instructor, turn in a one-page analysis of how your speech is adapted to the audience.

7. For one of your classroom speeches assigned by your instructor, turn in a one-page analysis of how you might change the speech if you were to give it to a different audience.

three

PREPARING SPEECHES

chapter 8

Types of Supporting Material

IV. Statements about facts: statistics
   A. Using statistics for clarity and interest
      1. Check the currency of the data
      2. Check the reliability of the source of the statistical data
      3. Be sure the statistics measure what they appear to measure
   B. Using statistics to prove
      1. Check the currency of the data
      2. Check the reliability of the source
      3. Be sure the statistics measure what they appear to measure
V. Opinions about facts: testimony
   A. Using testimony
   B. Evaluating testimony
      1. Is the authority competent?
      2. Is the authority trustworthy?
VI. Comparison and contrast

The meanings you and your listeners have for the words you use will never be precisely the same. Therefore, you must help your listeners understand what you say as accurately as possible. Concrete, specific, vivid details help them to visualize your ideas in terms of their own experiences and clarify your ideas for them.

All supporting materials are designed to provide meaning, but these materials are not things; they are statements about things. They carry meaning for the listener because they refer to something in the listener's experience: things, people, thoughts, ideas, beliefs, values. We speak of giving evidence to support a point. But you can't give "facts"; you make statements about facts. Gravity is a fact; the law of gravity is a statement about a fact. A definition of communism is a statement about communism. A college president's opinion on the pass/no-pass system of grading is a statement about that system.

Your purpose in using such statements is to make your listeners believe that through these supporting materials they are learning about reality.

CLARITY AND INTEREST

In choosing the supporting materials of your speech, you need to consider two qualities: clarity and interest. Your materials need to be clear so that they will convey your message. They need to be interesting so that they will be listened to. In a sense, the qualities of clarity and interest are antagonistic. Clarity increases as the listener is able to predict your meaning with greater certainty. Interest increases with novelty and change, when the situation is less predictable.

Clarity without interest will produce a speech that is dull and therefore difficult to listen to. Actuarial tables, for example, can be eminently clear, but they do not make good listening. On the other hand, there is harm in using materials that may be interesting in themselves but that add nothing necessary to clarify the ideas. A major artistic factor in all communication is striking a careful balance between what is dull but accurate and what is exciting but misleading. Try to find the point where you can strike a balance between clarity and interest, where your meaning is both interesting and clear.

Supporting materials may be classified into four categories: *Definitions* are used to clarify your meaning for words or concepts that may be unfamiliar, obscure, or different from the listeners'. *Statements about facts* are details found in the forms of examples and statistics. *Opinions about facts* occur in the form of the testimony of others. *Comparison and contrast* establish a relationship for the listener between the known and the unknown.

DEFINITION

A druggist labels a bottle of medicine so that there may be no confusion about the contents or the dosage. In a similar sense, language provides labels for ideas. The labels put on ideas, like the labels on bottles of medicine, should be recognizable, clear, and precise. But language is not always easy to use in speaking about complex or abstract ideas. "Democracy," "communism," "ecology," "feminism" are not "seen" in the same sense as "aspirin" or "vitamin C." When you use words like "aspirin" or "vitamin C," listeners recognize your simple denotative meaning, even though they may not have full insight into their chemical components. "Democracy," "truth," and "honesty," however, are abstract terms. These labels are used in a greater variety of meanings than are those of material objects. Too often listeners are confused because they do not understand the labels in the sense you use them. Consequently, an abstract, unfamiliar, or obscure term will need to be defined.

Types of Definitions

There are six kinds of definition which we will explain here: definition by classification and differentiation; by function; by example; by comparison and contrast; by figure of speech; and by usage, etymology, or history. One of these will be helpful to you, we are sure, in clarifying your meaning. Any one of them can help if it meets the requirements of a good definition by (1) indicating the sense in which you use a term and (2) bringing your meaning within the scope of your listeners' experience.

By Classification and Differentiation   The most common method of definition, the primary one your dictionary uses, is definition by classification and differentiation. The thing or idea to be defined is put into a class with which the listener is already familiar. Then, to restrict the meaning and eliminate ambiguity, the definition differentiates the thing defined from all other members of that class. For example, "Ullage [the term to be defined] is an amount of liquid [classification] required to fill up a partly empty container [differentiation]." The president of the World Bank has defined the poorest of the developing countries [the idea to be defined] as "those countries [classification] in which the per capita incomes are below $200 [differentiation]."[1]

By Function   You can define a term by explaining the use or function of what the term names. "The differential gear in an automobile divides the driving force of the engine between the two rear axles and lets the axles turn at different speeds when they have to."

Sometimes speakers will use a form of definition by function for persuasive purposes. Ronald E. Rhody, Vice President for Public Relations of Kaiser Aluminum, uses the phrase, "trial by television," to characterize what in his view is wrong with television reporting. He defines "trial by television" by its function, but for purposes of persuasion:

> "Trial by Television" is the relatively standard technique in which television production teams become the accuser, judge and jury of people and institutions with no real opportunity for the accused to get a fair hearing in the court of public opinion. Too frequently, the people in charge of those programs select story segments with their minds already made up, and proceed to choose the facts and quotes which make their case for them.[2]

Such a definition reveals clearly Mr. Rhody's opinion of television production teams, and the strength of his opinions probably makes them interesting to most people. It illustrates, moreover, that not all definitions are unbiased, and that the bias in them can be used to forward the speaker's persuasive goal.

By Example   On May 9, 1977, the Dean of the Law School of North Carolina Central University addressed the Rotary Club of Durham, North Carolina, on the subject of white-collar crime. In defining the term "white-collar crime," he gives examples to make clear what he means: "Webster defines it as a crime such 'as fraud, embezzlement, etc.' "

By Comparison and Contrast   In defining by comparison and contrast, you try to show your meaning for a term by likening it to something (comparison) and/or by differentiating it from something (contrast) with which your listeners are already familiar. In the same speech on "White-Collar Crime," Dean Harry Groves makes his meaning clear by contrasting white-collar crime with robbery and burglary:

> One characteristic that distinguishes white-collar crime from the kinds of crime most of us really fear is the absence of personal violence, the absence of physical threat. This is a very real difference in comparison say with robbery or burglary, both, like white-collar crimes, having the intent to deprive the rightful owners of their property. . . .
>
> The typical white-collar crime of embezzlement really does not compare with robbery or burglary because of the fear that the last two engender and the first does not. . . .[3]

Then, he compares the kind of embezzlement called white-collar crime with theft and shoplifting:

There are at least two other crimes with which embezzlement can, I think, be reasonably compared. . . . Ordinary theft and shoplifting compare with embezzlement because of the absence of threat or fear.[4]

By Figure of Speech   In most cases you will be concerned primarily with the clarity and precision of definitions. However, they can add interest value to what you are saying, and, as in the definition of "trial by television," they are not always solely denotative. Definition by figure of speech is one form of definition that is clearly connotative.

Carl Sandburg defined slang as "language that takes off its coat, spits on its hand and goes to work."[5] One speaker defined situation ethics this way: "Ethics, therefore, may seem to vary depending upon the situation. As Mark Twain once remarked, 'An ethical man is a Christian holding four aces.' "[6]

By Usage, Etymology, or History   A dictionary always reports the usage of a term:

showdown, *n.* 1: In poker, the play in which the hands are laid on the table face up. 2: Any action or disclosure that brings an issue to a head.

Professor Walter F. Stromer spoke on "The Mahatma and the Satyagraha: The Legacy of Gandhi," and used this definition by etymology and history to define the difficult Hindu term satyagraha:

Satyagraha comes from two Sanskrit words. Graha means "power" or "force." Sat means "truth," "essence," "being," "faithfulness," "honesty," "goodness," "keeping vows," plus many more ideas. Add to this the fact that for Gandhi, truth was tentative and relative, and you will understand why the term is not easy to define precisely. It is translated as "clinging to truth," or "soul force," or "truth force." We think of it as "nonviolent resistance." Gandhi would want us to be clear that the resistance was important because he had no intention of accepting passively whatever injustice came his way.[7]

Using Definitions

As you can see, the six kinds of definitions discussed above are quite different, although they all help to clarify the terms. Here are some general principles to consider in choosing what sort of definition to use.

A Dictionary Definition Is Not Always the Best   Beginning public speakers frequently turn to the dictionary for definitions. "Webster says . . ." is an often-repeated phrase used to introduce a definition. But remember, if you are interested in explaining how something works, a functional definition may be better. Even when a dictionary definition is appropriate, it may be more useful if you adapt it to your audience. "Intersession" is defined by one dictionary as "the time between two academic sessions or semesters." For your purposes it may be better to say that it is "the period in January between the autumn and spring semesters when the University provides a number of special short-term courses for credit." Such a definition is much more specific for your audience.

Use Terms That Are Close to the Understanding of Your Audience   Definitions that use terms the audience doesn't understand can be more confusing than no definition at all. If you have much more knowledge about your subject than your audience, you have to find terms they understand. The specialized vocabulary of any field (engineering, medicine, literary criticism, etc.) should be used ony for those who understand it.

Differentiate Biased from Unbiased Definitions   Definitions used for persuasive purposes, such as Ronald Rhody's definition of "trial by television," are not appropriate when your aim is to be informative or when your audience is likely to view the definition as unfairly biased. In short, such definitions are fine for listeners who generally agree with your point of view, but not for others.

Don't Insult Your Listeners   Frequently, you will be confronted with a difficult problem: Some of your listeners may not understand what a term means, but many will. So avoid comments such as, "I know that you don't understand this term, so let me define it for you." If your listeners do not understand the term, you scarcely need to tell them so. It is far better to put the responsibility on yourself: "To make myself clear, let me point out that by _____, I mean_____."

STATEMENTS ABOUT FACTS: EXAMPLES

Examples are the product of experience and observation, either yours or someone else's. Colorado State University is in Fort Collins. The Salinas Valley is an agricultural area in California. The Alaskan Gold Rush began in 1896. Ronald Reagan was reelected President of the United States in November 1984. All of these are statements about facts that may be used as examples to illustrate some point.

If you want to become a truly effective speaker, learn to use examples well. Think of the interesting speakers you have heard, whether on a public platform or in your own living room. Remember the many examples they used to illustrate the subjects they discussed.

Types of Examples

Examples may be real, secondary, or hypothetical, and brief or extended in length.

Real Examples   An example is a statement about an incident, person, or thing that you cite to illustrate a point. A real example is one that actually exists and is known to both you and your listener. It is real to you—you "know" it really exists from first-hand experience.

> ". . . a really great football team like, say, the Los Angeles Raiders."
>
> "When you visit a National Park—Yosemite, for instance. . . ."
>
> "A liberal politician such as Ted Kennedy. . . ."

All these are real examples because the speaker and the listener can attest to their existence. Similarly, to make his point, Lane Kirkland, President of the AFL-CIO, used examples with which his listeners were familiar, through the news at least:

> Yesterday, today and tomorrow, administrations are overtaken and driven by events outside their design, events which figure not at all in their campaigns for office.
>
> Lyndon Johnson had his Viet Nam; Richard Nixon his Watergate; Jimmy Carter his Khomeini; and Ronald Reagan should—but doubtless will not—profit by their example.[8]

Secondary Examples Because the personal knowledge that any speaker and any listener bring to the communication transaction is necessarily limited, many of the examples you will use are not drawn from your own experience. You accept them as being real on the credibility of someone else. You cannot usually testify to starvation in an African nation, brutality in a foreign jail, or the beauty of the French country-side. On all historical subjects except the most recent, you must use examples you obtain from others. Even if they are real to you, they will frequently not be to your listener. The French countryside you may have visited is made to seem more real to your listener because of your added credibility, but it is still secondary because the listener must depend on someone else for the example.

Sig Mickelson, President of Radio Free Europe, has had personal experience with the content of Soviet broadcasts to the United States, but probably you haven't. So to you his examples are secondary when he says:

> Soviet transmitters . . . are beaming 10 hours daily of short-wave broadcasts to us in English. *None of this is jammed.* And the content could hardly be described as factual and objective. An American listener—and they aren't very many—could recently hear, for instance, that the U.S. media are deliberately lying to him about life in the Soviet Union; that the United States Government has an offical policy of suppressing political dissent; that there are large numbers of political prisoners languishing in American jails; that members of the American Communist Party are arrested when they collect signatures to put their party on the ballot; that members of the United States Senate are lying and deceiving their constituents when they express concern over the Soviet military buildup (or when they vote funds for Radio Free Europe and Radio Liberty); that the Pentagon and the CIA were responsible for Legionnaire's disease in Philadelphia.[9]

Hypothetical Examples If an example describes an incident that has not actually occurred, but is yet possible, it is hypothetical. Stephen Horn, President of California State University at Long Beach, uses a hypothetical example to illustrate one of the problems with the amateur status of college athletics:

How many times have we heard the story of the coach who found the parents of some of these student athletes to be extremely sophisticated about the options available to their off-spring. Their conversation goes something like this: "Well, you know, coach, we had a visit the other day from someone from such-and-such University, and he offered. . . ." At this point you may insert whatever comes to mind: cash, cars, illegal job for parents or athlete—or any combination of the above.[10]

Extended Examples   On occasion, you will want to develop an example at somewhat greater length and in more detail than is possible in the brief form the example ordinarily takes. Such illustrations are called extended examples and may be hypothetical, real or secondary.

In the following extended example, Thomas P. Pike tells of his own experience to illustrate how serious a problem alcoholism can be in the "executive suite":

I had my first drink and got drunk when I was seventeen in 1926. I continued to drink heavily, but in a relatively controlled manner, and with serious problems until I was 27. Then, in 1936, I had the insanity to resort to morning drinking in a futile attempt to cure my king-size hangover with a bit of "the hair of the dog that bit me."

This was when I unknowingly crossed that invisible line from heavy drinking to uncontrolled drinking and became an alcoholic. Alcoholism had sneaked up on me like a thief in the night and seized me in its death grip. I became a compulsive drinker and completely lost control of how much or how long I drank once I started drinking.

The next ten years of my life were literally hell—an ugly nightmare of irrational living to drink and drinking to live. Like many alcoholics, I became a binge drinker . . . a periodic drinker, and suffered frequent blackouts. I got fired in 1937 when my lost weekends grew into lost weeks. This is now called excessive absenteeism. My employer, unlike some of you, had no enlightened employee alcoholism program. Instead of being counseled and referred to help, I was given the "old fashioned treatment" and summarily canned. It was a miracle that I didn't lose my wife, my sanity, and the new drilling company I had started after being fired.

Finally, in 1946, at the age of 37, after repeated hospitalizations and futile attempts at so-called controlled drinking, I became a hopeless alcoholic. I was bankrupt, mentally, physically, and spiritually. I had lost all my confidence and self-esteem. I loathed myself. A thousand nameless fears possessed me, and I was in a state of total demoralization and despair.

Then, the miracle happened. With the faith and loving help of my wife, Katherine, and the guidance of the late blessed Dr. John Doyle, I found a new and better way of life in the fellowship of Alcoholics Anonymous. I learned the facts and the truths about alcoholism which freed me from the bondage of booze (and believe me, this is another instance in which the truth can make you free).[11]

Using Examples for Clarity and Interest

In using examples there are some rules that you ought to remember:

1. Use extended examples only when the point to be described is an essential one. For minor points, brief examples are sufficient.
2. Use the best example you can find for the particular idea you are discussing. Unless examples are chosen carefully, the listener is thrown off the track, and after a few such instances may well give up listening.
3. Be sure that the necessary value characterizations are given with the example: The Los Angeles Raiders are not just *any* football team, they are a *great* one; while the Cottonwood High School Colts are a "typical high-school" team.
4. If necessary, use more than one short example for a specific point. A single example might enlighten part of the audience and not the rest, or may only partly enlighten the audience as a whole. A greater number and variety of examples will often clarify or prove when one example might fail and, incidentally, help to lend interest at the same time.
5. Use real examples whenever possible and give them the kind of detail that will make them seem more directly related to the listener's experience. Be specific as to time, place, and circumstance.
6. If real examples are not available, make secondary and hypothetical examples seem as real as possible.

Using Examples to Prove

When you use examples to prove a point in a speech, you not only choose illustrations for their value in achieving clarity and interest, you also select instances to meet three further criteria. If the answer to all three of the following questions is "yes," the examples may be considered acceptable.

Are the Examples Representative?   Examples must be typical, not exceptions to the rule. You may do all kinds of favors for a person, but the first time you refuse you may hear, "What kind of a friend are you? You never help me out when I need help." The person singles out what is perhaps the only atypical example in an otherwise clear pattern of behavior as the basis for an unfounded generalization. A specific instance must give a true picture of the situation it illustrates if it is to be effective as a means of proof.

Are the Examples Sufficient in Number to Give Clear Support to the Point You Are Making?   The number of instances that will be necessary is not the same in every case. One may be enough: The first sunburn you get on a cloudy day will establish the generalization that exposure to the sun is dangerous even on a cloudy day. On the other hand, it takes quite a number of baseball games to demonstrate which is the best team in the National League.

Are Negative Instances Accounted for?   You cannot get rid of negative instances, but you can put them in perspective for your listeners. You can do this in one of two ways: (1) You can show that they are not representative. Thus you might say, "Although there have been a case or two where a particular ski binding had to be replaced after one season, the vast majority of those bindings gave long-term service." (2) You can show that the negative instances aren't important. Henry A. Wallace, former Vice President, as a young man developed a strain of feed corn that had more corn to the ear than other strains. When experts complained that some of his corn had irregular rows of kernels, he said, "What's looks to a hog?"

STATEMENTS ABOUT FACTS: STATISTICS

Statistics are not just numbers. You may say, "There are 21 students in my public speaking class." That is a number, but it has no particular significance until it is shown in relation to something else—for example, that this number is greater than the 17 students per class average at your college. Statistics showing relationships among numbers are ordinarily used to compact large numbers of things, events, or people into some working relationships.

Lawrence J. Brady, Assistant Secretary of Commerce, used statistics to show how dependent the United States is on foreign sources for vital strategic materials:

> One of our major strategic weaknesses has been our dependence on the supply of critical minerals and materials which are primarily obtained from foreign sources. The potentially unstable area of Southern Africa and the untrustworthy suppliers controlling Siberia provide more than 99 percent of the world's reserves of platinum group metals; 98 percent of the world's manganese ore; 96 percent of the world's chrome; and 50 percent of the world's fluorspar, iron ore, asbestos, and uranium. Zaire and Zambia together provide 65 percent of the world's cobalt, a material for which the United States is more than 90 percent dependent on imports.[12]

Using Statistics for Clarity and Interest

When you use statistics in large numbers (roughly four or more digits), it is wise to round the numbers off. For instance, the 1980 population of New York State was 17,558,072, but if you wanted to use this in a speech, you would probably say, "In 1980 the population of New York State was a little over 17½ million." Even though 58,072 is a substantial number of people, "a little over 17½ million" is accurate enough for most purposes and much easier for the listener to remember.

After the numbers have been rounded off, they can be made still more meaningful by comparison. In 1977, President Jimmy Carter explained the energy crisis to the American people this way:

> The world now uses about 60 million barrels of oil a day, and demand increases each year about 5 percent. This means that just to stay even we need the

production of a new Texas every year, an Alaskan North Slope every nine months, or a new Saudi Arabia every three years.[13]

Percentages, fractions, and proportions all help to put the compacted examples we call statistics into a clear relationship with other facts. Statistics, then, can add clarity and interest if you round the numbers off and, by using comparison, show their relationship to other ideas.

When statistical data are used as illustrations to clarify an idea, it is important, of course, that they be accurate and meaningful as well as interesting and clear. When figures of this kind are used as evidence to support a claim, however, it is even more important that they be examined carefully.

Check the Currency of the Data   The date of compilation is one of the first things to ask about statistical information. Recency is of little concern, of course, in matters that change slowly or slightly if at all. A statement of the number of times a human heart beats per minute need not be doubted today just because the subject was studied years ago. The infant mortality rate in American hospitals does not change rapidly enough to demand a new study every day. If, however, you see a report on the number of jet fighter planes that Syria is supposed to have, you would want to know when the count was made. Air power is not static.

Check the Reliability of the Source of the Statistical Data   Completely apart from any interpretation put upon figures—the validity of any comparison between, let us say, the air power of Israel and of Syria—accurate reporting depends on the reliability of sources. You must ask: "Who made the statistical study?" "Did the information come from sources that may be intentionally misleading?"

Certain governmental agencies, such as the Bureau of Labor Statistics, are generally accepted as a source of honest reports. The Brookings Institution is a private economics research group that has earned general acceptance. But, as any television viewer can tell you, many so-called independent agencies are nothing more than sources of advertising copy.

Be Sure the Statistics Measure What They Appear to Measure   The most commonly used statistical measure is an average. You may want to know the average age of the student body, the average income of the members of a particular profession, or the average annual value of the agricultural production of Iowa or Illinois. But when you find such statistics, it is a good idea to ask how the term "average" is used. There are three kinds of averages: the mean, the median, and the mode.

The *mean* is a simple arithmetical average. To find it, add together the quantity of each item in a series and divide by the number of items. The *mode* is the figure that appears most frequently in a series. The *median* is the point above and below which half of the items fall.

According to the 1980 census, 15 of the United States have a population of 5 million or more. Here they are in order, rounded to a half-million:

California	23.5M	Michigan	9.5M
New York	17.5M	New Jersey	7.5M
Texas	14.0M	North Carolina	6.0M
Pennsylvania	12.0M	Massachusetts	6.0M
Illinois	11.5M	Indiana	5.5M
Ohio	11.0M	Georgia	5.5M
Florida	9.5M	Virginia	5.5M
		Missouri	5.0M

In this case the mean is 10.0M, a population that no state has. The median is 9.5, the figure for Florida and Michigan. The mode is 5.5, the population of Indiana, Georgia, and Virginia. Statistical measures like "average" are subject to scrutiny and interpretation. The old saying that "figures don't lie" is itself a generalization that bears investigation, although the remainder of the saying, "but liars figure," is above reproach.

OPINION ABOUT FACTS: TESTIMONY

Often the supporting material you use will contain statements by an expert on the subject. Such statements are called testimony. They are opinions about facts and depend for their strength on the credibility of the expert cited.

Patricia Roberts Harris, former Secretary of Health and Human Services, argued in September 1980 at Princeton University against the "Moral Majority," which she saw as a threat to the separation of church and state. In doing so she called on the testimony of Thomas Jefferson:

> What we need to remember is that this invasion of the political process by those purporting to act in the name of religion is neither new nor a matter for entertainment. Two hundred and one years ago, in 1779, Thomas Jefferson condemned such activity by religious leaders, saying in the preamble to a bill on religious freedom which he had introduced in the Virginia Legislature: "Our civil rights have no dependence on our religious opinions, any more than our opinions in physics and geometry; therefore, the proscribing of any citizen as unworthy of the public confidence by laying upon him an incapacity of being called to office of public trust . . . unless he profess or renounce this or that religious opinion, is depriving him injuriously of those privileges and advantages to which he has a natural right."[14]

Using Testimony

Using testimony in a speech makes it possible for you to tap the resources of generations of thought and expression. All that humankind has written and said becomes a vast reservoir from which you can draw the authoritative testimony of expert witnesses. You add clarity and interest to your attitudes and opinions with the thoughts and feelings of other people your audiences know, respect, and admire.

The privilege of using testimony in a speech is one that brings certain obligations. Honesty demands that you identify ideas and language that you have taken from someone else. This is not merely a moral injunction against plagiarism; two other considerations are involved. First, by failing to identify your source, you pass up the opportunity to add the credibility of your source to your own, and second, if a listener recognizes that the statement is not your own, it will tend to diminish your credibility as a trustworthy person.

If you are to get the maximal result from the use of testimony, you must identify the qualifications of the person you wish to quote. If, like Paticia Roberts Harris, you want to quote a well-known person such as Thomas Jefferson, then most adult audiences already know him as the author of the Declaration of Independence and third President of the United States. But what about someone not so well known? Here is an example from a speech by Jack D. Early, President of the National Agricultural Chemical Association, using Murray Weidenbaum as an authority in his speech against government regulation. Early makes a careful introduction of the testimony:

> If you can stand a frightening glimpse of the way government regulation is weighing heavily on *all* of American industry, pick up a copy of the new book called *The Future of Business Regulation* by Professor Murray Weidenbaum, Director of the Center for the Study of American Business at Washington Univer-

Testimony from people who are authorities in their fields may be used to support a speaker's position. (© Stewart, The Picture Cube)

sity in St. Louis. Professor Weidenbaum estimates that in 1979, federal government regulation—that's *federal* only—will cost business almost $5 billion in administrative costs.[15]

Putting directly quoted testimony into a speech may bring some awkward moments. To avoid these, it is generally wise not to use the words "quote" and "unquote" to identify the beginning and end of a direct quotation. Instead, identify the source of your material as thoroughly as the situation allows, and then let your voice (through pause, change in tempo, or other means) indicate which words are yours and which belong to your source.

Your use of testimony need not be in the form of a direct quotation, that is, word for word. It can be presented in your own words with an indication that the explanation or comparison has some respected person as its source. If the explanation of an authority is particularly clear, you may want to quote it *verbatim*, but, in general, putting the idea into your own words will keep it on the level of language used in your speech.

Regardless of the form, testimony is always opinion *about* facts, not fact itself. Consequently, the best use of testimony will reveal how the authorities cited arrived at their conclusions. Testimony that merely states an opinion asks listeners to accept the conclusion simply because they trust the source. It is far stronger to support this trust with the facts and reasons behind the judgment.

Evaluating Testimony

Before you decide to use a piece of testimony, you should ask yourself two questions about it:

Is the Authority Competent?   To be qualified, the persons whose opinions you use as supporting material should be speaking in an area of competence. A theologian is not usually an authority on biology. In addition to the greater potential for persuasion, it makes better sense for Lee Trevino, the professional golfer, to endorse Ram golf balls than Bridgestone tires. Look for sources whose competence will be clear to the listener. When you cite less well-known authorities, it is necessary to give the audience evidence of their competence.

Is the Authority Trustworthy?   Even a competent authority may not be considered thoroughly trustworthy. Henry Kissinger is one of the most knowledgeable persons in this country in the area of American foreign policy, but many people think he is biased on the subject. Biases, whether real or only imagined by the audience, will decrease the credibility of testimony.

COMPARISON AND CONTRAST

Comparison and *contrast* are not only used to define terms, they are also useful for the general clarification of ideas. Although they can be treated separately, they are in essence two sides of the same coin, two aspects of the same process. Comparison shows how one thing is *like* another; contrast shows how things are *unlike*. David P. Gardner, President of the University of California and Chair of the President's Commission on Excellence in Public Education, spoke about American education; he contrasted it with education in "all other industrialized societies."

> Compared with all other industrial societies, the U.S. has an extraordinarily nonselective educational system. In the United States, and virtually nowhere else until very recently, it is possible for a mildly persistent but singularly untalented student to complete high school, to attend a two-year college, and to transfer to some four-year institution and obtain a bachelor's degree. Virtually every other society places a series of checkpoints along this path so as to screen out the less able or uncommitted student. In Britain and France a series of examinations makes it unlikely that such a student would achieve a university place, and even in the unlikely event that it occurred, examinations at universities would screen out the student before graduation. In Germany, where as late as the mid-1960's only 9 percent of the relevant age group graduated from upper secondary school as compared with 75 percent in the U.S., this hypothetical student would probably not be admitted to the academic preparatory secondary school and, thus, would have no chance to go on to higher education.[16]

Walter Cronkite, arguing the right of reporters to protect their sources, compares the press with other professions:

> Critics of the press accuse reporters of trying to claim a privileged status above the rest of the citizenry. But the critics, who include many judges, and a majority of the present Supreme Court, are missing the point. We are not trying to assert *personal* privilege; we are trying to protect our ability to perform a critical social function—informing the public.
>
> There are other groups in our society which have important functions to perform, and which are granted special status, or "privileges," if you will, to perform them. Policemen, doctors, lawyers, ministers come to mind. The ordinary citizen is not allowed, in most American cities, to walk around with a gun on his hip, or prescribe drugs, or argue someone else's case before a court, or protect the confidentiality of a criminal confession. None of these "special privileges" seems to cause the courts any problem, perhaps because they rarely conflict with the "special privileges" which judges assume for themselves. But let reporters assert such privilege, and a judicial howl goes up.[17]

SUMMARY

Effective speaking is interesting and clear. Supporting materials supply clarity and interest by helping the audience visualize ideas concretely and specifically. The supporting materials used by speakers are of four types: (1) definition, (2) statements about facts—examples and statistics, (3) opinion about facts—testimony, and (4) comparison and contrast.

Definitions are necessary to clarify abstract, unfamiliar, or obscure terms. The most common method of definition, the one most used in the dictionary, is definition by classification and differentiation. In this form the thing to be defined is put in a general class and differentiated from other items in the class. You can also define by explaining the use or function of the thing being defined or by giving an example of it. Words and ideas can also be defined by using comparison and contrast or by figure of speech, usage, etymology, or history.

In defining terms you should remember that a dictionary definition is not always the best. Use terms close to your audience's understanding, differentiate biased from unbiased definitions, and don't insult your audience.

Statements about facts—examples may be *real* to you and your audience. Or they may be *secondary*—ones you have learned about without personal experience. *Hypothetical* examples are useful when a good real or secondary example is not available, and sometimes an *extended* example can be useful. Examples are used to provide clarity and interest, and they are used to prove.

Statements about facts—statistics are used to compact large numbers of examples for easier use. Numbers should be rounded off and should show a relationship to other ideas. Statistical data should be current and reliable. The measure used, such as the mean, median, or mode, should be carefully considered.

Opinions about facts—testimony provides the opinions of others to support your ideas. In using testimony you need to identify the ideas of others and sometimes clarify for your listeners who your authority is. Testimony can be paraphrased as long as you are true to the original intent. Testimony should come from an authority who is regarded by the audience as trustworthy and competent.

Comparison and contrast can each be used alone or with the other. The purpose of their use is to show how something is like and/or unlike something else.

NOTES

1. Robert S. McNamara, "The Dimensions of Poverty," *Vital Speeches of the Day*, **43** (May 15, 1977), p. 450.
2. Ronald E. Rhody, "The Conventional Wisdom Is Wrong: The Public's Right to Know," *Vital Speeches of the Day*, **49** (Nov. 1, 1982), p. 52.
3. Harry E. Groves, "White-Collar Crime," *Vital Speeches of the Day*, **43** (June 15, 1977), pp. 525–526.
4. Ibid., p. 526.
5. Quoted in *Life*, Dec. 15, 1941, p. 89.
6. Ben H. Warren, "Constant Values in a Changing World," *Vital Speeches of the Day*, **46** (Jan. 1, 1980), pp. 183–184.
7. Walter F. Stromer, "The Mahatma and the Satyagraha: The Legacy of Gandhi," *Vital Speeches of the Day*, **49** (Mar. 1, 1983), p. 301.
8. Lane Kirkland, "Free Trade Unionism and Collective Bargaining," *Vital Speeches of the Day*, **49** (Nov. 1, 1982), p. 37.
9. Sig Mickelson, "The Free Flow of Information," *Vital Speeches of the Day*, **43** (Mar. 1, 1977), p. 316.

10. Stephen Horn, "Ethics, Due Process, Diversity, and Balance," *Vital Speeches of the Day,* **43** (May 15, 1977), p. 463.
11. Thomas P. Pike, "Alcoholism in the Executive Suite," *Vital Speeches of the Day,* **46** (Jan. 1, 1980), pp. 166–167.
12. Laurence J. Brady, "The Need for New Directories in Defense of Industrial Policy," *Vital Speeches of the Day,* **49** (May 1, 1983), p. 422.
13. Jimmy Carter, "President's Proposed Energy Policy," *Vital Speeches of the Day,* **43** (May 1, 1977), p. 418.
14. Patricia Roberts Harris, "Religion and Politics: A Commitment to a Pluralistic Society," *Vital Speeches of the Day,* **45** (Nov. 1, 1980), p. 50.
15. Jack D. Early, "Agricultural Chemicals," *Vital Speeches of the Day,* **46** (Nov. 15, 1979), p. 93.
16. David P. Gardner, "Excellence and Equality of Opportunity: Education and Society," *Vital Speeches of the Day,* **49** (Jan. 1, 1983), p. 173.
17. Walter Cronkite, "Is the Free Press in America Under Attack?," *Vital Speeches of the Day,* **39** (Mar. 15, 1979), p. 332.

EXERCISES

1. Develop a one-point speech in which you support the one point with at least one instance each of three different types of supporting material.

2. From one of the other classes you are enrolled in, select a term you had never heard before. Define that term in a brief definition by classification and differentiation and by three other methods of definition. Decide which of the four methods has given the clearest explanation of the term. Decide which method was the least clear. Why do you think one method is better than the others for defining this term?

3. Make a survey of opinion among some group of students on campus. For instance, what do the men at the Sigma Chi fraternity house think about rock and roll? What generalization can you make from the statistics?

4. Develop three hypothetical examples, each of which has "the characteristics of a real example," to support a claim.

5. In one of the speeches in Appendix B, see if you can find examples of:
   a. Functional definition
   b. Extended examples
   c. Testimony
   d. Statistics
   e. Comparison and contrast

6. In one of the speeches in Appendix B, see if you can find places where the speech would be strengthened by additional supporting material. Explain in class what kind you would recommend and why.

chapter *9*

Finding Supporting Materials

To be a competent public speaker you must demonstrate to your audience that you know what you are talking about. Your competence is revealed through the kinds of supporting materials you use. Because you can't know in advance precisely what you will have to do to adapt to your audience, it is not enough to have what may seem to be adequate supporting material—you should have more than you think you will need. From a large store of examples, statistics, and testimony you can select those that best suit the audience and your subject and purpose. You will find supporting material in a variety of places. That is the subject of this chapter. We will look first at some nonpublished sources of information, then at how to use the library, and finally, at the methods of research.

USING NONPUBLISHED SOURCES

There are many reasons a good library is a valuable asset to a public speaker, and we will discuss them later in this chapter. But there are other resources that can also be useful, and will sometimes shorten your research time because they are easier to use. These include personal experience, the knowledge of experts, and information you get from radio and TV.

Personal Experience

The most obvious place to begin looking for information is in your *own personal experience*. Don't let this information go to waste. Anyone who has, for example, worked on an assembly line has absorbed countless minute details that could never come secondhand. Vivid recollection of these details can supply material that would not be found with the most meticulous research.

The greatest problem some speakers have in using personal experience is that they take it for granted. Personal experience has to be treated like any other source of information. Suppose that you want to give a speech about the Heimlich maneuver based on your own experience as a paramedic. Rather than just assume that because you know the material it will come to you as you prepare the speech, actually make notes. Think through the conditions that call for the maneuver, the steps to take, and any personal experiences that might be used as examples, and make a note of them. Then, after you look elsewhere for information about any controversy over its use or for authoritative information and diagrams on how it works, you will have a full set of notes from which to work. With such notes available you will be less likely to forget something important in preparing your outline.

Interviewing an Expert

One of the most important ways of finding information is to ask someone who knows the subject. That person need not be a stranger. You may have a friend who knows a lot about skiing, Yosemite Park, the effect of exercise, or growing corn in the Middle West. Frequently, someone in your own family can help you get information. Your mother or father may be a member of a profession or trade (such as a lawyer, stock-broker, electrician, cook) that deals with the problem you wish to discuss.

You may be surprised to discover how willing some expert, perhaps a faculty member or someone in the business community, is to grant you an *interview*. Remember, their fields of specialization are important to them, and they are usually pleased to find them of interest to others. However, you need to plan carefully and conduct the interview in such a way as to get maximum information.

Planning the Interview   Before an interview, learn as much as you can about the subject. Then ask for an appointment. Explain what information you want and why. This will permit the person you interview to think a little about the subject and your particular needs.

You also need to write out in advance eight or ten specific questions that cover all the essential areas you are interested in. Arrange them on sheets of paper with space for note taking after each question.

Make sure that you know the essential information about the person you are interviewing: name, occupation, title, important accomplishments. It may seem unnecessary even to mention these things; they seem so obvious. However, it is not uncommon for interviewers to fail to get such essential information and thus seem grossly unprepared to the person they interview.

Conducting the Interview   When you come for your appointment, be on time and be prepared to take notes. You may want to use a cassette recorder; most people won't object to it. But be sure to ask whether there is any objection. Some people are initially nervous when confronted by a recorder, but most soon forget that it is there.

Ask your questions one at a time and let your respondent answer fully. If the question doesn't get the response you expected, try rephrasing it or asking a more specific subquestion. Sometimes it helps, when one question seems unclear to the interviewee, to use other, more general questions and return to the unclear one later. Remember, even with careful preparation beforehand, it will take a while for you and the person you are interviewing to be comfortable with one another, and the initial questions are more likely to be confusing than later ones will be.

In the questioning, keep your objective in mind. You want to gain information. Don't argue with the person you interview. If you want a reaction to an opposition point of view, don't state it as your opinion (even if it is!). Say, "Some people say that offshore oil drilling is inevitably damaging to the environment. How do you respond to that argument?"

You will discover that if you prepare carefully, the questions you ask will provide you with much of the information you want. However, you will probably also discover new topics coming up. If they pertain to your subject you should pursue them with questions you didn't plan beforehand.

Don't overstay your welcome. If you asked for a half-hour of time, try to finish in that length of time. If you find yourself running out of time, look over your list of questions and turn quickly to the most important ones. One more matter: Before you leave, be sure to find out if the person objects to being quoted in the speech. Most will not, but you should respect the desire of those who do not want to be quoted. You can gracefully avoid naming your source by saying, "The vice president of a local bank told me. . . ."

After the Interview   Review your notes and your tape as soon as possible after the interview. They will be much clearer then than two or three days later. Select the material you can use and organize it along with the other information you will use in your speech.

Radio, Television, and Public Lectures

In many instances, radio and television programs offer data that would otherwise be unavailable. It is not likely that a college student could approach the U.S. President, for instance, and ask him for his views on federal aid to education, or continued support of Medicare. Yet the President's views are often communicated to the nation at large over radio and television. Some statements made under these circumstances will not appear in print, because most newspapers do not report the complete text of speeches or press conferences broadcast on radio or television.

Public lectures that are not broadcast are information sources less often available than broadcasts, but their content is often especially valuable. Unlike the interview, however, you can't always ask questions. And, unlike printed sources, you can't reread the material if you don't understand. To use this source you must be an especially careful listener. You may want to review Chapter 3 on listening effectively. The principles explained in that chapter will be quite useful to you in gathering materials from these sources.

USING THE LIBRARY

By far the richest source of speech materials (indeed, of knowledge of all kinds) is a well-supplied library. Yet for many students a library is a lost gold mine of fabulous wealth. They want the gold and are willing to work to dig it out, but they can't find the lode. A few nuggets fall into their hands by chance, but the real riches are never uncovered.

Each library has a systematic method of cataloging and arranging materials, and these methods must become familiar to the one who uses the library. If you do not understand the card catalog, the use of indexes, or the numbering system in your library, librarians are glad to explain them to you. They are in a very real sense teachers and are professionally trained for their jobs. They will be glad to help you find specific pieces of information and to help you familiarize yourself with the resources of the library. For the moment, however, we will look at the card catalog, which indexes the books in the library, and then at the special reference tools that can be used to find six kinds of frequently needed information: facts and statistics, brief articles, extended articles, biography, dates, and quotations.

The Card Catalog

In some libraries the card catalog is computerized. If your library has a computerized system, you may be able to find information in more ways than the conventional card catalog. No matter what the form, however, the mission of the catalog is the same, and the essential information retrieval systems are those described here.

The catalog is a device for locating books. It is alphabetically arranged, listing such bibliographical data as title, author, publisher, date of publication, and other pertinent information. Most books are entered in the catalog by author. (See Figure 9.1.) All but the most general are represented by title as well (see Figure 9.2), and these entries are alphabetically arranged. For nonfiction books, one or more subject entries (see Figure 9.3) will also be found. Title entries have the title at the top above the author's name, and subject entries have a subject designation above the author's name.

In most libraries the author and title entries will be found in one alphabetical file. The subject entries will often be in a separate file. If you know the name of the author or the title of a book, it will be easy to see whether your library has it. One caution: Be very careful about spelling. Ann M. Leech and Ann M. Lesch can be a long way apart in an author and title catalog. If you have difficulty finding a book you need, ask a librarian's help. However, these five filing rules will help you use the author and title section of the card catalog:

1. Names beginning with "Mc" are filed as though spelled "Mac."
2. Titles beginning with "A," "An," "The" (and their foreign equivalents) are filed under the first letter of the next word.
3. Titles beginning with "Mr." and "Mrs." are filed as if spelled out: "Mister" and "Mistress."
4. Titles beginning with numbers are filed as if spelled out: "1001"—"One Thousand One."
5. Titles of books beginning with personal names are filed after all author cards having the same name. Example: Title, Humphrey (written by Winthrop Griffith) follows all books written by authors whose last name is Humphrey.[1]

The subject catalog is made up of author entries with the subject at the top above the author's name (Figure 9.3). When you have found books on what seems to be the appropriate subject but they are not, other appropriate subject headings will be suggested. They are usually found near the bottom of the cards. They will help you to find the location of similar books in the subject catalog. At the end of each subject heading you will sometimes find an entry that tells you other places to look (see Figure 9.4). If you can't find what you need and even your best guesses don't pay off, consult a reference librarian, who can help you find related headings or different terminology.

When you find a book you think you need, write down the name of the author, the title, and the call number of the book. The call number tells you where the book is shelved in your library.

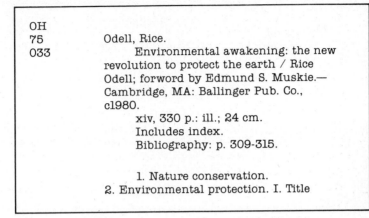

Figure 9.1   An author card.

Figure 9.2   A title card.

Figure 9.3   A subject card.

```
┌─────────────────────────────────────────────────────┐
│                                                       │
│           ENVIRONMENTAL PROTECTION                    │
│                                                       │
│                see also                               │
│                                                       │
│           AGRICULTURAL CONSERVATION                   │
│           AIR QUALITY MANAGEMENT                      │
│           CONSERVATION OF NATURAL RESOURCES           │
│           ENVIRONMENTAL ENGINEERING                   │
│           ENVIRONMENTAL IMPACT ANALYSIS               │
│           ENVIRONMENTAL IMPACT STATEMENTS             │
│           ENVIRONMENTAL LAW                           │
│           ENVIRONMENTAL POLICY                        │
│                                                       │
│                                                       │
└─────────────────────────────────────────────────────┘
```

Figure 9.4   A "see also" card.

Special Reference Tools

In addition to the general book collection, a library contains many other sources of information. Among these are standard reference works, magazines, newspapers, pamphlets, and government documents. In preparing speeches, you will probably find yourself using these sources at least as often as you use the general book collection.

For Basic Facts and Statistics   The *World Almanac,* the *Information Please Almanac,* and a number of other such volumes provide a vast amount of specific up-to-date information. The *Statistical Abstract of the United States* provides quantitative summary statistics (usually covering 15 to 20 years) on the political, social, and industrial organization of the United States. The *Statesman's Yearbook* gives statistics and facts on matters that concern the government, *Facts on File* is a weekly synopsis of world events, which, with its index, becomes a ready reference for a variety of information. The *Congressional Quarterly* gives a synopsis of federal legislation and the voting records of Senators and Representatives.

For Dates   Dictionaries supply many of the dates you will need. The *World Almanac* has a chronological listing of the events of the year previous to its publication. *The New York Times Index* provides the dates of events reported in the newspapers.

For Quotations   John Bartlett's *Familiar Quotations* is the best-known source of short quotations. It is arranged chronologically by author and has a fine index of topics as well. Another source of quotations, Burton E. Stevenson's *Home Book of Quotations,* contains more entries than Bartlett's book. It is arranged by topics.

For Biography   *Current Biography* is a publication that gives short, useful biographies of living persons. A wide variety of *Who's Who* books give brief

Standard reference works are good resources for speech preparation. (© Hankin, 1981, Stock, Boston)

biographical sketches. Webster's *Biographical Dictionary* contains very brief biographies of a great number of distinguished persons. The *Dictionary of American Biography* sketches the lives of historically prominent Americans, and the *Dictionary of National Biography* does the same for historically notable English citizens. The *Biographic Index* is helpful in locating more extended biographies. It is cross-referenced according to profession or occupation as well as the name of the persons listed; it indexes biographical periodical articles as well as books. In addition, the encyclopedias discussed in the next section contain biographies of notable persons.

For Brief, Authoritative Articles For an introductory discussion of a subject, you should go first to an encyclopedia. General encyclopedias such as the *Britannica* and the *Americana* give information on all phases of human knowledge, and their articles usually include references for further study. The *Britannica* is widely considered the best general reference in the humanities, whereas the *Americana* is thought to be stronger in science and technology.

Specialized encyclopedias are available for more thorough treatment of a subject. To list a representative group, we may mention encyclopedias of *Religion and Ethics, World History, Banking and Finance, World Arts and Sports*. Van

Nostrand-Reinhold's *Scientific Encyclopedia, The International Encyclopedia of the Social Sciences,* Grove's *Dictionary of Music and Musicians,* and the *Dictionary of American History* supply information in the specific areas their titles name.

For More Extensively Developed Articles   Although the basic sort of information we have discussed so far can be found in reference books such as almanacs and encyclopedias, more extensively developed articles will be found in magazines and scholarly journals. But such publications are useful only if you are prepared to use an index.

Periodical indexes are arranged by subject. The subject headings are often the same as those in the card catalog, so if you understand the use of the card catalog you should be able to find items in a periodical index. Remember, however, that indexes have specific time periods they cover. The most common index of magazines is the *Reader's Guide to Periodical Literature.* It indexes a large number of popular periodicals from 1900 to the present. Its entries are arranged in much the same fashion as the card catalog.

Except for the card catalog, the *Reader's Guide* is probably the most-used index in the library, but its limitations are too frequently overlooked. Because it indexes only popular magazines, it is of limited usefulness in investigating more specialized topics. There are too many specialized indexes to permit a complete enumeration here, but we list some that should prove useful. The *Social Sciences Index* and the *Humanities Index* are author and subject indexes to the scholarly journals in the social sciences and humanities. The *Business Periodicals Index* lists articles on business administration, public administration, and economics. The *Public Affairs Information Service* indexes a wide variety of books, periodicals, public documents, and mimeographed material in government, sociology, and business. The *Biological and Agricultural Index,* the *Education Index,* the *Art Index,* the *Music Index,* and the *Applied Science and Technology Index* catalog periodical literature in their special fields.

When you have found the author, title, periodical, volume, page, and date of an article from the index, you will want to check to see whether your library subscribes to the periodical in which it appears. Most libraries publish lists of their journals showing where they are located. Ask at the Reference Department for such a listing.

The New York Times is an especially useful source of information on current events. This newspaper prints complete texts of many speeches and documents of public interest. Its treatment of news items is ordinarily more extensive than that found in many other newspapers and in the news magazines. Most libraries subscribe to the paper and keep it on microfilm. *The New York Times Index* locates specific items in the paper and is an excellent reference tool. It can be used to find news items in other papers also, because most newspapers cover a story at about the same time.

You also need to remember that the U.S. government is the largest publisher in the world. You may want to look into the government documents in your library. They are all indexed through a series of special indexes which your librarian can provide. Government documents cover a wide variety of current topics and an amazing array of statistical information.

METHODS OF RECORDING DATA

The information you collect should be recorded on cards or slips of paper, about 4 × 6 inches. It is perfectly satisfactory to cut 8½ × 11 sheets of paper into four pieces and use these, or you can buy cards at any bookstore. Four items of information should be entered on these cards: (1) a label to identify the material, (2) the author, (3) the information you wish to use, and (4) the necessary bibliographical data. If you prepare note cards carefully, you will need to check the original source only once. Figure 9.5 shows an example of a note card.

Because the information you gather from all the sources we have listed may eventually find its way into the outline of your speech, you will want to make it as easy as possible to handle. Putting each item on a separate card makes it easy to rearrange the sequence of cards without excessive rewriting or checking back to your notes. When the rough draft of your outline has been prepared, you can decide where the data on each card fit into the outline. When you use note cards in this manner, much of the work of preparing an outline is done automatically, painlessly, and easily.

SUMMARY

An often overlooked source of supporting material is your personal experience. Frequently you have valuable knowledge and experience that others don't have. Use that experience when it is appropriate.

Information can also be obtained by interviewing an expert on your subject. Plan the interview and select questions in advance. Do some research to be sure you know some essential information before you go to the interview. During the in-

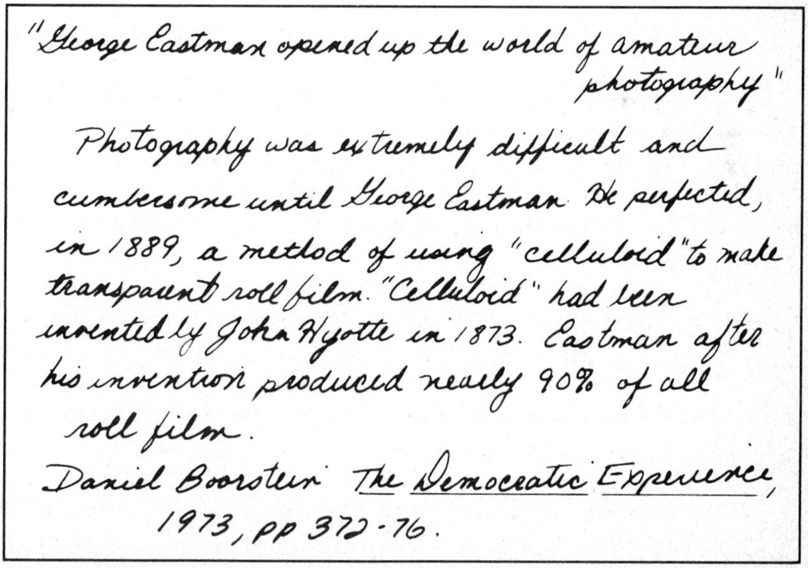

"George Eastman opened up the world of amateur photography"

Photography was extremely difficult and cumbersome until George Eastman. He perfected, in 1889, a method of using "celluloid" to make transparent roll film. "Celluloid" had been invented by John Hyatte in 1873. Eastman after his invention produced nearly 90% of all roll film.

Daniel Boorstein The Democratic Experience, 1973, pp 372-76.

Figure 9.5 A note card.

terview, be prepared to take notes or ask if you can use a tape recorder. Don't argue with the person you interview, and don't overstay your welcome. Review your notes as soon after the interview as possible. Radio, television, and public lectures can provide good information but, like interviews, they require careful note taking.

The library is probably the richest source of information. The card catalog indexes by author, title, and subject all the books in your library and tells you where to find them. There are also specialized reference works and indexes that can help you to find information. These will give you basic facts, statistics, dates, quotations, biographies, and brief authoritative articles. Indexes to magazines and journals help you to find more extensively developed articles. All the necessary information should be collected on cards so that it can be integrated into your outline and you won't have to go back to check the original source.

NOTES

1. Gwen Gittins and Carolyn Dusenbury, *Workbook in Library Skills* (Salt Lake City: Marriott Library, University of Utah, 1980), p. 11.

EXERCISES

1. Before you begin your next speech assignment, select two or three subjects and make a list on each to compare:
    a. How much personal experience you have with the subject
    b. Who you know that you could interview for further information
    c. What radio or TV programs you have heard on the subject
       If you had only these sources of information to draw on, which subject would you know best?
2. If you are not knowledgeable about your library, go there and take a tour to learn about the various resources and where they are found.
3. On one of your speech assignments, use the subject catalog to find three books pertaining to your subject.
4. On one of your speech assignments, use each of the six types of special reference tools and find one piece of information of each type. Turn in the list of what you found to your instructor.

chapter 10

Arguments and Values

C. Let the materials of the speech develop the warrant
  1. By direct argument
  2. By emphasizing the severity of the problem
  3. By the choice of examples
  4. By the choice of words
D. With an opposed audience, reexamine the warrant options care-fully
E. Don't overuse value appeals

When you speak to an audience, you are asking it to make some kind of change: for example, to understand something, or understand it differently, to give adherence to a new belief, or to abandon an old mode of conduct in favor of a new one, or to strengthen an already held conviction. In our culture, however, we are taught that we should have *reasons* for our behavior. One of your tasks, then, is to make arguments that serve as reasons to justify the claim of your speech. Arguments must be perceived by an audience as reasonable support for your proposal.[1]

What makes an argument acceptable, however, is not solely a matter of reasoning. Audience decisions are based as heavily on value judgments as they are on rational criteria. A second task, particularly in persuasive speaking, then, is to find ways to relate your speech claim to the value system of your audience.

This chapter will show you how to go about performing both of these tasks. It will explain how to develop several different kinds of arguments, how to avoid some of the major errors in reasoning, and how to use as avenues to persuasion the beliefs and values you share with the audience. Let's begin by looking at the way arguments work.

THE TOULMIN ANALYTICAL MODEL OF ARGUMENT

The following diagram serves as an analytical tool to understand your arguments and the arguments of others:[2]

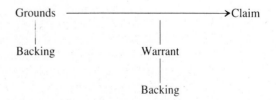

Let's go through the major elements of this model and see how easy it is to use it to analyze an argument.

1. You have a claim you want to prove. To justify it to someone, you give grounds for believing the claim.

(Grounds) ─────────────────────────────→**(Claim)**

The United States and the USSR have enough nuclear weapons to wipe out the human race.

(Therefore) An agreement between the United States and the USSR to limit nuclear weapons is necessary.

2. But the argument must show how this relationship between grounds and claim is rationally justified. That is, the argument must show why the grounds *warrant* the claim.

(Grounds) ─────────────────────────────→**(Claim)**

The United States and the USSR have enough nuclear weapons to wipe out the human race.

(Therefore) An agreement between the United States and the USSR to limit nuclear arms is necessary.

(Warrant)

(Since) Only an agreement between the United States and the USSR can prevent a nuclear wars.

3. Sometimes the grounds and/or the warrant of the argument need to be strengthened. In this case, you use *backing* (supporting material, beliefs, values, and credibility) to reinforce either or both.

(Grounds) ─────────────────────────────→**(Claim)**

The United States and the USSR have enough nuclear weapons to wipe out the human race.

(Therefore) An agreement between the United States and USSR to limit nuclear arms is necessary.

(Backing)

In 1984 the United States had 11,030 and the USSR had 9,710 strategic warheads.

(Warrant)

(Since) Only an agreement between the United States and USSR can prevent nuclear war.

(Backing)

No other nation has anything approaching what the United States and the USSR have.

Remember, this model is an analytical tool. It does not tell you the order of the parts in an actual argument. Nor does it tell you the best order for the parts. What it does is to lay out the parts of the argument so that you can tell where weaknesses may occur. Before we look at some of those potential weaknesses, we will examine each of the five forms your arguments can take.

THE FIVE FORMS OF ARGUMENT

Any argument you use will fall into one of five different forms: argument from authority, argument from sign, argument from cause, argument by generalization, and argument by analogy. Each can be diagrammed and tested by using the analytical model discussed above.

Argument from Authority

An argument from authority says that a claim should be accepted because it is the opinion of a credible source. If the audience does indeed accept the authority as credible and trustworthy, the claim will be warranted.

A student speaker, Rick Wallner of Colorado State University, made the following argument in a speech advocating a restricted use policy for our national parks:

> Many believe that if people want to enjoy the parks they shouldn't be stopped. What these people don't realize is that parks aren't playgrounds, they are preserves. This was spelled out in a letter written in 1918 by then Secretary of the Interior Franklin Lane to Stephen Mather, the first Director of the National Park Service. Lane wrote that "every activity of the Service is subordinate to the duties imposed upon it to faithfully preserve the parks for posterity in essentially their natural state."[3]

It would be diagrammed as follows:

(Grounds) —————————————————————→ **(Claim)**

Statement of Secretary Lane in 1918 that "every activity of the Service is subordinate to the duties imposed upon it to faithfully preserve the parks for posterity in essentially their natural state."

(Therefore) The national parks aren't playgrounds; they are preserves.

(Warrant)
(Since) Secretary Lane is an expert
on the National Park Service.

(Backing)
Lane set up the
National Park Service.

Chapter 8 explains in some detail the criteria for judging the credibility of any source cited as an authority. It would be a good idea to review that section of the chapter.

Argument from Sign

In an argument from sign, you observe directly some fact or condition. Using this as grounds, you make the claim that some other fact or condition, not immediately observable, exists. Medical diagnosis is sign reasoning. The physician looks for symptoms, conditions that are directly observable, which serve as signs from which the disease can be inferred.

Argument from sign always alleges a relationship between an observed sign and what it shows. It asserts that the observed phenomenon and the condition it signals always occur together, that the former does not occur without the latter. If the alleged relationship is accepted by an audience, and if the condition taken as a sign is known or believed to exist, the claim follows without question.

On December 8, 1941, the day after the Japanese attack on Pearl Harbor, President Franklin Delano Roosevelt delivered the famous speech in which he asked the Congress to declare that a state of war existed between the United States and Japan.

> Yesterday, December 7, 1941—a date which will live in infamy—the United States of America was suddenly and deliberately attacked by naval and air forces of the Empire of Japan. . . . The attack yesterday on the Hawaiian Islands has caused severe damage to American military and naval forces. . . .
>
> Yesterday the Japanese Government also launched an attack against Malaya.
>
> Last night Japanese forces attacked Hong Kong.
>
> Last night Japanese forces attacked Guam.
>
> Last night Japanese forces attacked the Philippine Islands.
>
> Last night the Japanese attacked Wake Island.
>
> This morning the Japanese attacked Midway Island.
>
> Japan has, therefore, undertaken a surprise offensive extending throughout the Pacific area. The facts of yesterday speak for themselves.

(Grounds) ————————————————→ **(Claim)**
The Japanese forces   (Therefore) The Japanese attack extends
have attacked   throughout the Pacific area.

(Backing)
Hawaiian Islands
Malaya
Hong Kong
Guam
Philippine Islands
Wake Island
Midway Island

(Warrant)
(Since) These diverse attacks are
signs that the attack is throughout the Pacific area.

Argument from Cause

When an occurrence or condition is the direct result of an antecedent occurrence or condition, the relationship between them is said to be that of cause and effect. The one that exists prior in time and operates to bring about the other is said to be the cause. The one that exists as a direct result of the first is said to be the effect. Arguments that support claims by causal reasoning may be developed in one of two strategic forms: *from cause to effect* or *from effect to cause.*

Cause to Effect   In a recent classroom speech, the speaker proposed that the state government should operate clinics to dispense narcotics at low cost to addicts. The speech contained these examples of argument from cause to effect: Lack of availability, plus the greed of peddlers, causes narcotics to be expensive. The expense of being an addict forces addicts to turn to crime for money to support their habits. The speaker argued further that the proposed clinics would reduce the cost of addiction, thus removing the cause of a large proportion of present-day crime, and would, at the same time, eliminate narcotics peddlers by removing their cause (the desire for profit).

(Grounds) ──────────────────────────▶**(Claim)**	
Free clinics would eliminate the profit motive in narcotics.	(Therefore) Free clinics would eliminate narcotics peddlers.

(Warrant)
(Since) Narcotics peddlers
exist only because of [are
caused by] profit.

Arguments of this kind move forward in time. That is, in reasoning from cause to effect, a speaker infers from one event or condition that a second event or condition will follow, the first (grounds) being the cause, the second (claim) its effect.

Effect to Cause   The second kind of causal argument moves backward in time from a given condition and attempts to establish a probable cause. This kind of reasoning determines why the Roman Empire fell, what causes juvenile delinquency, what causes a high divorce rate, or the cause of any other of the host of society's problems.

President Ronald Reagan argued from effect to cause in his address to Congress shortly after he took office in 1981:

> We know now that inflation results from all that deficit spending. Government has only two ways of getting money other than raising taxes. It can go into the money market and borrow, competing with its own citizens and driving up interest rates, which it has done, or it can print money, and it's done that. Both methods are inflationary.[4]

It can be diagrammed this way:

(Grounds) ──────────────────────────▶**(Claim)**	
Government has borrowed and printed money.	(Therefore) Government has caused inflation.

(Warrant)
(Since) Government borrowing and
printing money cause inflation.

Argument by Generalization

A generalization is a statement that makes a claim about all of the members of some class or group. What kind of group it is doesn't matter. It may be people ("college basketball players are tall"), objects ("cigarettes are harmful to your health"), or anything else that can be classified. The inference is made this way: "Every time I have had a cup of coffee after three o'clock in the afternoon, I have had trouble sleeping. Therefore, it is reasonable to accept the generalization that coffee will always keep me awake." This argument says that what is true of observed specific instances will also be true of all instances of the same class ("every time I drink coffee"), including those that have not been observed ("even in the future").

Notice that this hypothetical example about coffee is based on an argument from cause. This points to the fact that generalizations are grounded in causes and signs. One of the most important problems you will have in identifying an argument from generalization will be to differentiate it from sign or cause. The example of sign argument in Franklin Roosevelt's "Declaration of War Against Japan" illustrates the problem. He gives seven signs that Japan has "undertaken a surprise offensive throughout the Pacific." Thus, multiple signs are used to prove a single claim about Japan. To be a generalization, the claim must go beyond that and identify a general principle. The following example of argument by generalization is from a speech by Richard Erstad, a student at South Dakota State University, titled "What We Don't Know Can Hurt Us." Notice that its claim is a general principle.

> U.S. Congressman [now Senator] Paul Simon reports that of some 455,000 American soldiers stationed overseas, fewer than 600 can speak the language of the country in which they are located.
>
> At the time of the fall of the American Embassy in Teheran in 1979, only 6 of some 80 employees there had even a minimal training in the language of Iran.
>
> And when a young Russian tried to defect to the American Embassy in Afghanistan, in the fall of 1983, no one even knew what he was talking about, since no one in that Embassy was able to speak Russian.
>
> The list of incidents like these could go on and on.
>
> What does all of this seem to indicate? It would seem that when a crisis arises in some far, or not so far, corner of the world, we can only hope that the other side speaks English, because chances are, we won't be able to speak Chinese or Russian or Farsi. . . .[5]

This argument would be diagrammed as follows:

(Grounds) ──────────────────────────→	(Claim)
Only 600 American soldiers can speak the language of the country in which they are stationed.	Therefore, diplomats have weak foreign language skills.
Only 6 of the 80 employees at the American Embassy in Teheran could speak the language of Iran.	

In the fall of 1983 no one at the U.S. Embassy in Afghanistan could speak Russian.

(Warrant)
(Since) These examples justify the
generalization.

In every case, the generalization must be accepted by the audience or the
argument will fail. Many of the generalizations used in arguments are claims that an
audience already believes to be true: that all flavors of ice cream taste good, that
everyone needs a good education, or that tennis is good exercise. But if an audience
does not already believe a claim on which an argument depends, the claim has to be
proved. The proof of a generalization lies in the examples used as evidence. Chapter 8
explains how to select examples that will do the job.

A large number of examples is not always necessary to support a generalization.
It is quite possible that a single case in point might be enough to create belief in a
claim. In the example above, although there are three cases cited, the example of a
dramatic instance, like the fall of the American Embassy in Teheran, might have been
enough.

Argument by Analogy

An analogy is used to clarify an unfamiliar idea by comparing it to a similar idea with
which your audience is familiar. For example, you might say that the gills of a fish
serve much the same purpose as the lungs of an animal, or that a world federation of
nations would be quite like the United States in its political structure. "We all know,"
said Emerson, "that as the human body can be nourished on any food, though it were
boiled grass and the broth of shoes, so the human mind can be fed by any knowledge."

In an analogy you predict that because two things are alike in certain known
respects, they will be alike in other respects. Thus, you might argue that because
legalizing marijuana was successful in Oregon, it would work well in another state.

Here is a simple argument by analogy you probably would take for granted:

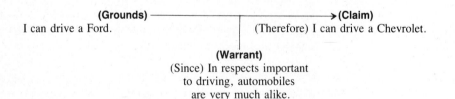

(Grounds) ⟶ **(Claim)**

I can drive a Ford.   (Therefore) I can drive a Chevrolet.

(Warrant)
(Since) In respects important
to driving, automobiles
are very much alike.

The chief benefit of drawing an argument by analogy is that it allows one to
profit from experience; the chief danger comes when some important difference has
been overlooked. The driver who has operated only late-model cars with automatic
transmissions will not be able to drive a car with a standard shift solely on the basis of
earlier experience.

Even if the audience accepts the grounds that the Oregon plan legalizing marijuana is a success, it can be expected to operate successfully in another state only if the two states are similar in respects that are important to the question. For an argument by analogy to be effective, the listener must believe that the similarities outweigh the differences. Oregon is like California. It is a state, on the West Coast, voted Republican in the last presidential election, has farmers, loggers, a port on a river, a capital city, and so forth. But it is also different. It is smaller, less populated, less industrial, and farther north. The crucial problem in analogy, therefore, is to identify for the audience a set of "significant" similarities and "insignificant" differences.

AVOIDING ERRORS IN ARGUMENT

The primary reason for diagramming an argument is to discover any errors in it and, by correcting them, to make the argument more effective.

There may be many things "wrong" with an argument. An audience can reject your argument simply because it doesn't believe your claim. But what we mean when we say "error in argument" is any flaw in the reasoning that lays the argument open to attack. Such errors are frequently called *fallacies*. These errors may be identified with the parts of the analytical model.

Claim Errors

A claim should provide a clear statement to which a listener can give an unambiguous response. Sometimes, however, a claim, whether it is justified by the argument or not, can make one or the other of two serious errors: It can beg the question or ignore the issue.

Begging the Question   A claim begs the question when the argument is circular: "I predict that before the snow flies we are going to have compulsory rationing of fuel oil in this country because as soon as it turns cold, the government is going to tell us all just how many gallons a month we can burn."

In this case the claim that we will have rationing of fuel oil this winter is quite clear, but the reasoning is circular because the grounds for the claim merely repeat the claim. The argument begs the question. In order for a claim to be acceptably reasoned, it must go outside itself for grounds.

Ignoring the Issue   This error is sometimes called *irrelevant conclusion*. It occurs when the claim that is supported by an argument is beside the point. Suppose you don't do well on a test and you go to the instructor to argue for a higher grade. You might say that some of the questions were ambiguous, that the instructor misunderstood your answers, that one or more of your answers were worth more points than they were given, or even that the instructor didn't add correctly. All of these arguments are at least to the point. But if your reason is that you studied hard, the instructor will say that your argument is irrelevant. "The issue is not whether you studied, but whether you knew the material."

Grounds Errors and Backing Errors

The grounds and backing in an argument are the evidence from which you expect an audience to infer the claim of the argument. Obviously, they must be acceptable to the audience. If an audience doesn't believe (G), "There is a shortage of oil," there is no reason it should accept (C), "Rationing is necessary." The same principle applies to backing for both grounds and warrant. The backing must be accepted by the audience or the argument will fail. To avoid errors in grounds or backing, review the tests for examples, statistics, and testimony in Chapter 8.

Warrant Errors

The only reason for an audience to believe, "Given the grounds, therefore the claim," is that some condition warrants the inference. Warrants that don't do this are weak. And they can be weak for one or both of two reasons: First, even though a warrant might completely justify the inference from grounds to claim, the audience simply doesn't believe it is true. For example:

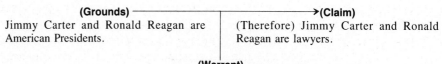

(Grounds) ——————————————→**(Claim)**
Jimmy Carter and Ronald Reagan are American Presidents. | (Therefore) Jimmy Carter and Ronald Reagan are lawyers.

(Warrant)
(Since) All American Presidents are lawyers.

The inference is clear, yet the argument is bound to fail because no knowledgeable audience would accept the warrant. Second, even if the warrant were accepted as true, it might not justify the inference from grounds to claim. For example:

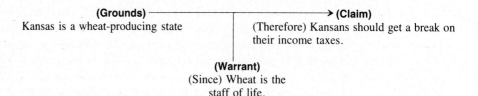

(Grounds) ——————————————→ **(Claim)**
Kansas is a wheat-producing state | (Therefore) Kansans should get a break on their income taxes.

(Warrant)
(Since) Wheat is the staff of life.

In arguments from sign, the sign relationship you allege in the warrant is the crucial point. To test for errors you need to examine the warrant in the light of three questions.

Is There a Reliable Relationship Between the Grounds and the Claim the Argument Makes? There may be a splendid correlation between the number of smogless days in Los Angeles and the number of days of rain in Phoenix, but a smogless day in Los Angeles is nonetheless a poor sign of rain in Phoenix. Perhaps you have heard it said that the birth of more boys than girls in any year is a sign of impending war. Such a condition is about as trustworthy a sign of coming war as left-handedness is of superior intelligence.

Do Changed Circumstances of Time or Place Weaken the Warrant by Altering the Relationship Between Grounds and Claim?   In the first half of the nineteenth century, the fact that a Southern farmer was wealthy would be a very reliable sign that he was a slave-owner. Today, such a relationship would be meaningless.

Is the Claim Supported by the Concurrence of Other Signs?   To say that someone who was seen in the vicinity at the time of a burglary is guilty of the crime is a weak argument. But to show, in addition, that the person was seen leaving the burglarized home and was arrested with stolen articles in possession is to offer further and more substantial signs of guilt.

When you test causal arguments, ask these questions:

Is There a Believable Causal Relationship?   A cause always precedes its effect in time. This one characteristic is often an occasion of the error called *post hoc, ergo propter hoc*—"after this, therefore on account of this." The fact that one event follows another does not mean that the second is the result of the first. Superstitions are good examples of faulty causal reasoning of this sort. "Oh, you broke a mirror. Seven years bad luck!" "I sprained my ankle when I stepped off the curb because I walked under a ladder just before it happened."

Even when a causal relationship might reasonably be expected, you may fail to notice that other causal factors intervene. Having the engine in an automobile overhauled should result in improved performance and economy of the car. But if you try to economize further by using paint thinner for fuel, you introduce another factor that will prevent the engine overhaul from having the desired effect.

Is the Cause-and-Effect Relationship Oversimplified?   Rarely, if ever, is cause-and-effect reasoning found in a simple one-to-one ratio. Most often, an effect has a whole series of contributing causes. It is quite common to say that a President *caused* a depression or a war. The tremendously complex nature of social ills makes oversimplification both a temptation and a danger. If, however, you can show that a President's policies made a substantial contribution to certain events, you are on more reasonable ground.

Not only must a warrant account for the presence of multiple causes, it must also account for the fact that a cause generates, or at least influences, multiple effects. If you argue that juvenile delinquency results from television violence, you may be ignoring the possibility that TV violence gives some people relief from tension, reduces aggressiveness for others, and has additional effects that some would believe good.

It is as important in an argument by generalization or by analogy as it is in arguments from sign or cause that the audience believes the warrant. Suppose you were arguing in defense of socialized medicine. If you pointed out a number of specific places where it has worked well and then claimed that it would therefore work well everywhere, that would be an argument by generalization. But unless the audience believes that programs of socialized medicine are pretty much alike, you can't use other nations' experiences as a warrant for the argument. Nor will that warrant justify the argument by analogy that because socialized medicine has worked well in Sweden it will be successful in the United States.

BELIEFS AND VALUES AS WARRANTS

To be effective, an argument must appear to be reasonable. The warrant is what gives the argument its justification. To be reasonable to an audience you must avoid errors in argument, and you must associate your claim through the warrant with the audience's system of beliefs and values discussed in Chapter 7.

Many quite different theories have been advanced to explain what causes a listener to accept a speaker's claim. Despite any differences, however, most of these theories are alike in one respect, at least: They recognize the importance of the principle of *consistency*. Human beings find it very difficult to live in a state of perceived inconsistency. Speakers have great impact on audiences either when they take advantage of an inconsistency the audience perceives, or, if the audience doesn't perceive it, the speaker creates the perception. "If you believe in honesty, why do you cheat on your income tax?" "If you know cigarettes harm you, why do you smoke?" "If you don't believe in prejudging people, how can you say that all politicians are crooks?"

In searching for a warrant, look for inconsistencies between beliefs and values, between beliefs or values and behavior, between personal beliefs or values and those of the peer group, between past or present behaviors and those you seek for the future. The warrants you construct will show listeners a way to relieve the tension caused by their perception of inconsistency.

Beliefs as Warrants

Because human beings have literally millions of beliefs, it would be impossible to sift through all of them in the search for warrants to support the claim of a speech. Luckily enough, you don't need to, because the subject matter of each individual speaking situation will automatically limit the possibilities to a relative few.[6]

Representative Elizabeth Holtzman of New York said in testimony before a House subcommittee on crime:

> . . . the average American does not feel safe walking the streets of most cities, many Americans do not feel safe in their own homes, and at least one out of every 20 Americans will be the victim of a serious personal or property crime this year.

It is clear, then, that we must make substantial improvements in Federal efforts to protect our citizens from crime.[7]

In her argument, clearly stated, is the very real perceived danger of crime and its effects on person and property. Do you see the challenge to possible inconsistency that she poses for the members of the committee? "How can you acknowledge the threat of crime in America without improving the federal effort to control it?"

Her argument when diagrammed looks like this:

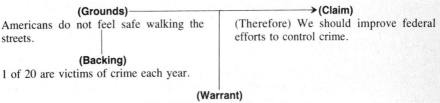

(Grounds)———————————————————→**(Claim)**

Americans do not feel safe walking the streets.

(Therefore) We should improve federal efforts to control crime.

(Backing)

1 of 20 are victims of crime each year.

(Warrant)

(Since) The federal government
has a responsibility
to control crime.

Both reasoning and values influence decisions. (Forsyth, Monkmeyer)

You may not agree with this claim, but if you don't agree, it is surely because you reject the warrant. To agree with her claim you must agree with her belief that the federal government has a responsibility for crime control.

Values as Warrants

Not only did Representative Holtzman base her argument on the *belief* that crime in the cities must be controlled, she also appealed to the *value* of personal security. What is true of her argument is true of every other: It is an important fact that there is no such thing as a valueless argument. Even when a speaker claims to have no motive, intends to give listeners "only the facts" or "to talk to sense to the American people," there are values operating.

Every sentence uttered expresses a belief and thus entails a claim. Every claim implies that there are reasons for believing it. Every argument advanced in support of a claim involves three varieties of proof: (1) the contention that the claim is a *reasonable* conclusion from the evidence, (2) the intention that it be consistent with the *beliefs* and *values* of the audience, and because the phrase, "I believe that . . .," is inherent in every claim, (3) the suggestion that the speaker is a *credible source*.

Values have a further utility in public speaking because there are times when an audience cannot be appealed to on the basis of a belief. When speaker and audience do not share specific beliefs, the speaker must appeal to broader value systems. Martin Luther King, Jr.,'s famous speech at the Lincoln Memorial in Washington, D.C., "I Have a Dream," was a major triumph for the extension of civil rights to blacks. Even though some members of his audience might disagree with him on some specific beliefs, they would find it difficult to reject his warrant, freedom, which dominates all the arguments of the speech. For the value of freedom is deeply imbedded in the American consciousness.

USING WARRANTS

Warrants should identify and resolve the inconsistencies between an audience's beliefs and its behavior. There are no magic rules for finding the most effective ones, but here are some suggestions that will help you.

Relate the Warrants Directly to the Claims of the Speech

Some listeners, unless they see clearly that the particular action you propose is consistent with their values, may take an action you do not desire. Suppose that you want to persuade your friends to support a proposal for a student-run judicial court to deal with those who violate university rules. The students, you argue, should set up such a system and run it to be sure that it is fair. If they don't, the administration will do it and the student voice will be lost. The value on which you base your appeal to your friends is their *freedom*.

But do your listeners understand the value warrant behind your claim? Is it their freedom that they see in the proposal, or students infringing on other students' freedoms? Or does your claim sound like a proposal to give the "usual bunch" new jobs and titles? If you don't make clear the relationship between the claim and the warrant, your listeners may be confused by your proposal and ignore the powerful value of freedom.

How explicit you need to be in making the value and the action desired quite clear will depend on the knowledge and preconceptions of your listeners. But you cannot assume that they will figure out what you mean, and you cannot leave the value or the action desired to chance.

Keep the Warrant Consistent Throughout the Speech

It is quite unusual for a single value or belief to be used as a general warrant throughout an entire message.[8] Multiple values in a unified value system are useful in meeting the problem of possible differences within audiences. Some audience members will have strong concerns for family security; others, although they are impervious to that appeal, put a high value on their own self-respect. One appeal reaches one listener and a second reaches another, and so both listeners may be persuaded. A single warrant may be based on more than one value. For example, when you tell a group at a service club that support for the Children's Camping Fund will benefit the community and at the same time increase the recognition of the club and its members, you are appealing to both social and personal values to win the support of the group. But these values must be consistent with one another. If a primary factor to be exploited in persuasion is a perceived inconsistency in your listeners, the last thing you want them to perceive is inconsistency in you.

Let the Materials of the Speech Develop the Warrant

A value is most effectively developed through the details of the speech, not by pointing it out. The old dictum applies well here: "Show, don't tell." The more concretely you establish a value, the greater is its capacity to serve as a warrant for arguments. Select the examples, statistics, comparisons, and contrasts with which your listeners can most readily identify.

Here are four ways in which you can use the materials of your speech to develop the warrant.

By Direct Argument Gary Hart, Senator from Colorado, told the Democratic National Convention in August 1984 that it must be a party of change, but of just and practical change. He argued these values directly:

> . . . to achieve our goals, our party and nation must disenthrall themselves from the policies of the comfortable past that do not answer the challenges of tomor-

row. The times change, and we must change with them. For the worst sin in political affairs is not to be mistaken, but to be irrelevant.

There are certain facts we must face. Compassion is based on justice. Justice requires resources. Resources flow from opportunity. Opportunity is produced by creative policies. And the creative policies of our times must come, and will come, from the new leadership of the Democratic Party.

Our party's greatest heritage is its willingness to change. We have failed when we became cautious and complacent. We have won America's confidence when we were bold and innovative.

Our party's great experimenter, Franklin Roosevelt, said it best at a critical hour at the dawn of his Presidency: "We will try something, and if it works we will keep it. If it doesn't, let's try something else."

By Emphasizing the Severity of the Problem   Even when the audience recognizes a need, the need will frequently not be strong enough to provide a basis for action. In such a case the need must be amplified in the listeners' minds. This can be a prime way to build an effective warrant.

Gloria Steinem believes that part of her job is to show women how severely they have been denied the value of self-respect. Speaking on the women's revolution to a mostly female graduating class at Vassar College, she said:

> With women, the whole system reinforces this feeling of being a mere appendage. It's hard for a man to realize just how full of self-doubt we become as a result. Locked into suburban homes with the intellectual companionship of three-year-olds; locked into bad jobs, watching less-qualified men get promoted above us; trapped into poverty by a system that supposes our only identity is motherhood—no wonder we become pathetically grateful for small favors.[9]

By the Choice of Examples   Presidential candidate Reverend Jesse Jackson addressed the Democratic National Convention on July 17, 1984. In his speech he used a series of hypothetical examples to develop the values of self-respect and optimism for slum youth:

> I told them [the youth] that like Jesus, I too was born in a slum. But just because you're born in the slum doesn't mean the slum is born in you, and you can rise above it if your mind is made up. I told them, in every slum there are two sides. When I see a broken window, that's the slummy side. Train some youth to become a glazer. That's the sunny side. When I see a missing brick, that's the slummy side. Let that child in the union and become a brick mason and build: that's the sunny side. When I see a missing door, that's the slummy side. Train some youth to become a carpenter: that's the sunny side. And when I see the vulgar words and hieroglyphics of destitution on the walls, that's the slummy side. Train some youth to become a painter and artist: that's the sunny side. We leave this place looking for the sunny side because there's a brighter side somewhere.

By the Choice of Words   If the language you use is more intense, it will influence the audience to perceive your conviction to be more intense (see Chapter 15). Such intensity, if not overdone, will tend to make your listeners more conscious of the warrant and its relation to your proposal.

There is no doubt that the words you choose can reinforce the belief or value you want to develop. Notice how Billy Graham uses intense negative words such as "friction," "conflict," and "warfare," and reinforces them by repetition as he builds in his predominantly Christian audience values centering in peace, security, and inner harmony, which, he says, the true Christian will find despite a life of friction and conflict:

> And the Bible indicates that the Christian life is a life of conflict and warfare. There are some people who promise that faith in God will remove all troubles and difficulties. This is not true. God has never promised to remove all our troubles, problems, and difficulties. In fact, sometimes I think the truly committed Christian is in conflict with the society around him more than any other person. Society is going one direction, and he is going the opposite direction. This brings about friction and conflict. But God has promised, in the midst of trouble and conflict, a genuine peace, a sense of assurance and security that the worldly person never knows (John 16:33). God has also promised new resources, new strength, through the indwelling of his Holy Spirit.[10]

With an Opposed Audience, Reexamine the Warrant Options Carefully

When you confront an audience that is fundamentally opposed to the claim you support, you can't always expect great success, but there are some things you can do to move them closer to your position. An opposed audience calls for a careful reexamination of purpose and warrant.

Shortly after Jimmy Carter won the Democratic party nomination for President in 1976, he was scheduled to speak to the American Legion Convention in Seattle, Washington. He had already announced his support for a proposal to pardon Vietnam War draft resisters and deserters. There was no way he could convince this powerful conservative veterans' group to agree with his position. So he built his own credibility and that of his party by identifying himself with the conservative values of the Legion (national security, thrift, self-respect, and tradition), and then put his amnesty plan in the context of those conservative values. While most Legionnaires did not support his proposal, some did, and many more admired him for his courage and his adherence to conservative values.

Don't Overuse Value Appeals

In one sense, this principle is a contradiction in terms, because an overused value is by definition of no value. The member of the college club or fraternity who sees all small crises as major catastrophes and the politician who sees every occasion as a time to defend "home, flag, and mother" lose effectiveness because listeners learn to discount what they say. At a time when the case demands powerful motivation, such speakers, like the boy who too often cried "wolf," will be ignored. In a situation where your objective is to get a substantial intellectual commitment, strong values such as fear appeals can reduce the attention listeners give to the message and turn their attention to more personal factors or even bring on a negative or boomerang effect.[11]

SUMMARY

In our society you are expected to give reasons when you ask someone to believe as you do. Construct rational arguments and link them to audience beliefs and values. Analyze the grounds and the warrant that are provided to justify a claim.

There are five forms of argument. Argument from authority justifies a claim by associating it with a person who is considered an expert. Argument from sign argues that one set of conditions points to another. Argument from cause may move from cause to effect or from effect to cause. Both are based on a belief that one of two conditions is caused by the other. Argument by generalization is grounded in examples that are believed to justify a general claim. Argument by analogy is a prediction that two things that are alike in certain known respects will be alike in another unknown respect.

It is quite useful to be able to recognize errors in the arguments of your opponents and avoid them in your own speeches. Claim errors and backing errors are characterized by violations of the tests of evidence discussed in Chapter 8. Warrants are weak when an audience will not believe them or do not justify the claim even if they are believed. Depending on the form of the argument used, there are specific tests that can be applied for warrant errors.

Beliefs and values serve as warrants. Use beliefs and values to exploit inconsistencies in an audience's thinking and to show the consistency between the basic understanding of the audience and your claims. Values are particularly useful because they can be used as a basis of appeal even when speaker and listener don't share beliefs.

In using belief and value warrants, there are five principles to follow: (1) Relate the warrant directly to the claim, (2) keep the warrant consistent, (3) let the material of the speech develop the warrant, (4) with an opposed audience, reexamine the options carefully, and (5) don't overuse value appeals.

NOTES

1. There is some dispute over the extent to which human beings are by nature logical. Some researchers point to the obvious failures of people to follow logical rules. Others note that even so, people are essentially logical. Still others say that such logicality is learned. Natural or learned, it is an important factor. See Mary Henle, "On the Relation Between Logic and Thinking," *Psychological Review,* **69** (July 1962), pp. 366–378; Daniel K. Stewart, "Communication and Logic:

Evidence for the Existence of Validity Patterns," *Journal of General Psychology,* **64** (Apr. 1961), pp. 297–305; and John Dollard and Neal E. Miller, *Personality and Psychotherapy* (New York: McGraw-Hill, 1950), p. 120.

2. The actual model introduced here is taken from Richard D. Rieke and Malcolm O. Sillars, *Argumentation and the Decision Making Process* (Glenview, Ill.: Scott Foresman, 1984), pp. 66–70. For the original diagram, see Stephen Toulmin, *The Uses of Argument* (Cambridge: University Press, 1964), pp. 94–113.

3. Rick Wallner, "Parks: Playgrounds or Preserves," unpub.

4. Ronald Reagan, "The State of the Nation's Economy," *Vital Speeches of the Day,* **47** (Mar. 1, 1981), p. 291.

5. Richard Erstad, "What We Don't Know Can Hurt Us," *Winning Orations of the Interstate Oratorical Association* (Mankato, Minn.: Interstate Oratorical Association, 1984), p. 87.

6. Malcolm O. Sillars and Patricia Ganer, "Values and Beliefs: A Systematic Basis for Argumentation," *Advances in Argumentation Theory and Research,* J. Robert Cox and Charles Arthur Willard, eds. (Carbondale, Ill.: Southern Illinois Press, 1982), p. 187.

7. Elizabeth Holtzman, Hearings Before the Subcommittee on Crime, Committee on the Judiciary, House of Representatives, 94th Congress, Second Session (Serial #42, part 1), p. 455.

8. Sillars and Ganer, op. cit., p. 188.

9. Gloria Steinem, quoted by permission.

10. "The Cure for Anxiety" by Billy Graham © 1957 Billy Graham Evangelistic Association.

11. For a discussion of fear appeals research, see Mary John Smith, *Persuasion and Human Action* (Belmont, Calif.: Wadsworth, 1982), pp. 230–232.

EXERCISES

1. Examine one of the speeches in Appendix B. Find and evaluate arguments from sign and analogy.

2. In the editorials of a news magazine or newspaper, find samples of argument from general principle and argument from cause. Diagram the arguments in the format of the Toulmin model. Supply any missing parts and assess the arguments.

3. Collect examples of arguments you hear in conversation and evaluate them as in Exercise 2. Here are some samples of what you might listen for:

a. "I didn't think you were at home. I didn't see your car in the driveway."

b. "My eyes are bothering me. I must have been studying too much."

c. "Don't make so much noise; you'll wake your mother."

d. "All the best television-viewing times are filled with crime dramas. Look at Saturday night's schedule."

Tell what kind of argument is used in each of the examples you find. Using the Toulmin model, explain how you would counter each of these arguments if you disagreed.

4. Examine one of the speeches in Appendix B. Come to class prepared to discuss the following:

    a. What are the most salient values of the speech?

    b. To what extent are they linked to specific beliefs?

    c. How effective do you think the values were with the audience?

    d. Do you think that the choice of values could be improved upon? Why? Why not?

5. Examine one of the speeches in Appendix B. Hypothesize that the speech might be given to two different audiences. What differences in effect might you expect and why?

6. What value and belief inconsistencies are most prevalent among persons like yourself? Develop some specific purposes for speeches that would be most likely to resolve them.

chapter *11*

Credibility

Aristotle said that he would "almost affirm" that credibility "is the most potent of all the means to persuasion."[1] That is an attractive idea. Some recent researchers have argued that credibility is the "dominant factor," and others have questioned such a conclusion.[2] There is a current emphasis in our society on the importance of image, charisma, personality, charm, and a host of other ill-defined characteristics, all of which refer to some aspect of credibility:

> "Ronald Reagan's image"
> "Michael Jackson's charisma"
> "Johnny Carson's personality"
> "Burt Reynolds' charm"
> "Howard Cosell's abrasive style"

Thus, popular notions are added to ancient theory and modern research to say that a speaker who is perceived as credible is more likely to have a message accepted.

THE NATURE OF CREDIBILITY

Every time you believe something because you hear it on the 6 o'clock news, you are giving credibility to the newscaster and the news team. Chances are that when you accept what a professor tells you or believe something you read, you are accepting the ideas because you trust the source from which they came. And when you reject an idea because it comes from someone you don't trust, a lack of credibility is at the base of your negative judgment. Credibility is, therefore, the image the audience has of a speaker which makes what the speaker says more or less believable. But note, it is not what a speaker has but what an audience gives. Credibility is assigned by the audience. Many voters in 1984 thought that Ronald Reagan was insensitive to the poor, that Walter Mondale was the tool of special interests, that Jesse Jackson was interested only in blacks, that Gary Hart was indecisive on issues. All of those opinions may have been false, but they were opinions that affected credibility.

Credibility does not stand alone. Too much of modern lore would have you believe that personality, not substance, is the source of persuasion. However, the source you trust also uses arguments you find reasonable in relation to the beliefs and values you already hold. And the process is self-supporting. You tend to see as most credible those persons whose values are the same as yours. So, over time, your estimation of a speaker's credibility is affected by your reactions to what is said and how it is said, and the effectiveness of what is said is affected by your estimation of the speaker's credibility.

An ancient term, *ethos,* was used by Aristotle to name this phenomenon. We mention it here because you will frequently hear it used even today. For Aristotle it meant the credibility a speaker generated through what was said in a speech. In this chapter we will consider the prior reputation of a speaker to be an important source of credibility as well. But for you, as a student speaker, *ethos* is still most important.

You cannot change your reputation with your classmates very fast; indeed, you may not have a reputation with them. You can, nonetheless, improve what you do in your speeches to maximize your credibility. That is the emphasis of this chapter.

CREDIBILITY FACTORS

There has been considerable research in recent years to identify those factors that cause audiences to give a speaker credibility.[3] That research has identified a variety of factors but two, which have been with us since Aristotle first defined the factors of *ethos,* emerge on all scales: trustworthiness and competence. A third, less important characteristic is dynamism.

Trustworthiness

Listeners tend to give credibility to people they feel can be trusted. Obviously, the characteristics that are signs of trustworthiness will vary with audience and subject. What characteristics cause you to trust someone? Honesty? Church affiliation? Income? Age? Experience? While some broad characteristics, such as honesty, may be generally valued in society, those characteristics are difficult for an audience to judge unless a speaker is well known. So you will need to build the idea of trustworthiness through what you say in your speech.

There are several ways to develop an image as a trustworthy person. One is to identify with the audience by linking the arguments and appeals in the speech with the beliefs and values that are important to the listeners. Another is to use language the audience considers appropriate. Adopting delivery, physical actions, and even dress characteristics that fit the audience's image of trustworthiness will also have a good effect.

Competence

Listeners tend to give credibility to people they feel are competent. Even if listeners have every reason to believe that someone is trustworthy, they may not see that person as competent on a particular subject. You may trust a friend to tell you the truth and to be competent to tell you where to get a good hamburger, but not competent to advise you on an algebra test. You may find your mother completely trustworthy and competent to advise you on financial matters, but not competent to advise you on music.

Judgments of competence may vary from one audience to another. One audience may find competent the person who engages in manual labor, whereas another sees competence as a function of higher education. Any audience must perceive you to be competent before it will consider you a credible speaker.

Listeners expect a speaker to demonstrate competence on the subject—at least to know more about it than they do. That is why it is important to make a thorough study of the subject and why there is a need for well-developed supporting material. An audience can only judge competence on the basis of what a speaker says.

Dynamism

A third factor has been identified by a number of researchers: dynamism, that is, *intensity* in language and voice, and physical activity. However, unlike trustworthiness and competence, it can be viewed as negative.[4] What may be "dynamic" to one person is too "pushy," "brassy," or "loud" to another. The overly aggressive salesperson is a good example of the negative quality of dynamism. Although you can't imagine saying, "I didn't like him because he was too trustworthy," or "She's competent, so she must be wrong," it is not strange at all to think of a remark like, "I don't trust him, he's too pushy."

Relationship Among Factors

In addition to variety in the ways people define each of the factors of credibility, there is a variability in the relationships among them. Suppose an audience finds you highly trustworthy but not particularly competent, or vice versa. This not unusual situation illustrates again the complexity of credibility. Credibility is not a simple matter of respecting and trusting someone in general. Credibility emerges from the listener's perceptions of all of the elements of the communication situation: speaker, occasion, subject.[5] In addition, impressions of competence and trustworthiness may change during the course of the speech, depending on the subject you are discussing and how you approach it.

Trustworthiness, competence, and dynamism, and especially the first two, are characteristics that are admired by audiences. Your problem, as a speaker, is to utilize your past experience and your present knowledge to create for the audience an image of believability. Before we look at how you do this, however, let's consider the kinds of credibility that are available to you.

KINDS OF CREDIBILITY

There are four ways in which you can generate credibility: by your reputation, by direct statements, from secondary sources, and through indirect means.

Reputation

Although the three kinds of credibility we will discuss subsequently are all part of the speech you deliver, reputation is not. Aristotle specifically excludes reputation from his concept of *ethos*. It refers to that credibility which speakers have before they begin to speak and is based on their past actions. Reputation may be altered by the other forms of credibility, but only over time. At the beginning of a speech, you are stuck with your reputation—and it can play a great role in determining your effectiveness.

Chances are that when you address your class, you don't have a reputation with them. There are probably groups, however, to which you are known and with which you can draw on your reputation. Perhaps your club, church group, or a small number of close friends will accept what you say because your reputation is good with them. Individuals in your class may believe you because they know you. But for many in the class, you have no reputation, and when you speak to them, you will need to build other forms of credibility.

Direct Credibility

Some speakers will make direct references to themselves to gain credibility. They will tell their listeners about aspects of their character that should make them believable: "Listen, I wouldn't cheat you," "You ask Sam, he will tell you I'm a right guy," "I promise you I will do everything in my power to see that you are happy."

One of the most famous speeches in recent times with direct credibility as its major characteristic was a speech delivered on September 23, 1952, by former President Richard Nixon. Then a senator and a candidate for the vice presidency, he appeared on television to defend a fund that had been raised for him by wealthy Californians. In that speech, Mr. Nixon made heavy use of direct credibility:

> I worked my way through college and, to a great extent, through law school. And then in 1940, probably the best thing that ever happened to me happened; I married Pat—sitting over here. We had a rather difficult time after we were married, like so many of the young couples who may be listening to us. I practiced law; she continued to teach school. I went into the service.
>
> Let me say that my service record was not a particularly unusual one. I went to the South Pacific. I guess I'm entitled to a couple of battle stars. I got a couple of letters of commendation but I was just there when the bombs were falling and then I returned. I returned to the United States and in 1946 I ran for Congress.

While Mr. Nixon's speech was immediately effective with some people, it is widely believed that it hurt his credibility in the long run because his overt attempt to increase his credibility had a quite contrary effect on some people, making them suspicious of him. Efforts to build credibility directly must be carefully monitored to avoid suggesting that you are interested only in yourself.

Secondary Credibility

Secondary credibility depends for its strength on the trustworthiness and competence an audience ascribes to someone the speaker associates with a proposal. All testimony has favorable secondary credibility or it is worthless. You would surely never quote someone in whom your audience has no confidence or, worse still, distrusts.

Ronald Reagan came to the presidency as perhaps the most conservative candidate in modern times. To increase his credibility in his speech accepting the nomination in 1980, he associated himself with Franklin D. Roosevelt, a Democratic President with strong liberal credentials:

> And the time is now to redeem promises once made to the American people by another candidate, in another time and another place. He said: "For three long years I have been going up and down this country preaching that government—Federal, state and local—costs too much. I shall not stop that preaching. As an immediate program of action, we must abolish useless offices. We must eliminate unnecessary functions of government.
>
> "We must consolidate subdivisions of government and, like the private citizen, give up luxuries which we can no longer afford." And then he said:
>
> "I propose to you my friends, and through you, that government of all kinds, big and little, be made solvent and that the example be set by the President of the United States and his Cabinet."
>
> That was Franklin Delano Roosevelt's words as he accepted the Democratic nomination for President in 1932.
>
> The time is now, my fellow Americans, to recapture our destiny, to take it into our own hands. And to do this it will take many of us, working together. I ask you tonight, all over this land, to volunteer your help in this cause so that we can carry our message throughout the land.[6]

His conservative Republican supporters would not be offended by the statement, although FDR is not one of their heroes. More important, to be elected Reagan needed the support of moderate Republicans and Democrats, so for those listeners Franklin Roosevelt added secondary credibility to his candidacy.

In 1976, when former Congresswoman Barbara Jordan became the first black woman to deliver a keynote address at a national nominating convention, she made extensive use of direct means to build her credibility. But in her conclusion she turned to secondary credibility:

> Now, I began this speech by commenting to you on the uniqueness of a Barbara Jordan making the keynote address. Well I am going to close my speech by quoting a Republican President and I ask that as you listen to these words of Abraham Lincoln, relate them to the concept of a national community in which every last one of us participates: "As I would not be a slave, so I would not be a master. This expresses my idea of democracy. Whatever differs from this, to the extent of the difference is no democracy."

Indirect Credibility

In developing indirect credibility, speakers do not directly associate their proposal with their own or someone else's qualifications. Instead, credibility is enhanced by anything in the speech that identifies the speaker with arguments, values, and salient beliefs in which the audience has confidence. Even the use of language the audience admires or impressive delivery techniques add to this kind of credibility.

It is not possible to give a specific example of indirect credibility, because everything you do in your speech affects your credibility indirectly. If your audience wants specific evidence and you give them only opinion, that will hurt your credibility. If they see a problem as complex and you say it is simple with a simple answer, that will hurt your credibility. If you mispronounce words and use inappropriate language, you will hurt your credibility with an educated audience.

DEVELOPING CREDIBILITY

There are, of course, many ways to use credibility, and different audiences and situations will call for different approaches. But there are six general principles for gaining credibility:

1. Be temperate in showing trustworthiness, competence, and dynamism.
2. Build credibility indirectly.
3. Use the credibility of others to support your own.
4. Sometimes candor will disarm a hostile audience.
5. A chairperson's introduction can build your credibility.
6. Carefully analyze your potential credibility.

Be Temperate in Showing Trustworthiness, Competence, and Dynamism

Although you must show your listeners that you are worth listening to, you have the potential for injuring your credibility if you create the impression that you are too self-centered. However, if direct statements about credibility are introduced in a not-too-obvious way, they tend to increase the listener's willingness to believe what you say. Frequently, you can avoid the problem of injury to your credibility through direct references to your experience by specifically downgrading your experience humorously.

Former Secretary of State Henry A. Kissinger was a man who had earned a reputation with much of the press as being egotistical and close-mouthed with the news. When he delivered an address to the National Press Club in Washington, D.C., on January 10, 1977, shortly before he left office, he used this introduction:

> I am grateful for this opportunity to appear before you today. It is almost like coming home, for we have so much in common: a reluctance to see our names in print, a uniform appreciation of the goodness of mankind, total subordination of ego, a basic reliance on working within the system, and, above all, humility.[7]

Direct, heavy-handed attempts to impress listeners with one's own qualifications, or to deny any personal advantage from a proposal, like the salesperson who keeps denying any personal reason for making a sale when the customer knows about commissions, can be injurious. It is common sense to avoid any statements which suggest to your listeners that you mean to manipulate them and to avoid statements that imply you are what your listeners know you are not.

Build Credibility Indirectly

Much of your credibility is built on the fact that through your thoroughness, accuracy, and careful thought you *show* that you are competent rather than *tell* listeners that you are. In a very real sense, all the factors of the speaking situation go together. Credibility helps to make argument, evidence, and value appeals more believable and thus more persuasive. Conversely, when you organize clearly, support reasonably, and use language well, you strengthen your audience's image of your competence. Your trustworthiness, for example, can be enhanced by revealing shared experience, religious background, social origins, or friendships better than it can by claiming directly that you and your listeners are alike. Even though you may have the experience on which to build credibility, you can still make sure you have carried on adequate study and research and use it to demonstrate your competence.

Indirect credibility is also developed by the way you dress, use your voice, and act physically. In general, you should behave and dress in a way that will not be seen

Credibility is gained through a number of factors. (Alper, Stock, Boston)

as odd to the audience (unless, of course, oddness is your credibility objective). It is a small concession to a conservative audience that you dress conservatively in order to establish credibility with them.

Use the Credibility of Others to Support Your Own

To a large extent, quotations from sources that rank high in the estimation of your listeners help to make you more believable. "Mr. Dressler, the registrar, says that the average grade at our university is 2.7 not a C." "Even the coach admits our football program is in trouble." "Dean Reynolds told me that the University is thinking of phasing out the industrial engineering program."

Sometimes Candor Helps to Disarm a Hostile Audience

So much emphasis is placed on not offending hostile listeners that you may think it is always best to hide your true views from them. But many speakers are so successful through candor that this technique cannot be ignored. Sometimes the audience knows your views in advance, and to hide them would be foolish. It is best in such circumstances to be candid. Senator Edward M. Kennedy is regarded by conservatives as the epitome of the liberalism they reject. Yet on October 3, 1983, he spoke to the students of Liberty Baptist College, whose President is Dr. Jerry Falwell, leader of the "Moral Majority." To disarm his hostile audience, Senator Kennedy used candor in his introduction about his differences with Reverend Falwell:

> I have come here to discuss my beliefs about faith and country, tolerance and truth in America. I know we begin with certain disagreements; I strongly suspect that at the end of the evening some of our disagreements will remain. But I also hope that tonight and in the months and years ahead, we will always respect the right of others to differ—that we will never lose sight of our own fallibility—that we will view ourselves with a sense of perspective and a sense of humor. After all, in the New Testament, even the disciples had to be taught to look first to the beam in their own eyes, and only then to the mote in their neighbor's eye.
>
> I am mindful of that counsel. I am an American and a Catholic; I love my country and treasure my faith. But I do not assume that my conception of patriotism or policy is invariably correct—or that my convictions about religion should command any greater respect than any other faith in this pluralistic society. I believe there surely is such a thing as truth, but who among us can claim a monopoly on it?[8]

Candor in that case built credibility, contradicting the all-too-prevalent notion that a politician is one who skirts the issues. There are grave dangers in hiding your biases. When a listener discovers that there is covert bias, that is the time when the most damage is done to your credibility.[9]

A Chairperson's Introduction Can Build Your Credibility

The chairperson's introduction can build the credibility of a speaker by giving relevant facts that will be significant to the audience. A chairperson who is better known to the audience than you are can frequently do a better job of building credibility for you than you can yourself.[10] But even the chairperson who is not better known can be a real help with a carefully prepared introduction of a speaker. When you are called on to introduce a speaker, remember to plan your introduction carefully with the speaker's credibility in mind.

Analyze Your Potential Credibility Carefully

One of the reasons you need to analyze your audience carefully is to discover possible links between you and the audience that will make you more credible to them. Consider possible similarities of ethnic background, home town, school ties; in short, experiences that create a bond between you and your audience. The references you make to experiences you have had need not call attention to the similarity—they need only draw on it.

"When I was growing up on a farm we learned. . . ."

"I learned a lot from high school sports. . . ."

"Inner-city life can be very rewarding. . . ."

"Because my mother was such a good cook I learned to love Jewish food. . . ."

All of these kinds of references have particular strength because they are verifiable— even obvious. Simply claiming that you share beliefs and values with an audience is not.

SUMMARY

Credibility, the image an audience has of a speaker, is an important part of making what the speaker says more believable. It works together with the arguments, the beliefs, and the values in any speaking situation.

There are three factors of credibility. Signs of trustworthiness, competence, and dynamism make a speaker more credible to listeners. These factors will be perceived through different characteristics, however, depending on the subject and the situation. Also, it should be realized that dynamism, unlike the other two, is not always positive. A dynamic speaker may be perceived negatively, as too pushy.

There are four kinds of credibility that convey the credibility factors of trust, competence, and dynamism. Reputation is the credibility you have before the speech. The other three are generated during the speech. Direct credibility occurs when you tell your listeners specifically about your trustworthiness and competence. Secondary credibility occurs when you associate the credibility of others with your own. Indirect credibility is the credibility you gain by the way your audience responds to the arguments, values, language, and delivery of your speech.

There are many ways to develop credibility in specific situations. Six general principles are discussed in this chapter: be temperate, build credibility indirectly, use the credibility of others, sometimes use candor, use a chairperson's introduction, and analyze your potential credibility.

NOTES

1. *The Rhetoric of Aristotle,* trans. by Lane Cooper (New York: Appleton-Century-Crofts, 1932), p. 9.

2. James C. McCroskey, *An Introduction to Rhetorical Communication* (Englewood Cliffs, N.J.: Prentice-Hall, 1978), p. 67; Mary John Smith, *Persuasion and Human Action* (Belmont, Calif.: Wadsworth, 1982), pp. 221, 225.

3. Kenneth Andersen and Theodore Clevenger, Jr., "A Summary of Experimental Research in Ethos," *Speech Monographs,* **30** (June 1964), pp. 59–78; Kenneth Andersen, *Persuasion: Theory and Practice* (Boston: Allyn & Bacon, 1978), pp. 238–242; Kim Giffin, "The Contribution of Studies of Source Credibility to a Theory of Interpersonal Trust in the Communication Process," *Psychological Bulletin,* **68** (Aug. 1967), pp. 104–120; McCroskey, op. cit., pp. 68–71; Jack L. Whitehead, Jr., "Factors of Source Credibility," *Quarterly Journal of Speech,* **54** (Feb. 1968), pp. 59–63.

4. Velma J. (Wenzlaff) Lashbrook, "Source Credibility: A Summary of Experimental Research," Paper presented to the Speech Communication Association Convention, San Francisco, Dec. 1971; Gerald R. Miller and John Basehart, "Source Trustworthiness, Opinionated Statements and Responses to Persuasive Communication," *Speech Monographs,* **36** (Mar. 1969), pp. 1–7; W. Barnett Pearce, "The Effect of Vocal Cues on Credibility and Attitude Change," *Western Speech,* **35** (Summer 1971), pp. 176–184.

5. Jesse G. Delia, "A Constructivist Analysis of Credibility," *Quarterly Journal of Speech,* **62** (Dec. 1976), pp. 361–375; Jo Liska, "Situational and Topical Variations in Credibility Criteria," *Communication Monographs,* **45** (Mar. 1978), pp. 85–92.

6. Ronald Reagan, "Republican National Convention Presidential Nomination: Acceptance Address," *Vital Speeches of the Day,* **46** (Aug. 15, 1980), p. 646.

7. Henry A. Kissinger, "My Valedictorian Address," *Vital Speeches of the Day,* **43** (Feb. 15, 1977), p. 265.

8. Edward M. Kennedy, "Tolerance and Truth in America," Text provided by Senator Kennedy.

9. Judson Mills and Elliot Aronson, "Opinion Change as a Function of a Communicator's Attractiveness and Desire to Influence," *Journal of Personality and Social Psychology,* **2** (1965), pp. 173–177.

10. Andersen and Clevenger, op. cit., p. 64.

EXERCISES

1. Consider some prominent public speaker you have heard recently. In what way did the speaker's reputation affect your reception of the ideas? What did the speech do to confirm or deny your opinion of the speaker? Write a short paper explaining your reactions.

2. Which do you consider more important to a speaker's effectiveness: credibility, or the ability to use value appeals? Why?

3. Examine one of the speeches in Appendix B. How well does the speaker develop credibility according to the principles discussed in this chapter?

4. Choose one of the following well-known persons and write a short paper explaining what factors in that person's reputation would influence your classmates positively or negatively.

Ronald Reagan	Michael Jackson
Geraldine Ferraro	Elizabeth Taylor
Edward Kennedy	Robert Redford
Marie Osmond	Jesse Jackson
Caspar Weinberger	Lee Iaccoca
Andre Gromyko	Francis Ford Coppola

chapter *12*

Organizing the Outline

I. Elements of organization
    A. Relationships
    B. Sequence
II. Achieving good organization
    A. Unity
    B. Coherence
III. Purpose of the outline
IV. Types of outlines
    A. Scratch outlines
    B. Briefs
    C. Rhetorical outlines
        1. Complete-sentence outlines
        2. Topic outlines
V. Techniques of outlining
    A. Parts of the outline
        1. The introduction
        2. The body
        3. The conclusion
    B. Showing relationships and sequence
        1. Subordinate ideas
        2. Coordinate ideas
        3. Symbols of subordination and coordination
    C. Checking the outline
        1. Accurate subordination and coordination
        2. Formal correctness
        3. Content completeness of informative speech outlines

VI. Important technical principles
    A. Each heading an assertion
    B. Each heading a single assertion
    C. Only one symbol per heading
    D. No overlapping headings
VII. Revising the outline

Even though it is possible to talk about subject matter and organization as separate entities, it is impossible to separate them in fact. That is, it is impossible to have one without the other. Just as every painting must have composition and every statue must have shape, the subject matter of a speech must have some kind of organization. Organization is an important factor in determining how an audience will understand a speech. Analysis of the subject and the audience suggest what the best order is likely to be.

In this chapter we will explain how to put the organization of a speech into outline form. Outlining is an important part of speech preparation because outlines are related to organization, because good organization brings desirable order, and because a reasonable order is an important help toward success in speaking. Let's begin by looking briefly at some elements that are basic to organization.

ELEMENTS OF ORGANIZATION

When you were born, your understanding of the world was seriously limited by a lack of experience and by the fact that your nervous system was not yet well developed. As time passed, and you gradually began to sort out and to classify people, objects, and events, you gained two important perceptions: first, that there were *individual* "things" separate from you and distinct from one another, and second, that similarities and differences among these things made them belong to groups or classes. And that is when you began to reason, because fundamental and essential to any kind of reasoning is the ability to perceive and assign relationships.

The number and kind of relationships you assign is limited only by your ability to see them. Some things are taller, shorter, or longer than others in size; above, below, to the right, or to the left in space; sooner or later in time. People also have relationships to each other, such as employer–employee, husband–wife, mother–daughter, older–younger, richer–poorer. All of these relationships and countless others are important to the degree that they help to bring some kind of *organization* into the world.

Organization is necessary for a second reason. Human beings don't like chaos. Random events are unpredictable; in order to be comfortable, people need to make predictions they can depend on. Thus they look for order in their world. They will certainly look for it in the speeches they hear. Organization, therefore, is necessary because it is *expected*.

The subject matter of a speech cannot be communicated all at once. It has to be broken down into single ideas that can be delivered one at a time. From the moment speech preparation begins, therefore, questions about *what* to say and *in what order* to say it arise simultaneously.

Answering these questions requires two kinds of decisions: first, how the various ideas and materials of the speech are *related,* and second, the *sequence* in which to present these related elements.

Relationships

The world makes no sense if people, objects, and ideas are perceived as isolated random events. Rather, they must be seen in relation to other individual events. This implies, of course, that every piece of material in a speech—each idea, claim, definition, statistic, example, quotation, no matter what—should have some relationship to every other element. If any item doesn't have a specific and clear relationship to the others, it doesn't belong in the speech at all.

Sequence

Determining in what order or sequence to present the materials goes on simultaneously with deciding how the individual pieces of material are related to each other.

ACHIEVING GOOD ORGANIZATION

Unity and *coherence* are always important criteria in judging the quality of composition, either written or oral. Unity is a characteristic of subject matter, and coherence is related to structure. Let's see what unity and coherence are and how organization helps to achieve and maintain them.

Unity

Unity in a speech is a necessary and desirable quality that occurs when all of the ideas are related to each other as members of a single entity. Without it, the elements of a speech would be random events, unrelated to each other, and it would be impossible to put them into any meaningful communication.

There are two principal ways in which the unity of a speech can be harmed. The first is to have more than one subject or one purpose. Consider this statement of purpose: to inform the audience about nuclear energy as an alternative source of power and some of its serious drawbacks. This purpose would require two speeches: one informative, to explain the use of nuclear energy as a source of power; and the other persuasive, to prove the value claim that it has serious drawbacks.

Look at another example. Some automobiles have air bags that inflate automatically in case of a collision. These air bags could be the subject of any number of speeches: to describe how they work, to show their life-saving capabilities, to explain the controversy over their value, to argue their superiority over conventional seat belts, to persuade the audience to buy them, to name only a few. Some of these potential speeches, moreover, would clearly be informative, others persuasive. Any of these subjects and purposes would do perfectly well given the right audience and the proper occasion, but a speech that tries to handle two or more of them at the same time is very likely to make a listener think, "Now I wonder what that was all about."

The second principal way to lose the unity in a speech is to digress from the subject. There is a real temptation to insert material that just happens to come to mind, not because it has any necessary bearing on the subject, but because it is interesting or amusing. It makes no difference whether the digression is ad lib ("That reminds me of a story") or whether the material is deliberately included when the speech is prepared, the result is the same—the unity of the speech is impaired.

Unity alone, however, does not ensure understanding because, even if all the parts belong together, unless they are arranged in an appropriate order, there is no guarantee that the communication will be accurate and efficient. Thus, coherence is a second important need.

Coherence

A group of individual elements has unity if all of them are related to a single entity. But in order for the elements to be coherent, they must fit together in a consistent, rational pattern. When a pair of dice stops rolling, they will be in some spatial and numerical relationship to each other. But this kind of order is random and accidental. It would be like trying to build a watch by shaking up the pieces in a sack. The resulting jumble would have unity, because all the parts belong to a watch, but it would have no coherence whatsoever. A horse and cart have unity as a transportation system, but if the cart is put before the horse, the coherence is pretty poor.

Relate the notion of coherence to speaking. No matter how badly garbled a message may be, it will still communicate *something*. It is even possible that the audience will understand it correctly. But when sense-making is the result of chance, it is inherently unpredictable. Speakers want to be as sure as possible of the response they will get. Therefore, if an audience has to understand in a few minutes a speech that has taken days or even weeks to prepare, an organization that ties all of the ideas together into a coherent package makes it more likely that the audience will understand it accurately.

Moreover, the efficiency of communication will be increased because the audience doesn't have to work as hard to understand when ideas are presented in a coherent order. The easier it is to understand a message, the greater is the chance that interest will be maintained and the greater is the chance that the audience will listen at all.

PURPOSE OF THE OUTLINE

An outline shows the sequence of ideas in a speech and the relationships among them. The way it groups related materials shows the unity and coherence in the speaker's ideas. In other words, an outline is a blueprint of a speech.

In addition to helping organize a speech, an outline is useful in delivering it. It helps to ensure against the danger of omitting anything significant and, at the same time, it preserves unity and coherence by ensuring against the temptation to ramble.

TYPES OF OUTLINES

There are several different kinds of outlines, and each is helpful when used for the right purpose. But only one is of interest to us, so we will mention the others only briefly.

Scratch Outlines

A scratch outline is a "laundry list" of random notions related only vaguely to each other and to the subject and purpose of a speech. It can be useful for writing down ideas about a topic in the early stages of preparation, but a final outline should be better developed than this. Using a scratch outline invites inadequate topic analysis and poor development of the subject, and it provides a poor set of notes for use in delivery. When someone is unexpectedly called upon to speak, and has very little time for preparation, jotting down some notes in a scratch outline can serve a useful purpose.

Briefs

The most elaborate of all outline forms is called, strangely enough, a *brief*. A brief is an argumentative outline and contains *all* of the arguments that a speaker can discover, both *for* and *against* a claim. It is most useful in situations like debate, where speakers confront many of the opposing arguments. Moreover, preparing a brief helps to ensure complete analysis of a claim.

Rhetorical Outlines

A brief suffers, in a somewhat different sense, from a problem of the scratch outline; that is, because of its all-inclusivesness, it is a sophisticated sort of laundry list. A rhetorical outline, on the other hand, contains only the materials that will help to prove a case for a specific audience. Similarly, a rhetorical outline for an informative speech includes only what is necessary to accomplish its specific purpose. A rhetorical outline is by far the most useful in both preparation and delivery.

All three kinds of outlines vary in completeness of content, but rhetorical outlines vary also in the amount of language they contain. This ranges from the sketchiest kind of "topic" outline to the "complete-sentence" outline that is virtually a manuscript of the speech.

Complete-Sentence Outlines   A complete-sentence outline avoids one of the biggest problems with scratch outlines—inadequate development of ideas. Writing a complete sentence requires thinking it through before setting it down in final form. A significant disadvantage is that a complete-sentence outline is likely to become a manuscript of the speech or, at least, a document that in delivery needs only a transition here and there. Delivery is a lot less likely to be spontaneous under those conditions.

Topic Outlines   At the other extreme is the topic outline. Its headings are no more than a few words that call to mind the ideas to be discussed. There are several factors to weigh in judging the usefulness of either form. Complete-sentence outlines promote thorough analysis of ideas but tend to make delivery less spontaneous. Topic outlines, on the other hand, ensure spontaneity, but require a firmer grasp of materials and foster the temptation to memorize the speech.

The two outlines are identical in the way they show relationships and sequence. For example, here is part of the outline of a speech advocating passage of a federal slum-clearance bill. This section was meant to demonstrate the seriousness of the problem.

Complete sentence form	Topic form
I. Slums are a serious problem in American cities.	I. Slums a serious American problem
A. Decay has occurred in major American cities.	A. Decay
1. Areas more than 40 years old have decayed.	1. In spots 40 years old
2. 27 percent of nonfarm residences do not meet federal standards of structure and sanitation.	2. 27 percent unsound, unsanitary
B. There is an insufficient number of dwellings for the population.	B. Insufficient housing
1. More than 1.5 persons per room is considered by sociologists to be overcrowding.	1. Overcrowding at 1.5 per room
2. 6 percent of America's dwelling places house more than 1.5 persons per room.	2. 6 percent hold more than 1.5 per room
C. Slums create financial problems: 15 percent of Los Angeles residents live in slum areas.	C. Financial problems: 15 percent in slums
1. They contribute less than 3 percent of the city's tax income.	1. Give less than 3 percent of tax income
2. They consume 33 percent of the city Health Department's budget.	2. Use 33 percent of Health Department's budget
3. They require more than 33 percent of the city's law enforcement budget.	3. More than 33 percent of law enforcement budget

One final consideration: There is no absolute rule that forbids making a proper rhetorical outline in either of the two forms we have described and then in addition preparing a separate set of notes to use in delivery. All of these approaches to speech preparation have their advocates and their critics. Your instructor will tell you what is required.

TECHNIQUES OF OUTLINING

Parts of the Outline

All well-organized speeches have three identifiable parts: a beginning, a middle, and an end. They are mirrored in speech outlines in what are called, respectively, an introduction, a body, and a conclusion.

The Introduction   The introduction catches attention and arouses interest in the subject. It also contains a subject sentence, which says what the speech is going to be about, and it includes any necessary background information.

The Body   The body of the outline follows the introduction. It contains the subject matter of the speech organized in accordance with your purpose to inform, persuade, or entertain.

The Conclusion   In the conclusion, you bring the speech to an appropriate close.

In skeleton form, an outline looks like this:

SPECIFIC PURPOSE: _____
INTRODUCTION
   I. [Attention and interest material]
  II. [Subject sentence]
 III. [Background material, when required]
BODY
   I. [First main heading]
     A. [Supporting material]
     B. [Supporting material]
  II. [Second main heading]
    [And so on]
CONCLUSION
   I. [Summary, if used]
  II. [Concluding remarks, as needed]

Manuscript Speech

Showing Relationships and Sequence

The symbol that marks each heading (I, II, A, B, 1, 2, or the like) shows the relationship of that heading to others in the outline. The symbols used and the degree to which a heading is indented indicate its superior, subordinate, or coordinate rank.

Subordinate Ideas   If one heading is used to explain, prove or otherwise support another, it is subordinate to the other.

I. A main head is superior to its subheads.
A. Each subhead is subordinate to its main head.

Both the indenting of the subhead and the use of a different symbol series indicate the subordination to the eye. In the outline, subordinate headings *always follow* the main head.

WRONG
I. Supporting materials, [therefore]

A. Main idea

RIGHT
I. Main idea [which we understand because]

A. Supporting material

I. 27 percent of nonfarm homes do not meet federal standards of structure and sanitation, [therefore]
A. Decay has occurred in major American cities.

I. Decay has occurred in major American cities, [which we understand because]
A. 27 percent of nonfarm homes do not meet federal standards of structure and sanitation.

Coordinate Ideas   If two or more headings support the same larger heading, they are said to be coordinate. In the following illustration, headings A. and B. under I. are coordinate with each other, and so are A. and B. under II. Note also that I. and II. are coordinate because together they support the speech claim.

I. First main head

A. Support for I

B. Further support for I

II. Second main head

A. Support for II

B. Further support for II

[And so on]

I. Decay has occurred in major American cities.
A. Areas older than 40 years are allowed to deteriorate.
B. 27 percent of nonfarm homes do not meet federal standards of structure and sanitation.
II. Number of dwellings is insufficient for the population.
A. Sociologists consider more than 1.5 persons per room overcrowding.
B. 6 percent of America's housing has more than 1.5 per room.
[And so on]

Symbols of Subordination and Coordination   The symbols used to show subordination and coordination are purely arbitrary, but the following pattern is widely used:

    I. First main heading
        A. Support for I
            1. Support for A
                a. Support for 1
                    (1) Support for a
                        (a) Support for (1)
                        (b) Further support for (1)
                    (2) Further support for a
                b. Further support for 1
            2. Further support for A
        B. Further support for I
    II. Second main heading
        [And so on]

Checking the Outline

As the outline develops, check it frequently for accurate subordination and coordination, for formal correctness, and for content completeness.

Accurate Subordination and Coordination   Because the major purpose of making an outline is to show how the ideas are related, accuracy in subordination and coordination is an absolute requirement. In a speech to support the claim that Los Angeles is facing a crisis in transportation, the speaker organized a section of the outline this way:

    I. Traffic congestion is at a breakdown point.
        A. More than 600,000 automobiles enter and leave downtown Los Angeles
            every 24 hours.
            1. Most carry only one person; the average is 1.4 persons per car.
            2. More than half come and go from 7 to 9 A.M. and from 4 to 6 P.M.
            3. Rush-hour traffic is mainly one-way.
                a. Morning traffic is mostly inbound.
                b. Evening traffic is mostly outbound.
            4. Cars are expensive to operate.
        B. Adequate parking facilities are unavailable.

This outline says that 4. is subordinate to A. and helps to support it. But the idea that cars are expensive to operate (4.) has no direct connection with how many automobiles enter and leave downtown Los Angeles every day (A.). Nor does the fact that it's expensive to drive a car help to support the claim (I.) that traffic is at a breakdown point. In no reasonable sense, then, is 4. subordinate to either A. or I. Instead, the idea that cars are expensive to operate directly supports the basic speech claim (that there is a crisis in transportation). Because it has the same purpose as I. (traffic congestion), subhead 4. is really coordinate with I. and should become II. in the outline. The corrected outline would then read:

I. Traffic congestion is at a breakdown point.
  A. More than 600,000 automobiles, etc.
    [And so on]
  B. Adequate parking facilities are unavailable.
II. Cars are expensive to operate.

Formal Correctness   Making sure that the speech outline is formally correct will eliminate many of the problems of subordination and coordination. And the formal correctness of any speech outline can be checked by a simple and mechanical method. To check the formal correctness of a persuasive speech outline, add a connective such as *for, since, because, for the reason that* at the end of each heading *that is followed immediately by a subordinate point.* Add the word *and* to each heading *that is followed immediately by a coordinate point or by a superior heading.* The skeleton looks like this:

The speaker's claim should be accepted *for the reason that*
  I. Argument I. helps to prove the claim. [Argument I. should be accepted *for the reason that*]
    A. Helps to prove I. [Point A. should be accepted *for the reason that*]
      1. Helps to prove A. *and*
      2. Also helps to prove A. *and*
    B. Along with A. also helps to prove argument I.
      [B. ought to be accepted *for the reason that*]
      1. Helps to prove B. *and*
      2. Also helps to prove B. *and*
  II. Argument II. along with argument I. also helps to prove the speech claim. [Argument II. should be accepted *for the reason that*]
  [And so on]

Checking an outline by this method is quite simple. For instance, it makes very good sense to say:

  I. Traffic is at a breakdown point [*for the reason that*]
    A. More than 600,000 automobiles enter and leave Los Angeles every day, [*and*]
    B. Parking facilities are inadequate.

But within the context of this argument, it makes no sense at all to claim that:

  A. 600,000 automobiles enter and leave [*for the reason that*]
    1. *and*
    2. *and*
    3. *and*
    4. Cars are expensive to operate.

The formal correctness of an informative speech outline is tested by mentally adding in front of subordinate points such connective phrases as *for example* and *that is to say*. In coordinate positions use such words as *moreover, furthermore,* and *in addition.*

When either informative or persuasive speech outlines are tested this way *and they make sense,* it is reasonably certain that they are formally correct.

Content Completeness of Informative Speech Outlines   In addition to checking its formal correctness, an informative speech outline can also be tested by a system of "adding" ideas. Coordinate headings taken together should add up to no more and no less than their superior heading. Here is an example in skeleton form.

SPECIFIC PURPOSE: To inform the audience about _____
    I.
        A.
        B.
            1.
            2.
    II.
        A.
        B.

Now, "add up" the ideas contained in the above headings:

I.B.1. + I.B.2. = I.B.

I.A. + I.B.   = I.

II.A. + II.B. = II.

I. + II.   = Specific purpose

Let's see how this works in an actual example:

SPECIFIC PURPOSE: To explain the operation of the Electoral College
    I. Alexander Hamilton's mistrust of the common man
    II. Method of selecting electors determined by states
    III. Number equal to each state's congressional delegation
    IV. Electors nominated by parties
    V. Electoral College injustices

The outline is faulty for two reasons: In the first place, the five points of the outline add up to *less* than the specific purpose because the speech does not explain the operation of the Electoral College. Second, because the first and last points are not part of an explanation of how the College operates, they make the outline add up to *more* than the specific purpose sets forth. The example given here pertains to the relationship of main points to the specific purpose. The same principle applies to lower levels of subordination as well.

IMPORTANT TECHNICAL PRINCIPLES

Applying these principles will not only make it easier to construct well-organized outlines, it will make the speeches they represent hang together better and, at the same time, it will help to avoid a number of logical problems that would plague the outlines if the principles were ignored.

Each Heading an Assertion

Each of the headings in an outline should express an assertion. This means that a heading cannot be a question. The trouble with questions in an outline is that there can be no clear relationship between a question and either a subordinate or a coordinate point. Because a question makes no definite claim, it cannot be proved and it cannot be used as supporting material to clarify or to prove. An outline should answer questions, not ask them.

WRONG: How serious is traffic congestion in Los Angeles?
RIGHT: Traffic congestion in Los Angeles is at a breakdown point.

We are aware that rhetorical questions can be an effective element of style, and our discussion of oral style in Chapter 15 will show how they can be used artistically. Nothing we are saying is intended to deny that. Rather, the point here is one that we made in discussing traditional rhetoric in Chapter 1. *Disposition* (organization) and *elocution* (style) are different functions of language. The purpose of the outline is to reflect the *organization* of the speech (relationships and sequence). It is not intended to be a mirror of the *style*.

Each Heading a Single Assertion

An outline should show the relationships among the *individual* ideas. It cannot do this correctly unless each of the headings makes one and only one assertion.

WRONG
I. A six-year traffic survey in Los Angeles demonstrates the interesting paradox that approximately the same numbers of people daily come into and out of the downtown area but that traffic has increased 20 percent.

RIGHT
I. A six-year traffic survey in Los Angeles demonstrates an interesting paradox.
A. Approximately the same numbers of people daily come into and out of the downtown area.
B. Yet traffic has increased 20 percent.

Only One Symbol per Heading

To label a single heading in the outline both I. and A. or both A. and 1. suggests that a subordinate point is its own main head, which is clearly impossible. It brings to mind the old song, "I'm My Own Grandpa." When a double symbol is used, it ordinarily means that the speaker has recognized a series of points that seem coordinate and senses that they need a common superior heading but hasn't decided what it is.

WRONG
    I. A. Decay has occurred in major American cities.
        B. 27 percent of nonfarm homes do not meet federal standards of structure and sanitation.

RIGHT
    I. Slums are a serious problem in America.
      A. Decay has occurred in major cities.
      B. 27 percent of nonfarm homes, etc.

No Overlapping Headings

A speaker advocating the repeal of child labor laws argued that other cities in the nation might receive the benefits Philadelphia got from the work-school program initiated to combat labor shortages in World War II. Here is a part of the argument in outline form:

    I. In Philadelphia, the wartime work program was of great value.
      A. It helped reduce the number of school dropouts.
      B. It taught initiative and responsibility.
      C. Young people gained a new sense of importance from contributing to the family's resources.
      D. Discipline problems at home and at school decreased.

Notice that subpoint B. overlaps both C. and D. Instead of being coordinate with B., these two points are really pieces of evidence to show that B. is true. When they are outlined correctly, they will be subpoints 1. and 2. subordinated under B.

REVISING THE OUTLINE

The first outline of a speech is usually not strong. Often it is little more than a scratch outline of ideas that seem to have some bearing on the subject and some relationship to each other. In beginning to think about a subject, a speaker usually lacks enough detailed information to see clearly the best way to relate the ideas. As information and ideas grow, however, new relationships develop and less useful ones are discarded. A constant examination of the outline will be necessary, even to the actual moment of speaking.

SUMMARY

Although it is quite usual to talk about subject matter and organization as if they could be separated, in fact, they cannot. Neither substance nor form can exist independently. But speech organization is not always effective. *Good* organization makes clear the *relationships* among the ideas, arguments, and supporting materials, and it also shows the *sequence* in which they will be presented. Good organization is characterized by *unity* (a harmonious oneness among the parts) and *coherence* (a rational ordering of the parts).

An outline is a blueprint for a speech. There are several different kinds of outlines, each of which has its proper use, but a rhetorical outline is the one that will usually serve best.

The parts of an outline reflect the parts of the speech. There is an introduction, a body, and a conclusion. The introduction serves to catch attention and arouse interest, to tell the audience what the subject and purpose are, and to give them any necessary background material. The body of the outline organizes the subject matter of the speech. The conclusion brings the speech to an appropriate close.

Structurally, an outline uses subordination and coordination to show the relationships among the elements of the speech. Subordinate headings clarify or prove some other (superior) heading. Headings are coordinate when they support the same superior heading. Subordination and coordination are shown by the use of symbols and indentation.

The quality of an outline can be tested by checking it for accurate subordination and coordination, formal correctness, and, in the case of informative speech outlines, completeness of content.

Keep these technical principles in mind:

1. Each outline heading should make an assertion.
2. Each heading should contain no more than one assertion.
3. Use only one symbol for any one heading.
4. There should be no overlapping among the headings.

Frequent revision of the outline will be necessary, even to the actual moment of speaking.

EXERCISES

1. Using the following points, make an outline for the body of a speech showing subordination and coordination by the use of correct symbols and indentations. First find your main heads (there are two of them); then look for the subheads; and then proceed to further levels of subordination.

SPECIFIC PURPOSE: To inform the audience about the major activities open to students on a college campus.

1. Students attend classes
2. Pamphlets
3. There are extracurricular activities
4. Plays

  5. Students plan and attend their own social events
  6. College football team
  7. College fencing team
  8. Volleyball
  9. They take tests
10. Periodicals
11. Students have a variety of cultural activities outside the classroom
12. College track team
13. Art exhibits
14. Softball
15. Dances
16. College basketball team
17. The primary activities on a college campus are curricular
18. Books
19. College wrestling team
20. Golf club
21. Parties
22. College baseball team
23. Students use the library as a source of information
24. Clubs and fraternities have a league
25. They write papers and deliver speeches
26. Maps
27. Touch football
28. Concert series
29. Tennis club
30. They listen to lectures by the instructor
31. Students attend athletic events as spectators and participants
32. Swimming club
33. Intercollegiate athletics
34. Lecture series
35. Minor sports
36. They engage in class discussions
37. Major sports
38. Afterschool sports are available
39. Intramural athletics

2. Read one of the speeches in Appendix B. State the specific purpose of the speech and then outline it. Discuss with your class what you learned about organization from this exercise.
3. Write a short paper to attach to the statement of purpose and outline you have made for the speech in Exercise 2. In this paper evaluate the organization of the speech based on what you learned from outlining it.

chapter **13**

Introductions, Conclusions, and Transitions

I. Introductions
  A. Principles for gaining attention
    1. Intensity
    2. Change
    3. Unity
    4. Familiarity
    5. Novelty
    6. Repetition
  B. Putting attention factors to use
    1. Show the importance of the subject
    2. Show the importance of the occasion
    3. Use startling statistics
    4. Ask rhetorical questions
    5. Use quotations
    6. Tell a story
  C. The subject sentence
  D. Background material
II. Conclusions
  A. Summarizing the main points
  B. Characterizing the subject
  C. Telling a story
  D. Restating a proposed plan
  E. Using a quotation
  F. Developing an analogy
  G. Showing the importance of the subject and/or occasion
III. Maintaining clarity: transitions

Now that we have examined (in Chapter 12) some of the general principles of organization and outlining, let's turn to the central subject of this chapter: introductions, conclusions, and transitions. The body of a speech carries the main burden of communication, but because of the inherent ambiguities of language, the normal self-centeredness and short attention span of audiences, and the inevitable distractions in any speaking situation, speeches need all the help they can get in order to be interesting, clear, and effective. That's why introductions, conclusions, and transitions play such a vital role in the success of a speech.

INTRODUCTIONS

A speech introduction performs three very important tasks. First, it helps to *gain attention*. Second, in the subject sentence it tells the audience what the speech is about. Third, it conveys any necessary *background material*.

Principles for Gaining Attention

In most cases, listeners have only a vague notion of what a speaker is going to say and little active interest in it. Despite this, speakers are tempted to rush into the subject of the speech. As a result, speeches in class often begin like this:

"My purpose today is to tell you why the inflation index is misleading."

"You have to be careful how you choose a health club."

"Since grades interest us all, perhaps you'd like to hear about the history of the grading system."

Although none of these openings is likely to command enthusiastic attention, notice that the third example is a bit different from the other two. The speaker seems to be at least aware of the need to arouse the interest of the audience. By way of contrast to these openings, look at the following introduction. It was used by a student who wanted to talk about acupuncture. It catches attention, includes a touch of humor, looks as though it would arouse curiosity, and relates the subject to a value of universal interest: health.

If someone ever put a tack on your chair and you sat on it, unless you're one of the dead-end kids you'd know it. Could it be that that person was trying to improve your health? "Not likely," you say and you are probably right. But many people claim that there is a way that puncturing you can improve your health. It's the ancient Chinese practice of acupuncture. Let me tell you about the medical controversy acupuncture has aroused.

Some theorists consider attention to be the central factor in successful communication.[1] But it isn't easy to hold attention, because listeners are constantly being bombarded by all sorts of stimuli. People can't attend to several things at one time and perceive all of them clearly. Instead, they pay attention to the stimuli that are most prominent.[2]

Many conditions influence a listener's tendency to pay attention to one message rather than another. People who place a high value on horses, football, or classical music will pay attention when their valued subject is discussed. No matter what the subject, however, there are several factors that will help draw the attention of an audience: *intensity, change, unity, familiarity, novelty,* and *repetition.* These factors ought to be used throughout the speech, but especially in the introduction. To perform their function properly, they must be pertinent to the speech and appropriate to the audience and the occasion.

Intensity   Among a group of stimuli, listeners tend to respond to those that are most intense. The stimuli a speaker conveys must be the most intense in the room. And they must be louder than the general babble. The speaker's case must be stated more forcefully than that of any competitor.

A startling statement can be used to gain attention in the introduction. The story is told that the eminent nineteenth-century clergyman, Henry Ward Beecher, began a sermon on a hot day by mopping his brow with his handkerchief and saying, "God damn, it's a hot day!" [*pause*] "I heard a man say that just a few minutes ago." With that opening, Reverend Beecher began to develop his theme—on cursing and swearing. Intensity of this sort, however, can go wrong. It did for a student who wanted to talk about the problem of rape. She began her speech by blowing a police whistle as loud as she could and literally screaming, "RAPE!" To be sure, she caught the attention of her audience, but the most startling thing was that she caught the attention of a great part of the rest of the campus, including the security officers.

Change   Sustained and unvaried intensity can lose attention. People pay more attention to a change in the nature and intensity of stimuli than they do to a continuous level of stimulation. When you are studying and someone starts typing nearby, it attracts your attention because the sound is different from the stimuli you have become used to. Soon, however, the noise of the typing fades into the background and you don't hear it any more.

Not all changes command attention. For example, someone speaking in a sing-song pattern will make vocal changes but, once a listener recognizes the pattern, the rhythmic changes command as little attention as a monotone. If, at certain points in a speech, the speaker seems more intense, argues more carefully, or strengthens the value appeal, the audience will pay closer attention.

Unity   In Chapter 12, using other words, we defined unity as the quality a speech has when all of its parts belong there. It is not only an essential characteristic of good organization, it is required in all other aspects of speech making as well. It must be as strictly maintained in the introduction as in any other part. The most important way to do this is to be sure that the interest factor of the introduction points to the subject of the speech. For example, some speakers take pride in their ability to tell jokes. But a joke is a good interest factor only when, in both substance and mood, it directs the attention of the audience to the subject and purpose of the speech. Otherwise, no matter how funny it is, the joke is intrusive and damages the unity of the speech. As a result, it distracts the attention of the audience from the proper subject.

Familiarity Familiar ideas command attention. When ideas are unfamiliar, listeners' minds will begin to wander, to look for more understandable stimuli in which they are already interested. A subject, therefore, has to be related to what is familiar to the audience. "You may not know or care what a transmission is, but if your car didn't have one, you wouldn't be in class today." "The food you get in a Chinese restaurant is not what the people in China eat." In each of these cases, the speaker is trying to link the subject to something that is familiar to the audience.

Novelty Something novel will almost always attract attention. A speaker brings a strange machine to class. The members of the audience say to themselves, "I wonder what that is all about." Although novelty will get immediate attention, it must be linked to the familiar if interest is to be sustained. Listeners will stop paying attention to something if they become aware that it has nothing to do with their interests.

Able public speakers make clear transitions between ideas. (Forsyth, Monkmeyer)

Repetition   Since attention span is short and listeners are continually being attracted by competing stimuli, it is quite common for the ideas of a speech to be forgotten, even those that have been stated forcefully. Judicious repetition of ideas and phrases will strengthen the speech. One way to use repetition is through parallel sentence structure and phrasing. In one section of his Annual Message of January 1936, President Franklin Delano Roosevelt used 14 questions in a row beginning with the word "Shall." Ten of the 14 began with the words, "Shall we say?" Everyone is familiar with the repetition of words and phrase patterns that Lincoln used in the Gettysburg Address, "That government of the people, by the people, and for the people shall not perish from this earth."

Putting Attention Factors to Use

Look now at some examples of how to use these attention factors in beginning a speech.

Show the Importance of the Subject   A student speaker began a speech on acid rain this way:

> Rain can be a real inconvenience to any of us. It might cut short a softball game, eliminate a tennis date, ruin our hair or sop up our clothes. But, there is a new kind of rain falling in the United States and Canada which may have a devastating impact on our environment and on our future. It's called acid rain.

Show the Importance of the Occasion   Here is an example of how a speaker could take advantage of the occasion:

> December 7, 1941, was a day which Franklin Delano Roosevelt said would "live in infamy." That was the day when Japanese air forces bombed Pearl Harbor and involved us in World War II. Well, today is December 7, 1986, forty-five years later. It is an appropriate anniversary for us to ask a question about the current status of our warning system. How open are we to another Pearl Harbor attack? Do we have a defense warning system? Yes, we do and it is called the Early Warning System.

Use Startling Statistics   To take advantage of a situation wherein the audience isn't aware of the true state of affairs, a speaker can use startling statistics. Here's an example:

> Single parent families only constitute about eight percent of all American house-holds. But since 1970 while all households increased by 32 percent, single parent families have increased by 102 percent. Nine out of ten single parent families are headed by women. The median income of these single parent families headed by women is only $9000 per year. Perhaps it's time we looked more carefully at this growing phenomenon and learned more about what sets such families apart from the rest of America.

Ask Rhetorical Questions   A rhetorical question is one that is directed at an audience but that the audience is not really expected to answer. One method of getting attention is to ask rhetorical questions in the introduction. For instance, the introduction in the example given just above could be handled this way:

> Did you know that single parent families have increased since 1970 more than three times faster than all other households? Did you know that nine out of ten of such families are headed by a woman? Does it shock you to learn that their median income is $9000 per year? Can we ignore any longer this growing phenomenon in America?

Use Quotations   A striking quotation will arouse interest, particularly when it is something said or written by a well-known person. The following introduction to a speech on dog training is an example of how it might be used.

> Lord Byron, one of England's greatest poets, wrote this epitaph:
>
> > "Near this spot are deposited the remains of one who possessed beauty without vanity, strength without insolence, courage without ferocity and all the virtues of man without his vices." That epitaph was for his dog. And most dog owners know that a dog can truly be a better companion than a lot of the people we know. But a dog can also be a great nuisance and a real trial if not properly trained. The difference between the dog you wish you didn't have and the one Byron describes may be a matter of investing a few moments of your time each day while the dog is still a pup. A few simple commands are not difficult for you to teach your dog, and they will make your relationship much better.

Tell a Story   A story is an interesting way of introducing a speech, especially when it recalls some experience the audience has had.

> A friend of mine had a crush on one of the prettiest women in the freshman class. He was in two courses with her, but could never find the right moment to introduce himself. One day in the cafeteria he ended up standing in line right behind her. Because he felt so self-conscious, his voice froze, and as they moved along the serving counter he felt yet another opportunity slipping away.
>
> > Suddenly the girl turned to him and pointed at a selection. "Do you know what this is?" she asked.
> >
> > "Y-yes," he replied, "that's Don MacKensie. Hi, I'm macaroni salad."
> >
> > Surely you've had similar, though perhaps not quite as embarrassing, situations. What is it about the way our brain functions that accounts for differences between what we say and what we want to say?[3]

We have examined only a few of the countless ways to begin a speech. All of these attention-getting devices are at least potentially useful. But any decision about which one to use should be determined solely by the subject, the audience, and the occasion of the speech. Not one of them is worth the time it takes to deliver it unless it is appropriate to all three of these elements of the speaking situation.

The Subject Sentence

After you have won the attention of an audience, you must direct it to the subject of your speech. If the statement of purpose expresses the speech claim clearly and precisely, it will serve admirably as a guide in speech preparation. But because its style is not suited to good oral communication, it won't appear in the speech. Instead, a *subject sentence* will tell the audience what the speech claim is. This, in effect, is the statement of purpose cast into the sort of sentence one might use in conversation.

STATEMENT OF PURPOSE: To inform the audience about the caste system in India.

This statement of purpose would become a subject sentence somewhat as follows:

SUBJECT SENTENCE: We can get a better insight into the culture of India if we have some understanding of how the caste system operates in that country.

Background Material

When an audience is not familiar with the subject at hand, it may be necessary to orient them to it. For example, the captive breeding program to save the California condor, an endangered species, received a good deal of publicity a few years ago but today many people know nothing about it. A speech on the subject would probably need some background such as the following:

The California condor is the world's largest bird. In the past it soared over all the Pacific coast. Today it is confined to a small nesting area near Ventura, California, in Los Padres National Forest. By 1983 its numbers had declined to slightly more than 30 birds, with no more than a dozen able to reproduce. Consequently, a controversial program was undertaken to take eggs from nests in the wild and raise the birds in captivity.

This gives the listeners an idea of what the program is about and prepares them to be informed about the controversy surrounding it.

Background material, however, should be limited to a few sentences. If more background information than this is required, it would be better to revise the statement of purpose and make the background material the subject of the speech.

CONCLUSIONS

The conclusion brings a speech to an appropriate close and, at the same time, helps to ensure that its purpose has been clearly achieved. Clarity, however, is a minimal requirement. The conclusion can also lend a personal touch by adding a story, a joke, or a quotation that illustrates the overall idea. The conclusion is the last chance to make sure that the audience has understood the central idea of the speech. There are several ways of doing this.

Summarizing the Main Points

The conclusion of a speech to inform draws together the main ideas and the supporting materials, to ensure that the audience has a unified and coherent overview of the subject as a whole. The conclusion should therefore contain at least a restatement of the subject sentence and a restatement of the main ideas. In short, it should be a summary of the speech. This much is needed to assure clarity. A student, talking about the way dolphins communicate among themselves (and with human beings), concluded the speech this way:

> We see, then, that dolphins have big brains, bright minds, sharp ears, and their own built-in version of a sonar system. Not only do they communicate rapidly and effectively among themselves but they graciously condescend, so it seems, to communicate with us even to the extent of learning some of our language.
>
> We like to consider ourselves expert communicators but we still have prejudices and people don't know very well how to touch each other and say, I love you. Maybe knowing something about dolphins will sharpen, highlight, and make more effective our research into the mysteries of human communication. Anthropologist Ashley Montague puts it precisely and simply when he says, "Dolphins have large brains. Possibly they will some day be able to teach us what brains are for."

A speech to persuade, on the other hand, does not as often close with a summary of ideas or arguments. More frequently, it will have a climactic ending that summarizes only in the sense that it is the final outcome of all that has gone before.

It would be untrue to say that there is such-and-such a number of ways a persuasive speech can be brought to a close. The only limit to the variety of conclusions possible is the number of speeches possible. Despite the wide variety that one finds in the conclusions of actual speeches, however, a unifying thread of similarity may be found in all of them: the tendency to *characterize* the central claim of the speech in some way that will thrust it home. A sampling of conclusions chosen almost at random from recent issues of *Vital Speeches of the Day* shows a few of the different ways speeches end. Notice that in each case a specific technique can be recognized.

Characterizing the Subject

Historian Sue Mansfield was arguing that war and preparation for war among industrialized nations is caused not by greed, glory, or revenge, but by fear, and she claimed that fear exerts a dangerous influence on military strategy and tactics. Her conclusion sums up the point she was making in an almost allegorical fashion:

> I saw a cartoon recently in which three togaed figures are shown meeting up among the clouds. The first says to the second, while pointing to the third, "I'd like to introduce Mars, the God of Defense." Obviously, the artist hoped to play on our sense of the absurdity of recent escalations of nuclear weapons in the name of a seemingly innocuous and sane defensiveness. Unfortunately the joke is not as funny as it was meant to be. If any of you have ever seen a six-pound mother cat take on a dog five times her size and weight, prepared either to eliminate him or die in the attempt, you will understand the seriousness of fear. Indeed, the Goddess of Defense—and she has I suggest no favorites among the nations of the world—may well be more dangerous in the long run than the greedy, calculating God of the warriors.[4]

Telling a Story

Wayne C. Anderson is a business executive who is responsible for relations between his company and the federal government. In a speech discussing the significance of consumer-related issues, he concluded his remarks with a story to emphasize the central point of his speech:

> I'll close with a true story that I believe sums up why all of us devote the enormous energy we do in our profession to our responsibilities. And then I'll be happy to take your questions.
>
> Several years ago I experienced one of those beautiful memories parents truly cherish. We had put the children to bed about an hour earlier, and after my wife and I talked about the day's events, over some coffee and tea, I opened the briefcase to tackle the daily evening ritual of "homework." That night in preparation for a trip to Brazil, I was reading some background reports about that part of the world. To clarify a point, which frankly I have since forgotten, I decided to tiptoe into my oldest son's bedroom, he was about 7 at the time, to get a globe that was on his bookshelf. I carefully and quietly opened the door to his bedroom and by relying on the light in the hallway, proceeded to sneak into his room and without a sound (I thought) took the globe from the shelf and headed for the door. About 2/3 of the way across the room, my son sat straight up in bed and asked, almost apologetically, "Dad, where are you going with my world?"
>
> It's a question that keeps re-occurring to me even today as I ponder the great issues of the day and what I can do about them. Perhaps one of the reasons I feel so strongly about our responsibilities in the business/government relationship is because of my sense of duty implicit in the question.
>
> I understand next month the issue management association will celebrate its second birthday. Congratulations and best wishes for many more—and to you, its members, from whatever discipline you represent, I look forward to working with you and share with you the hope of answering the question—where are you going with my world![5]

Restating a Proposed Plan

Business executive John B. Fery spoke to the Executives' Club of Chicago. His central idea was that although business planning in the decade of the 1980s is much more difficult than it was in the 1950s, 1960s, and 1970s, managers are nonetheless expected to guide their companies in the right direction. He concluded his speech not with a summary of the *arguments* he had used, but with a brief restatement of the *plan of action* he had proposed. Repeating the plan would tend to remind the audience of the reasons that supported it. Notice, incidentally, the parallel structure of his language. This stylistic device is discussed in Chapter 15.

> To sum up, then. We can mitigate the downside potential of an uncertain future;
>
> By committing ourselves, at least implicitly, to a long-term strategic view of the future;
>
> By remaining flexible, both financially and operationally, so that we can respond appropriately to a changing environment;
>
> By understanding clearly, based on experience and other sources of information, what drives our business; and, finally,
>
> By building upon our strengths—that is, continually infusing the latest technologies into our manufacturing processes and tapping more fully that very critical competitive asset—our people.
>
> As Peter Drucker has said, managing the fundamentals of a business also means managing for tomorrow—no matter how uncertain. Fundamentals *are* obvious, but, quoting Drucker now, "How many managements work on them? How many even *think* of them? I'd like to leave you with the thought that there's no more appropriate time for working on fundamentals than our present Age of Uncertainty.
>
> Thank you.[6]

Using a Quotation

The speaker cited in the example just above included a brief quotation in his conclusion. Speakers quite frequently use quotations that sum up, characterize, and give impact to a subject; the more eminent the source, the greater the impact. For example, James C. Miller, III, Chairman of the Federal Trade Commission, told members of the American Bar Association that the best approach to restoring long-term industrial growth was to keep the government out of the business of controlling industrial policies. This is the way he ended his speech:

> In conclusion, it was Thomas Jefferson who said:
>
> No, my friend, the way to have good and safe government, is not to trust it all to one, but to divide it among the many, distributing to everyone exactly the functions he is competent to [perform]. . . . It is by dividing and subdividing [the powers of government] from the great national one down through all its subordinations, until it ends in the administration of every man's farm by himself; by

placing under everyone what his own eye may superintend, that all will be done for the best. What has destroyed liberty and the rights of man in every government which has ever existed under the sun? The generalizing and concentrating all cares and powers into one body. . . .

In sum, I strongly believe that if we are to preserve our democratic heritage, we must always be on guard against the unwarranted centralization of power. By even the most optimistic assessments, the prospective gains from any interventionist reindustrialization program do not justify the attendant losses in individual liberties and threats to our democratic institutions.

Thank you very much![7]

Although it is not evident from reading the conclusion alone, in the conclusion Miller identifies *for the first time* the values on which he has based his appeals: individual liberty and the preservation of democratic institutions.

Developing an Analogy

Bank executive Thomas C. Theobald used an analogy as a concluding device:

I think of business in the international arena much as the Olympics. In the Olympics, country does not play against country. One player plays against another player, one team against another team. When three winners stand on the steps to receive the gold, the silver, and the bronze medals, those three winners, individually, have won their championships, and the three winners nearly always represent three different countries, countries with different cultures, different approaches, even different rules.

As businessmen in a world business Olympics, we are proud of our individual nationalities—but we are competing like the long-distance runner, in a world competition, where individual performance will win the day.[8]

Showing the Importance of the Subject and/or Occasion

John Brademas, President of New York University, concluded a speech by reminding his audience of the *significance of the subject*. Because the speech was the keynote address of a meeting, and because it is a primary function of a keynote address to impress upon the audience the seriousness of the business at hand, it was quite appropriate for him to end the speech in this fashion. He said:

I hope that in the remaining sessions of the Forum, and after you have returned to your universities, you will give these matters [of financing graduate-level education] your full attention. A great deal is at stake for no less than the future of America in this century—and the next—depends on the strength and quality of our institutions of graduate scholarship, research and teaching.[9]

MAINTAINING CLARITY: TRANSITIONS

A language device that has enormous utility for helping an audience see the unity, coherence, relationships, and sequence in a speech is called *transition*.

Transitions have been variously described as uniting ideas, joining them, cementing them. Although it may seem paradoxical, they also hold them apart. These two opposing functions of transitions, joining together and at the same time holding apart, are necessary for the reason that the transitions literally stand between two separate ideas. The job the transition does is to maintain the separateness of the two parts and to show at the same time that they are related. It says to the listeners, "The idea just discussed has a bearing on the one that's coming up right now. I'm supposed to show how the two are related to each other without confusing them with one another."

No one needs to be told that transitions are necessary. Everyone seems to use them instinctively. The trouble lies in the kind of transitions that are used. Virtually meaningless expressions like "and," "uh," "ok," "also," are tiresomely repeated by speakers who feel the need for indicating a movement of thought but don't know how to say clearly from where to where the thought is going to move.

Confusing gaps can occur if a speaker fails to make adequate connections when moving from one point to another. Look at this outline of the introduction to a speech:

I. Everyone who drives the highways faces a problem.
II. The problem is as old as the highways themselves.
III. Billboards are undesirable.
  A. They are esthetically displeasing.
  B. They create so much clutter that they defeat their own purpose.
  C. They can be dangerous.
IV. [SUBJECT SENTENCE] Let's look at the three major attempts at federal regulation of billboards:
  A. The Bonus Act of 1958
  B. The Highway Beautification Act of 1965
  C. Amendments to that Act in 1978

Although the subject is not likely to have a great inherent interest value, it could, with an imaginative and adequately developed interest factor, command the attention of the audience. In the opening comments, this speaker used the device of suspense in order to arouse the curiosity of the audience. But look at the awkward gap between Sections II. and III. of the outline. The value claim that billboards are undesirable does not follow smoothly from the notion that some undisclosed problem has a long history. A transition is needed to pave the way between the two ideas.

Again, look at the unbridged span between Section III. and the subject sentence. Although it seems reasonable to say that billboards are undesirable because they are esthetically displeasing, self-defeating, and dangerous, it is not likely that the audience will be able to move easily from there to the idea of federal regulation. Some transition is needed to bridge the gap.

In general, transitions appear in one or the other of two forms. In the first case, they merely indicate the sequence of ideas. There are many familiar variations of this kind: "First, second, third." "Not only, but also." "Let me turn now to another point." The second kind of transition is considerably better and should be used whenever there is a significant movement between ideas. It is also somewhat more elaborate in that it not only shows the sequence of ideas but includes an internal summary. An *internal summary* is a repetition or a restatement of a part of the material previously discussed. Such a brief recap serves as a convenient bridge between the ideas or parts of the speech. In the illustration above, for example, a transition between the heading III.C. and the subject sentence might be, "Because of these undesirable characteristics, there have been attempts at governmental regulation."

SUMMARY

The introduction and the conclusion of a speech are both necessary and helpful in achieving clarity and getting the audience involved in the subject of the speech. Transitions help to maintain both clarity and interest.

Introductions are more likely to gain attention when they are marked by such characteristics as intensity, change, unity, novelty, familiarity, and repetition. Some of the ways a speech introduction gains attention and arouses interest are by showing the importance of the subject and the occasion, using startling statistics, asking rhetorical questions, using quotations, and telling a story. The introduction also contains a subject sentence, which tells the audience what the speech is about, and it provides any necessary background material.

A conclusion brings the speech to an appropriate end. Most often an informative speech will conclude with a summary of the central idea and the major supporting points. Persuasive speeches will also on occasion summarize the arguments adduced in support of the speech claim, but they tend more often to *characterize* the subject in some way, tell a story, restate the plan proposed, use a quotation, develop an analogy, or stress the importance of the subject and/or occasion.

Transitions form a bridge between consecutive ideas. They maintain clarity by showing where the speech has been and where it is going.

NOTES

1. James A. Winans, *Public Speaking* (Englewood Cliffs, N.J.: Prentice-Hall, 1917), p. 194.
2. Paul Bakan, *Attention* (New York: Van Nostrand Reinhold, 1966), p. iii; Magdalen D. Vernon, "Perception, Attention and Consciousness," in *Attention,* ed. Paul Bakan, pp. 38–39.
3. Robert K. Blechman, "Campus Comedy," *Reader's Digest,* Sept. 1984, p. 100. Reprinted with permission.

4. Sue Mansfield, "Strategy, Fear and the Atom," *Vital Speeches of the Day,* **50** (Mar. 1, 1984), p. 308.

5. Wayne C. Anderson, "Issues Management," *Vital Speeches of the Day,* **50** (Mar. 1, 1984), p. 311.

6. John B. Fery, "Managing in an Age of Uncertainty," *Vital Speeches of the Day,* **50** (Jan. 1, 1984), p. 169.

7. James C. Miller, "Reindustrialization Through the Free Market," *Vital Speeches of the Day,* **50** (May 15, 1984), p. 464.

8. Thomas C. Theobald, "Rediscovering America," *Vital Speeches of the Day,* **50** (May 1, 1984), p. 432.

9. John Brademas, "Graduate Education in America," *Vital Speeches of the Day,* **50** (Apr. 1, 1984), p. 377.

EXERCISES

1. Examine two of the informative speeches in Appendix B. How effective do you think the introductions are? What differences in technique do you see between them? What alternative ways can you think of to introduce those subjects to a college student audience?

2. Examine two of the persuasive speeches in Appendix B and answer the same questions as in Exercise 1.

3. Select an informative speech by one of your classmates and suggest how you might have tried to gain attention had you delivered the speech. Why is your method better than the one your classmate used?

4. Write a short paper explaining the conclusion of a recent speech you gave and why you concluded as you did. Explain either why that was better than some other possible conclusions or how you would improve the conclusion were you to give the speech again.

5. Listen to several speeches in your class and note the kinds of transitions used. Compare the speakers on how often they omit transitions, or use transitions that only indicate order, and how often they make internal summaries.

four

COMMUNICATING SPEECHES

chapter *14*

Dealing with Anxiety

   I. Don't blame yourself
  II. Realize the importance of experience
 III. Choose situations with a high potential for success
 IV. Concentrate on the message
  V. Prepare thoroughly
 VI. Adopt a conversational attitude
VII. Consciously play the role of the confident speaker
    A. Walk briskly to the platform
    B. Look directly at the audience
    C. Use a good attention factor in the introduction
    D. Control the rate of delivery
    E. Keep your nervousness to yourself
VIII. Be a good listener

Chances are good that you have some anxiety about the public speaking situation. If so, you are not alone, because about 75 percent of the people in your speech class believe that this is an important problem.[1] A group of 3000 Americans were interviewed in 1973, and 41 percent of them said that they were more afraid of speaking before a group than they were of any other one of the things that people normally fear, such as heights, loneliness, or ugly bugs.[2] Even seasoned professional entertainers, actors, and lecturers are not immune to "stage fright." Indeed, many successful speakers and performers realize that nervousness is a natural part of getting ready for a public presentation. It is much like the athlete who has to be "psyched up" to have an outstanding day. Being tense and nervous before a speech is perfectly normal. It is something you can expect.

Anxiety, of course, can be very troublesome to a speaker even though it is expected. Anxiety may mean butterflies in the stomach, stumbling over words, vocalizing pauses (injecting "uh" and "er" without regard to meaning), trembling hands and knees, or being unable to look directly at members of the audience. And the symptoms can differ from one speaking situation to another. In your church group you may feel no nervousness, but in a speech that is to be graded it may be a problem. Nervousness may also differ with the topic or the nature of the communication called for.[3]

One reality that should help to put your nervousness into proper perspective is that you rarely actually look or sound as bad as you think you do. There is even evidence that in some situations people who show serious anxiety problems are actually accepted better than those who don't.[4] Remember also that frequently your symptoms of anxiety are not perceived. Again and again we have heard students comment on their nervousness only to have the other students say that they didn't notice anything.

Here are some practical suggestions to help you deal with anxiety.

DON'T BLAME YOURSELF

Speakers who find themselves displaying anxiety will frequently make the problem worse by becoming angry with themselves. But the physical manifestations of nervousness cannot be controlled easily. If you understand how powerless you are, you may be able to stop blaming yourself and thus reduce the psychic feedback. You cannot will away the anxiety no matter how much pressure you put on yourself. As a matter of fact, paying attention to the problem sometimes makes it worse.

REALIZE THE IMPORTANCE OF EXPERIENCE

Just as unhappy experiences can condition you to fear public speaking, so can favorable experiences condition you to enjoy it. Eliminating as much of the mystery as possible will help you to attain this goal. It is best to know what effective public speaking is, and to study the methods of organizing speeches, supporting them, and delivering them. In the locker room, the hallway, or at the dinner table you are continually making speeches. It is your perception of a speaking situation rather than the situation itself that makes it threatening. Making a good speech requires nothing you cannot master. You can have the kind of experiences that build confidence. Each favorable experience will reinforce the others.

Some people have such serious anxiety that it is genuinely disabling. They need professional help.[5] But for most people, a well-developed program of speech preparation and presentation, such as the course you are now enrolled in, is very effective in reducing the problem.[6]

CHOOSE SITUATIONS WITH A HIGH POTENTIAL FOR SUCCESS

Research evidence shows that students who suffer from anxiety have a tendency to do one of two things: choose the simplest or the most difficult speaking situations.[7] Those who choose difficult tasks, it is believed, do so because they won't be criticized for failure. Whether it is deliberate or accidental, this tactic should be avoided. Instead, do everything you can to make yourself successful. Choose a subject you know well and in which you have considerable interest. Limiting your task helps to maximize the possibility of success. There is plenty of time to try challenging subjects after you have had some success.

CONCENTRATE ON THE MESSAGE

We are convinced that the most important way to deal with anxiety is to focus your attention on the communication task before you rather than on any emotional problems you have. Concentrating on the message you want to convey will help you take your mind off the personal anxiety you feel.

PREPARE THOROUGHLY

It seems obvious that anxiety will attack you if you aren't sure of what you want your speech to do or whether the speech will do it. In the presence of these uncertainties, you will be insecure about how the audience will react. Careful preparation is the only realistic solution to this problem. Study your speech subject well. Understand your topic and build a broad background of information around it.

There are certain laxities that effective speaking does not allow: "I'm not too sure about this, but I think it is pronounced. . . ." "I understand that Professor Kernaghan has a different view on this, but I couldn't find his book in our library." "I had to work late last night, so I didn't have a chance to check all the facts." These confessions merely say that you are not expert on the subject. Listeners ask, "Why should I listen?" Confidence in speaking grows from knowing that you are well prepared and seeing that your audience realizes you are qualified to speak.

Thorough preparation includes a careful analysis of your audience. The more you know about your listeners, the more familiar they will become to you and the less threatening. Believe this. It's the best advice the present chapter can give: When you

Doing the homework—studying methods of organizing, supporting, and delivering speeches—
helps a speaker achieve a favorable speaking outcome. (© Kruse, Jeroboam)

are sure of your audience and sure of your subject, you will be confident of your
ability to meet the demands of the speaking situation.

ADOPT A CONVERSATIONAL ATTITUDE

It is helpful to think of public speaking as conversation. People speaking to a group of
friends in informal surroundings have little trouble saying what they want to say. If
you think of public speaking as something enormously greater and more formal than
private conversation, you burden yourself with pressures that are not part of the
informal situation. The more you can think of public speaking as conversation, the
easier public speaking will be. The same direct, friendly, enthusiastic kind of
communication that is so enjoyable in a friendly get-together is what makes public
speaking effective.

CONSCIOUSLY PLAY THE ROLE OF THE CONFIDENT SPEAKER

There is much value in deliberately adopting a pose of good adjustment to the
speaking situation. Psychologists believe that accepting a role often makes one do

things that are compatible with it. For example, you will become more composed if you consciously adopt the body set and delivery of one who is composed. Actors have long recognized that audiences tend to do and feel what they see being done and felt. When they see someone in pain on the stage, they "feel" pain. When the actor is happy, they "feel" happy. This reaction is called *empathy*. It is useful to a public speaker. If listeners perceive an alert speaker, they will tend to be alert. The speaker, seeing a favorable audience response, tends to become more confident.

Here are a few specific actions you can practice to help give you the appearance and the feeling of emotional control.

Walk Briskly to the Platform

Walk directly and resolutely to the speaker's stand and put down your notes. Don't slouch or shuffle along the way. Don't fumble with your papers or clothing.

Look Directly at the Audience

When you reach the speaker's stand and have your notes assembled before you, look directly at the audience for a brief time before beginning your speech. Think of this as a moment when you "meet" the audience and make your first friendly contact with them. During the speech, concentrate on looking directly at the members of the audience. Speakers who seem unable to look directly at their listeners signal their anxiety. Eye contact is perhaps the most important factor in good delivery. It will be discussed in more detail among the visual elements of delivery in Chapter 17.

Use a Good Attention Factor in the Introduction

Your introduction may set the tone for the reactions you will get to the rest of the speech. For this reason, you will want to get off to a good start. Make sure to plan an opening that will arouse the interest of the audience; then deliver it as you planned it. Don't let any anxiety you feel rush you into the main body of the speech so that you lose the interest value of the attention factor. Attention factors are discussed in Chapter 13.

Control the Rate of Delivery

When nervous fear strikes you, your first wish is to get the unpleasant experience over with as soon as possible. This reaction is understandable because the human organism always tries to avoid unpleasant stimuli. Your effectiveness can be hurt by the perfectly normal desire to escape an unpleasant situation. To avoid this reaction, control the rate of your delivery. Talk more slowly than you might be inclined to, especially at the beginning of the speech.

Keep Your Nervousness to Yourself

No matter what happens, don't tell your audience that you are nervous. Far too many speakers do this, as a defense. They try to break the ice by saying something like, "Well, I hope you're more relaxed about this speech than I am." Or, when they fumble with words or have muscle spasms, they look self-conscious or apologize or giggle. You might be able to gain sympathy this way, but you won't win respect.

If you tell listeners about your troubles, they may give you sympathy, but they will deny you the very important goal you seek—support for your ideas. Listeners can feel sympathy for a speaker in distress, but they will not follow one who finds it necessary to lean on them.

If you are obviously nervous, your listeners know it without having to be told. When you have difficulty, empathy makes the audience suffer with you. Furthermore, there is reason to believe that feeling sympathetic makes an audience uncomfortable. This discomfort can easily turn to annoyance directed at a speaker who seeks sympathy. If you fight out the problem, your audience will react favorably to your perserverance. Many will admire you for doing what they feel they cannot do.

BE A GOOD LISTENER

In Chapter 3 we discussed how to be a good listener so that you can learn more from the speeches of others. You can also help speakers overcome their problems with anxiety by practicing those principles of good listening. Focus your attention on the speaker. Establish eye contact and react to the ideas expressed. Not only will you get more out of the speech, you will also help the speaker feel that someone cares and appreciates the speech. This is a good application of "Do unto others as you would have others do unto you."

SUMMARY

If you have problems with nervousness (and probably 75 percent of all people do), remember that you never actually look or sound as bad as you think you do; the symptoms of your anxiety are frequently not even noticed.

There are several ways you can relieve the tension of communication anxiety: (1) Don't blame yourself, (2) realize the importance of experience, (3) choose situations with a high potential for success, (4) concentrate on the message, (5) prepare thoroughly, (6) adopt a conversational attitude, and (7) play the role of the confident speaker. The way you do this is to walk briskly to the platform, look at the audience, develop the introduction, control the rate of delivery, and keep your nervousness to yourself. Finally, when you are in an audience, be a good listener. Help others to have a satisfactory speaking experience.

NOTES

1. Raymond Ross, *Speech Communication* (Englewood Cliffs, N.J.: Prentice-Hall, 1974), pp. 91–92. Estimates of the percentage of beginning speakers who have a problem serious enough to require special therapy vary between 5 and 20 percent. Gerald M. Phillips, "Reticences: Pathology of the Normal Speaker," *Speech Monographs,* **35** (Mar. 1968), p. 42; James C. McCroskey, "The Implementation of a Large-Scale Program of Systematic Desensitization for Communication Apprehension," *Speech Teacher,* **21** (Nov. 1972), p. 260.

2. *London Sunday Times,* Oct. 7, 1973.

3. Linda C. Lederman, "High Communication Apprehensives Talk About Communication Apprehension and Its Effect on Their Behaviour," *Communication Quarterly,* **31** (Summer 1983), pp. 233–237; Judee K. Burgoon and Jerold L. Hale, "A Research Note on the Dimensions of Communication Reticence," *Communication Quarterly,* **31** (Summer 1983), pp. 238–248.

4. James C. McCroskey and Virginia P. Richmond, "The Effects of Communication Apprehension on the Perception of Peers," *Western Journal of Speech Communication,* **40** (Winter 1976), pp. 14–21.

5. For a summary of the major clinical approaches to serious speech apprehension, see Susan R. Glaser, "Oral Communication Apprehension and Avoidance: The Current Status of Treatment Research," *Communication Education,* **30** (Oct. 1981), pp. 321–341.

6. Michael Weissberg and Douglas Lamb, "Comparative Effects of Cognitive Modification, Systematic Desensitization, and Speech Preparation in the Reduction of Speech and General Anxiety," *Communication Monographs,* **44** (Mar. 1977), pp. 27–36.

7. Kim Giffin and Shirley Masterson Gilham, "Relationship Between Speech Anxiety and Motivation," *Speech Monographs,* **38** (Mar. 1971), pp. 70–73.

chapter 15

Improving Oral Style

I. Language and meaning
  A. Denotation
  B. Connotation
  C. Syntax
  D. Context
  E. Emotional coloring
II. Clarity
  A. Avoid ambiguity
  B. Avoid vagueness
  C. Avoid meaningless qualifiers
  D. Avoid abstract terms
  E. Avoid general terms
  F. Provide transitions and internal summaries
III. Propriety
  A. Avoid shoptalk
  B. Avoid slang
  C. Avoid taboos
  D. Avoid formal English
IV. Simplicity
V. Originality
VI. Vividness
  A. Simile and metaphor
  B. Overstatement and understatement
  C. Irony
  D. Antithesis

E. Parallel structure
F. Rhetorical questions
G. Climax

The outline of a speech has been likened to the skeleton of a human body. In much the same sense that the human skeleton must have ligaments, muscles, and nerves to function, a speech needs the sinews and flesh of language to become a complete and living thing.

At least one further comparison can be made. The muscles of the body are either weak or strong, flabby or firm. Language, too, is either weak and flabby or firm and strong. In this chapter, we shall see how language is used to give life and strength to a speech by adding to the skeleton of the outline the firm, strong muscles of effective oral style.

LANGUAGE AND MEANING

The substance of a speech cannot be transplanted directly into the minds of an audience. It requires some kind of language as a medium of transmission. By language we mean all of the visual and auditory symbols, verbal and nonverbal, that are used to transmit messages.

Verbal symbols are words. *Nonverbal* symbols of language, as the name implies, are not words. For example, shaking a clenched fist says something quite specific to a large part of the world's population, but it is not a word. A skull and crossbones printed on the label of a bottle tells you something important about the contents as quickly as the verbal symbol "Poison." The star of David and the cross are almost universally understood symbols. *Verbal* language, however, is the primary means by which human beings communicate ideas.

Although word symbols stand for things, *words in themselves have no meaning*. The answer to the apparently simple question, "What does *slip* (or *hand*, or *sack*, or *pool*) mean?" is equally simple: "Nothing!" The meanings are not in the words; they are in the people who use them.

But a listener's meanings are never precisely the same as a speaker's. That is because meaning exists only in somebody's mind and it is peculiar to the person who has it. Hence for a word to evoke exactly equivalent meaning in two people, their brains would have to be identical, cell for cell, synapse for synapse, and nerve for nerve. In addition, each of the two people must have had exactly the same experiences with what the word names, must have precisely the same understanding of it and exactly the same emotional attitudes toward it. These conditions obviously cannot be met.

However, individuals, their words, and their thinking, shape and are shaped by the cultural atmosphere in which they live. As a consequence, people who use words in common have also had many experiences in common and share many overlapping meanings for these words. Communication is impaired, therefore, only to the extent that dissimilarities in people's meanings cause confusion.

For example, if someone proposes to tell a group how to make raisin cookies, each person in the group will have a somewhat different meaning for "raisin." Even so, the object that the word names is likely to be understood in pretty much the same way by everybody in the audience. One person might buy muscat raisins and another white raisins, so their cookies would not be exactly alike, but that difference isn't terribly serious.

In other cases, confusion arising from different meanings could have very grave consequences. The superintendent of a highway construction crew says, "Make sure that everyone is out of the area before you set off the dynamite." In giving a message of this kind, the superintendent will take great pains to satisfy himself that the dynamite crew has very much the same meaning he does for the terms, "make sure," "everyone," and "out of the area."

The way any verbal communication will be interpreted is determined by five properties that are inherent in the language of the message: *denotation, connotation, syntax, context,* and *emotional coloring.* Understanding the roles of these factors helps a speaker to choose precise language, to arouse desired emotional responses in the audience while avoiding unwanted ones, to ensure that the language is correct and the meanings it conveys will not be confused.

Denotation

An "automobile," a "monarchy," and a "unicorn" are, in varying degrees, difficult to designate by pointing out. And they certainly can't be carried around to show someone. Yet, for one reason or another, it may be necessary to talk about them. A word, then, is used as a symbol to *denote* (designate or stand for) what it refers to. The word becomes a way of pointing to what it names. But what about "unicorn"? Can that word be used to refer to anything—something outside the user's mind? The answer is, "Yes, the word unicorn denotes a small, horselike animal with a single horn in the middle of its forehead."

"Show me one."

"Don't be silly. I don't think there ever has been, is now, or ever will be a single instance of a unicorn anywhere in the world. But if there were one, that one, and any other like it, would be what the word would denote."

Connotation

Two users of a language can share very much the same denotative meaning for any number of symbols in the language—say, for example, "socialized medicine," "environmental protection," or "draft registration." But in addition to this denotative meaning, each individual has meanings that cannot be shared exactly by any other person. These meanings are internalized, personalized, attitudinized, and reflect each one's value judgments about the object or condition named. They are not the result of any relationship between words and *reality,* as in the case of denotations. Instead they grow out of the relationships *people* have with words and things. They are called *connotations.*

The more aware speakers are of the connotations their *listeners* have for the language of a speech, the better their chances will be of choosing the most effective words. You might be surprised, for example, by the great difference between the connotations you and any listener have for terms such as "feminist," "black power," "ecology," or "nuclear weapons."

Syntax

Syntax is the way a sentence is structured in accordance with the grammatical customs of a language. And the relationships among the words give clues to meaning. Zsa Zsa Gabor's answer to the question, "What would you do if a man were unfaithful to you?" was, "Darling, him I would shoot in the legs." The structure of her sentence is out of the ordinary for the English language, and yet there is no question about her meaning. In fact, it is the kind of locution audiences have come to expect from all the Gabor sisters and it is probably a part of what makes them charming entertainers.

It is wiser, however, to use the syntax accepted in the language and expected by the audience. The man who began a speech by saying, "The use and abuse of animals for pleasure and knowledge has existed since the beginning of time which it isn't ethical to do," ran a double risk: his meaning was in danger of being confused because of his muddy syntax and, more important, he was in grave danger lest the audience think him not worth listening to because he was ignorant.

Context

Syntactical meaning is elicited by the way words are placed in a sentence. It is a function of grammar, of the relationship of words to other words. *Contextual meaning,* on the other hand, is evoked by the subject matter that the words encode. Many words are ambiguous in that they can be taken in any of several senses. Even when they are used in correct sentences, they can be misunderstood. Have you ever seen a dog run? Of course! But are you sure? Sometimes the word "run" denotes an enclosure where dogs can exercise without the need of a leash. So we ask again, have you ever seen a dog run? Maybe, maybe not. Only when the question is put into the clarifying context of other, explanatory words will it say what the user intends.

Emotional Coloring

In some instances, language is used to report facts with as little emotive coloration as possible. Informative speeches, for example, are meant to communicate ideas in such a way that they will be *understood* and *remembered.* The language should be objective. To the extent that the language is also interesting, it will serve well.

But language is used to transmit more than fact and opinion, because, at times, understanding and retention are only a part of the goal. In persuasive speaking particularly, language has the additional function of creating attitude and influencing the emotional reactions of the audience. *Emotionally colored language* is instrumental in creating in an audience the attitudes and beliefs the speaker wants it to have.

Language, however, also has great power to deceive, because it can encapsulate into a single word a whole complex of attitudes and reactions. When that word is honorific, it is called a "euphemism" ("plump" rather than "fat"); when the word is pejorative, it is "name-calling" ("ward heeler" rather than "politician"). Both euphemism and name-calling have bad reputations and, for the most part, rightly so. They are two widely used substitutes for good evidence and sound argument. And that's the danger of emotive language. When attitudes and feelings are separated from evidence and reasoning, the results most often disadvantage the speaker and the audience as well.

But there is a proper use for emotional coloration in language. One's values are part of the truth as one sees it. Given a clear and correct understanding of the subject, the kind of language that will communicate it accurately and efficiently is quite justified.

Sensitivity to language brings awareness of the subtle shading of ideas and the emotional coloration it can achieve. Moreover, it will make you aware of your own linguistic practices. Don't be content with a word or phrase that is only an awkward approximation of what you mean. Let's examine the characteristics that oral style must have in order to carry to an audience the exact shades of meaning: clarity, propriety, simplicity, originality and vividness.

CLARITY

Everyone has a personal way of using language. And every profession or activity seems to evoke a distinctive style as well. Commentators and news reporters on TV use language in a distinctive way. Novels differ from poetry and plays. And oral style, our concern here, is distinguishably different from writing.

Writing is directed to the eye. But although comprehension is important, there is generally little need to grasp a written message instantly. Ordinarily it is possible to examine a page at leisure, to think about the ideas, and to absorb them at any comfortable rate, or to reread a passage the number of times understanding requires and interest allows. In short, the goal of a writer is to make ideas *ultimately* intelligible to a reader.

A listening audience, on the other hand, has no time for leisurely consideration of the speaker's ideas. Listeners cannot go back to rehear. If they pause to reflect, they break the chain of the speaker's organization, lose connection with the movement of ideas, and are left behind. Consequently, good oral style must make ideas *instantly* clear.

No criterion of good style can be more basic than clarity. It is the starting place, the first step. Clear language is easily understood because it is free from obscurity and confusion. Without clarity no explanation can be understood, no argument can be persuasive, no humor can be funny, no speech can be effective. To provide clarity, avoid its enemies: ambiguity, vagueness, meaningless qualifiers, abstract terms, and general terms. To preserve clarity, use transitions and summaries between major points and ideas.

Avoid Ambiguity

One of the enemies of clarity is ambiguity, that quality of language that makes an expression susceptible of more than one interpretation. That is, a statement is ambiguous when either of two meanings is possible and the context does not make clear which is intended. As often as not, it can be a source of fun.

> "I like teaching more than my wife."
>
> "The restaurant is famous for its *pate de fois gras* made from goose livers and its fine chef."
>
> "We are sorry to report that our past president, Mrs. Gertrude Sturtevant, is at home recuperating from an operation."
>
> "A few young people swam in the chill night air."

These are examples of *grammatical* ambiguity, so-called because of imprecise grammatical construction. In another form of ambiguity, the *context* fails to make clear which of the potential senses of a word is meant. For example, the lawyer who phoned his wife to say he would be late for dinner because he was delayed by a bar meeting was guilty of (deliberate?) ambiguity.

Often, however, ambiguity is no fun at all for the one who is guilty of it. And the cost in embarrassment can sometimes be painfully high. In August 1984, an ambiguity in an early draft of the Republican party platform caused laughter in the media, glee among the Democrats, and a problem for the platform committee. The troublesome language was a statement promising to "oppose any attempts to increase taxes which would harm the recovery." Does the statement say that any tax increases which would *not* harm the recovery could be made? Or does it say that *any* tax increase would be harmful to the recovery? The stylistic problem (but not the political one) was solved by inserting a comma after the word "taxes." Then the intention (not to raise taxes) became clear.

Avoid Vagueness

When both the syntax and the context of an expression are precise, the likely causes of ambiguity are removed and the meaning is usually clear. But this is not the case with another great enemy of clear language—vagueness. Vagueness is found in words themselves, not their contexts. A vague word is one whose denotations are so broad that, no matter what its context, it will be imprecise if left unaided. You could condemn "gambling" but not fret about church bingo parties. You could denounce "undemocratic nations" and let your listeners decide whether South Africa belongs in that group. If you deplore "corruption" in "unions," then you can let your listeners stigmatize Local 4321 unfairly. This kind of vagueness is not good communication. If you mean to talk about Senator Kennedy, Cranston, or Hart, say so. Don't talk about "some liberal politicians." The more specific you are, the more you can be sure that your meaning is clear. When language is vague, it encourages an audience to grasp a meaning not intended at all. The way to avoid vagueness is to use words that are concrete, specific, and precise.

To be precise is to choose the right words—those that express an idea exactly. They eliminate vagueness by putting the idea sharply into focus, thus minimizing the chance of being unclear. John Tagg, a free-lance writer who has taught both speech and writing, sternly criticizes the careless, vague, and imprecise kind of language that people try to excuse with, "Oh, you know what I mean." He says:

> When we get right down to it, the "you know what I mean" attitude bespeaks a helpless and hopeless fatalism. The obvious question in response to it is "If I know what you mean, why do you bother to tell me? If I have to ignore your words to get your meaning, why go to the trouble of speaking?" And the answer is usually either a shrug or an outright admission that there really isn't any point to this report, or paper, or speech, or conversation.[1]

Good oral style uses precise language to make ideas instantly and accurately intelligible. But no idea can be conveyed precisely unless it is precisely in mind. For precise language, then, the first requirement is a precise idea.

Avoid Meaningless Qualifiers

Many words give the impression of qualifying or quantifying when they really don't. For example, what is meant by saying that someone is "fat," "thin," "tall," "short," "middle-aged," or "old"? The terms are so relative that they need to be referred to some criterion or scale. The images listeners get from terms like these vary widely, and they will ordinarily differ widely from the idea the user intends to convey. How many is "some," "few," "several"? How much is "lots," or "very"? Whenever possible (and this should be nearly always), make the information precise.

Avoid Abstract Terms

It is tempting to use abstract terms because this is easier than making clear distinctions among a number of overlapping cases, all of which are comfortably covered by the abstract term. By their very nature, abstract terms are vague because they refer to no tangible object. Of course, there are times when it is necessary to talk about abstractions, such as *justice, honesty, democracy, virtue,* and the like, but to do it without defining them or giving clear examples makes the concepts vague.

Avoid General Terms

A comedian, whose name we have forgotten, makes fun of what he calls, "the vague specific." There are good examples of it in many of the phrases speakers like to use: "Authorities agree. . . ." Other examples are easy to find: "a noted physicist (chemist, lawyer, theologian, whatever)," "a large Midwestern city," "government sources." What you say will be much clearer if you are precise; that is, *name* the authority, the city, the source, *describe* the research, *give* the audience the statistics that support the claim.

Provide Transitions and Internal Summaries

An excellent way to make sure that audiences understand accurately is always to let them know where they are, how they got there, and where they are going next. There is no better way to do this than with transitions and internal summaries. We discussed them in Chapter 13.

PROPRIETY

Propriety in language is the quality of being proper and fitting; of being appropriate to the listener, the subject, the time, and the place. In daily life, speech practices are constantly adjusted to different audiences. No two listeners are exactly alike: The boss, neighbors, casual acquaintances, total strangers, and old friends are all addressed differently. Automatically and unconsciously, audience analysis precedes the selection of words, sentence structure, and figures of speech. That a woman would talk to her husband in the same way she speaks to a sales clerk is highly unlikely. No one uses the language of the *Congressional Record* in casual conversation, nor does anyone signaling an S.O.S. use scientific or technical terminology.

Choice of language, then, is habitually determined by audience and occasion, and the ability to adapt to those two elements of the speaking situation is a necessary ingredient of effective communication. Four kinds of language usage are likely to cause problems of propriety: shoptalk, slang, taboos, and formal English.

Avoid Shoptalk

Many occupations and activities have what amounts to a private language, a jargon that may be incomprehensible, or at least strange, to anyone not part of the activity.

An "RV" is a "recreational vehicle," and the term denotes a conveyance such as a "Winny" or an "Airstream." It may be a "cab over," a "fifth wheel," or a simple "camper shell" on a "pick-up." If an audience is familiar with these vehicles, the jargon is no problem; in fact, it can make the communication more efficient. If not, it is better to avoid it. Although shoptalk can provide useful verbal shortcuts that are understandable to people in the shop, its limitations are apparent. The jargon of the trade is useful mainly for talking to the trade.

Avoid Slang

Language is constantly changing, and slang often represents its leading edge. Creative people, looking for fresh, sharp, colorful, or humorous ways to express ideas, invent new words and use old words in new ways. The resulting expressions either survive to become a part of the standard language, or they grow stale and die out.

The problem with slang is its transient nature. The middle-aged folks who try to keep up with the young people's slang usually find that the expressions have changed and they are using slang that is already out of date. Columnist Thomas H. Middleton recently made the point almost poignantly when he took a good-natured poke at himself and the difficulty of keeping up with slang. He said in part:

> One of the most depressing side effects of the "empty nest syndrome"—that sense of loss that sets in when the kids have grown up and moved out and started their own lives—is that you begin to lose touch with the sometimes wonderful, always arresting, language of youth. . . .
>
> The most recent linguistic fad among the young that I'm familiar with is "Really," and that might be passé by now. I feel quite out of touch. "Really," the last I heard, had a meaning I'd never associated with it before. It was used to express simple agreement: "Good movie!" "Really!"; acceptance: "More ice cream?" "Really!"; I suppose that it's the modern equivalent of the "And how!" and "You said it!" out of my own youth.[2]

Slang should be used only when it is clear and does not obscure what it is meant to convey. Even when it is clear, it will be inappropriate if the occasion calls for more formal English.

Avoid Taboos

Certain tribes avoid naming their gods for fear of offending them, but they will still talk about them by circumlocution. Talking around subjects is a common way of avoiding linguistic taboos. Two terms with precisely the same denotation often flourish side by side because one of them has connotations that make it improper in public discourse. Familiar examples are words that refer to the functions of reproduction and excretion. Whatever the taboos of an audience, violating them exposes a speaker to reproof and a consequent loss of effectiveness.

One audience can differ so greatly from another that it is hard to know what any particular group might consider profane or obscene. A word such as "damn" or "hell" might offend one group, whereas another wouldn't flinch from language a lot stronger. The most practical rule is, don't take a chance. It's true, of course, that words in and of themselves can't hurt anyone, but it's arrogant to feel free on that account to use any language whatever.

Profanity, vulgarity, and obscenity may shock and be effective, but they are more likely to be counterproductive. There is evidence to show that although language that is judged to be obscene by a general American audience will make a speaker seem more dynamic, it will also decrease the listener's estimate of the trustworthiness and competence of the speaker.[3]

Avoid Formal English

At another extreme from shoptalk, slang, and linguistic taboos is formal English. This is the proper style for the speaking situation that requires formality in tone and precision in usage. In a Supreme Court proceeding, business report, or research report, for instance, informality would be inappropriate.

Informal English admits a large number of words and sentence constructions that formal English excludes, words and forms that are customarily found in the casual speaking of educated people. Since people are at ease with this language, you should feel quite comfortable using it. Dictionaries label some informal English words "colloquial," as indeed they are, but the term should not connote inferiority or incorrectness. Informal English is found in communications aimed at general listeners and readers: speeches, magazine articles, newspaper columns, and the like. This is the language that will be appropriate in virtually all of the speeches you will be called upon to make.

SIMPLICITY

A naive but common misconception is that "big" words are better because they are somehow more impressive than their ordinary counterparts. Acting on this misconception, speakers often sound pompous when they mean to be dignified. Few things are more damaging to one's purpose than feeble elegance. Francis Bacon scoffed at the narrow-minded preoccupation with style that led to what he called "delicate learning." Henry David Thoreau, whose own style is marked by economy and simplicity, said that long words have a paralysis in their tails. Far from being an elevated variety of English, self-conscious formality is pretentious and unnatural.

The term "gobbledygook" was coined by former Representative Maury Maverick to label writing or speaking that is pompous, wordy, involved, and full of long, Latinized terms. Gobbledygook is almost totally destructive of clarity. What did the college administrator mean who listed these aims for education?

> . . . the development of intellectual consistency, the creation of aesthetic awareness, the liberation of the personality, the awakening of nonverbal and nonrational sensibilities to amplify adult experience, and the structure of an insight into the eternality of human aspiration and frustration.

Simplicity is not only a matter of using short, forceful words, but also as few words as will do the job. Language should demand as little effort as possible on the part of a listener. Therefore, economy of expression is important. Ideas sometimes require complex language, but only what is necessary is useful.

ORIGINALITY

Originality in style is, in part, a skillful use of variety that helps to avoid monotony. It brings freshness and vigor to language by avoiding cliches, hackneyed phrases, and figures of speech that are tired from overuse.

William H. Whyte, Jr., built a composite business speech out of 60 badly overused expressions and constructions. It "lends a powerful, straight-from-the-shoulder effect to ambiguity and equivocation," but it says nothing. Look at an excerpt from that speech:

Cooperation—An Opportunity and a Challenge

It is a pleasure and a privilege to be here with you today. These great annual meetings are always an inspiration to me, and doubly so today. After that glowing introduction by our toastmaster, I must confess, however, that I would like to turn the tables and tell a little story on Chuck. When I say it's about the nineteenth hole and a certain gentleman whose baritone was cracked, those of you who were at the Atlanta conference last year will know what I mean. But I won't tell it. Chuck Forbes is too good a friend of mine and, seriously, I know full well we all realize what a tower of strength his yeoman service has been in these trying times.

Yes, gentlemen, trying times. So you'll pardon me if I cast aside the glib reverberation of glittering generalities and the soothing syrup of sugarcoated platitudes and put it to you the only way I can: straight English.

We're losing the battle!

From every corner the people are being weaned from the doctrines of the Founding Fathers. They are being detoured from the high-speed highways of progress by the utopian highwaymen.

Now, the man in the street is a pretty savvy fellow. Don't sell him short. Joe Doakes may be fooled for a while, but in the end he wants no part of the mumbo jumbo the global saboteurs are trying to sell him. After all, he is an American.[4]

But avoiding the trite, the stale, and the hackneyed is not the only way to be original. Another, paradoxically, is through imitation. Imitation can take all sorts of forms. Composers write variations on the themes of other composers. Imitations in the form of burlesques, parodies, and lampoons are the source of comedy in writing, speaking, and in the theater. The story is told of the great Greek orator Demosthenes that he copied Thucydides' history of the Peloponnesian Wars eight times so that he could master its style. The famous parent of the quotation from the speech of Lane Kirkland cited in Chapter 8 is a speech by Patrick Henry:

> Tarquin and Caesar each had his Brutus, Charles the First his Cromwell and George the Third—[Pause]—may profit from their example!

Kirkland composed this variation on Henry's theme.

> Lyndon Johnson had his Vietnam; Richard Nixon had his Watergate; Jimmy Carter his Khomeni, and Ronald Reagan should—but doubtless will not—profit by their example.

VIVIDNESS

Even clear, appropriate style can be improved by making it more *vivid*. A vivid style is one that heightens the impact of the ideas because of the ways in which it deviates from the usual denotative usages and from common sentence patterns. The catalog of stylistic devices is far too long to consider here; literally hundreds of them have been identified and defined. We will discuss only a few of the most common of these "figures of speech": simile and metaphor, overstatement and understatement, irony, antithesis, parallel structure, and rhetorical questions.

Simile and Metaphor

The simile and the metaphor are the most common figures of speech. Both are formed by likening one object to another, but they do it in different ways. A *simile* ordinarily indicates the comparison with a word such as *like* or *as*. When a sportscaster described the way spectators left a stadium during a dust storm, he said it looked "like a mob scene being sandblasted off a billboard." This fine simile makes a vivid picture because the elements being compared are not too closely related. If he had compared the dust-driven spectators to people running indoors from a rainstorm, he would have had a dull simile. Columnist Jack Smith said that Los Angeles during the 1984 Olympic Games was like a house that had been readied for important guests.

A *metaphor* is also based on a comparison, but it says that one thing is not just *like* another, it says that it *is* the other. Among the pointed and powerful metaphors Jesse Jackson used in his speech to the Democratic Convention in July 1984 was his description of graffiti as the "hieroglyphics of destitution."

Overstatement and Understatement

Both overstatement and understatement will appear again in Chapter 20 when we discuss the use of humor in speeches. Overstatement and understatement, however, are useful stylistic devices even when amusement is not the goal.

Overstatement attracts attention to an idea by using a stronger word or statement than is necessary to convey an idea. Former governor, presidential candidate, and UN ambassador Adlai Stevenson was one of the truly great stylists of this century. In the following excerpt from one of a series of lectures he gave at Harvard University, we have italicized several examples of the figure of overstatement:

I am not a historian, but I doubt if anyone will dispute the *incomparably* dramatic qualities of the twentieth century. . . . In 50 years, distance has been *obliterated* by a technological revolution that has brought *all mankind* cheek to jowl, and that has released the creative and obliterative power of the atom. . . . National independence and democracy have scored *spectacular* victories and suffered *shocking* defeats. . . . Two new *colossi,* the United States and the Soviet Union, have *suddenly* emerged. Ideas, on which the West has had an export *monopoly* for *centuries,* are now flowing out of the East and colliding *everywhere* with our Western ideas.[5]

Hyperbole is the name given to the kind of exaggeration that is used for dramatic effect. It is an acceptable figure of speech and is not likely to cause confusion or lack of clarity. No one will take literally a statement such as, "My car is as old as the hills," and the hyperbole adds a degree of vividness to the expression. But this is noticeably different from a grossly exaggerated statement that is intended to deceive.

The vocabulary of advertising, for instance, uses the kind of exaggeration that destroys accuracy. "Big" isn't *big* enough, so advertisers use, in progression, "gigantic," "colossal," and even, ultimately, "supercolossal." This kind of thinking, for example, leads the manufacturers of toothpaste to identify as their "large" size the smallest tube available through retail channels. When the superlatives have been exhausted, what next? To exaggerate for emphasis has been called an American trait. But it fails to achieve its effect when it is overused, just as the habit of using too much spice makes normally seasoned food seem flat.

Understatement, on the contrary, calls attention to an idea by deliberately saying less than what might be said. To say that some out-and-out crook is "not the most scrupulous person I know" is to understate the case.

Irony

An *ironic* statement is one in which the intended meaning is the direct opposite of what the statement actually says. For example, "I'm very fond of Professor Kingston. I especially like the way he tears my work to shreds right in front of the class."

Irony is often found in company with either exaggeration or understatement. In the following passage, the nineteenth-century Republican orator, Robert G. Ingersoll, combines understatement, overstatement, and irony to argue *in favor of* using gold rather than silver as our monetary standard. There is also a touch of wry humor in the passage. But that is not surprising since all three of these devices are not only instruments of style, they are forms of humor as well.

In 1816 Great Britain demonetized silver, and that wretched old country has had nothing but gold from that day to this as a standard. And to show you the frightful results of that demonetization, that government does not now own above one-third of the globe, and all the winds are busy floating her flags.

Antithesis

Antithesis, the opposing or contrasting of ideas, is not only widely and commonly used today, it is among the oldest of the consciously practiced rhetorical techniques.

Perhaps the most famous instance of antithesis in the speeches of modern times is in John Fitzgerald Kennedy's inaugural address: "Ask not what your country can do for you. Ask what you can do for your country." In accepting the Republican presidential nomination in 1964, Senator Barry Goldwater stated his conservative position with an antithesis that aroused quite a political controversy: "I would remind you that extremism in the defense of liberty is no vice! and let me remind you also that moderation in the pursuit of justice is no virtue!" In a speech to the nation in February 1977, President Jimmy Carter said: "Our nation was built on the principle of work not welfare—productivity, not stagnation."

Parallel Structure

Parallel structure highlights and emphasizes a series of related ideas by phrasing them in expressions that are similar in language and construction. One of the best-known examples is the familiar set of phrases in Lincoln's Gettysburg address: "Government of the people, by the people, for the people." Jesse Jackson, in the conclusion of the speech mentioned earlier in this chapter, said, "Our time has come," 10 times. And this sentence was the closing words of the speech.

An excellent use of parallel structure can be seen in a speech on the federal deficit by bank president Fred Shaw. At the time he spoke (April 1984), the budget deficit for that year was estimated at $185 billion.

Our annual deficits and the total debt we have established are so enormous that they are difficult for most people to comprehend.

I would like to take a moment to try to put the amounts into perspective.

What's a billion?

To spend a billion dollars, a shopper would have to spend a hundred dollars a minute—each and every minute—for 19 years.

A billion seconds ago America was reeling from the surprise attack on Pearl Harbor.

A billion hours ago, Christ was still living.

A billion years ago, man had not appeared on earth.

A billion federal budget dollars ago was only yesterday.[6]

Rhetorical Questions

A question is *rhetorical* when it does not ask the audience to give a direct answer. The question does not elicit an overt response (although on any given occasion an audience might be excited or aroused enough to volunteer an answer); instead, it is meant to add vividness to an expression. A direct question, even one that requires no direct answer, attracts the immediate, personal attention of an audience to a degree that a statement often will not.

As both of the following examples show, when a speaker uses more than one rhetorical question at a time, they can be expressed in a parallel structure.

In the speech cited just above, Fred Shaw said:

> Take a minute to think about whether you receive some sort of government benefit.
> —Are you a farmer earning thousands of dollars for not planting a crop?
> —Are you a small business man taking advantage of government loans?
> —Are you a parent with a child in college who receives a government subsidized loan?
> The list could go on and on.[7]

Jeanne Kirkpatrick, while still U.S. Ambassador to the United Nations, addressed the Republican National Convention in August 1984. In her speech she used this series of rhetorical questions. Here again, the questions are also an excellent example of parallel structure:

> Ask yourself:
> What would become of Europe if the United States withdrew?
> What would become of Africa if Europe fell under Soviet domination?
> What would become of Israel if surrounded by Soviet client-states?
> What would become of Asia if the Philippines or Japan fell under Soviet domination?
> What would become of Mexico if Central America became a Soviet satellite?
> What, then, could the United States do?

There is no question that all of the language devices we have discussed here can add vividness to a speech. But a word of caution: They can be used to excess. When they are, the style becomes not vivid but flamboyant, flowery, and weak. Like poor delivery, style can call attention to itself rather than to the substance of the speech.

Climax

Chapter 19 mentions the ancient dispute about the placement of arguments in the body of a persuasive speech. The question is whether to put the strongest argument first, last, or elsewhere. The best way to answer that question is with another, "What kind of effect do you want?" But speaking from a *stylistic* point of view, the questions won't arise because, in every case, a speech should *end strong*. In an informative speech, the point at hand, no matter which one, or in a persuasive speech, no matter what the relative strength or weakness of an argument, that point, or that argument, should be dressed in clear, appropriate, vivid language. And the ending should never be weak, but strong.

Daniel Webster closed his "Reply to Hayne" defending the Union against secession before the Civil War with this stylistically vivid climax:

> When my eyes shall be turned to behold, for the last time, the sun in heaven, may I not see him shining on the broken dishonored fragments of a once glorious Union; on States dissevered, discordant, belligerent; on a land rent with civil feuds, or drenched, it may be, in fraternal blood! Let their last feeble and lingering glance, rather, behold the gorgeous ensign of the Republic . . . blazing on all its ample folds . . . that sentiment dear to every true American heart—Liberty and Union, now and forever, one and inseparable.

SUMMARY

The minimum requirement for effective speaking is good quality in substance, organization, and delivery. But a truly superior speech will also be clothed in a strong, handsome style. Human beings communicate through the verbal and nonverbal symbols of the language by means of which they communicate their ideas.

The way an audience will interpret a speech is determined by its understanding of what the words denote, by its connotations for these words, by the syntax of the language, and by the context in which the ideas are placed. The ability of language to lend emotional coloration to ideas, when it is not used as a substitute for reasoning and evidence, will add great force to the style.

Good oral style makes ideas instantly clear and, at the same time, maintains a high level of attention and interest in the audience. The style that does this best is marked by clarity, propriety, simplicity, originality, and vividness.

The way to provide clarity is to avoid its enemies: ambiguity, vagueness, meaningless qualifiers, abstractions that are not defined, and general terms. To preserve the clarity of a speech, provide transitions and internal summaries between each major point to the next.

Propriety in style demands that language be suited to the audience, the subject, and the occasion. Using shoptalk to the uninitiated, unfamiliar or outdated slang, language that is taboo, or inappropriately formal English will diminish the propriety of style.

Vividness is to style what seasoning is to food. The right spices in the right amount add zest and tang, but too much spoils the flavor. The spices of style are figures of speech: simile and metaphor, overstatement and understatement, irony, antithesis, parallel structure, rhetorical questions, and climax.

NOTES

1. John Tagg, "Wielding Words to Say Something," *Los Angeles Times,* Dec. 14, 1983, Part V, p. 2.

2. Thomas H. Middleton, "Youthspeak is Aw-RI-I-GHT!" *Los Angeles Times,* Feb. 29, 1984, Part V, pp. 1–2.

3. Robert Bostrom, John R. Basehart, and Charles M. Rossiter, "The Effects of Three Types of Profane Language in Persuasive Messages," *Journal of Communication,* **23** (Dec. 1973), pp. 461–475; Velma Lashbrook, "Source Credibility: A Summary of Experimental Research," paper read to the Speech Communication Association, Dec. 1971.

4. William H. Whyte, Jr., "The Language of Business," *Fortune,* **42** (Nov. 1950), p. 114, © 1950 Time, Inc. All rights reserved.

5. Adlai E. Stevenson, *Call to Greatness* (New York: Harper & Row, 1954), p. 109. Italics added.

6. Fred Shaw, "The Federal Deficit," *Vital Speeches of the Day,* **50** (Apr. 15, 1984), p. 406.

7. Ibid., pp. 407–408.

EXERCISES

1. While at work, or at a student hang-out, or at a meeting of a departmental club or some other special group, make a list of the words you hear that are not used in general society. Translate each of the words into language appropriate for a general audience.

2. Select an essay written in "formal" English style and convert one or more paragraphs into acceptable informal, oral style.

3. Note examples of vague terms used in classroom speeches (meaningless modifiers, abstract words, general words) and show how they may be made more precise through illustration and definition.

4. Write down trite expressions in one round of classroom speeches and suggest a phrase that expresses each idea more vividly.

5. Examine one of the speeches in Appendix B and write a short paper discussing the kinds of figures of speech used (or lack of them). Explain how specific figures improve or detract from the effectiveness. Explain how the speech might have been improved with more or fewer figures of speech.

6. In your next classroom speech, use two or three figures of speech to make it more vivid.

chapter 16

Using Visual Aids

Although oral language is the primary means of communicating, the visual element can make you a more effective speaker. Therefore, in this chapter we will show the use of visual aids to improve effectiveness.

TYPES OF VISUAL AIDS

Many devices can be useful if they are appropriate to the particular task they are expected to perform. The following list identifies a number of classes into which visual aids may be grouped:[1]

1. Actual objects
2. Models
3. Pictures (photographs, drawings)
4. Symbolic representations (maps, graphs, diagrams, charts)

Actual Objects

In explaining some object, displaying the object itself will help an audience visualize what is said. Putting aside considerations such as size, the actual three-dimensional

Visualization of a diagram helps the audience understand the point a speaker is making. (©Blotnick, 1983, Omni-Photo Communications)

object will often be a more useful visual aid than any representation of it. For example, in a speech about styles of headwear as manifestations of cultural differences, a number of actual hats of different kinds (a fez, a beret, a shako) would be useful visual aids. The photo shows an actual object used as a visual aid.

For a variety of reasons, however, even if specimens, samples or artifacts are available, the actual objects are not always best to use. As one writer puts it, "They are too large, too small, too expensive, too dirty, too dangerous, too delicate, or they come out only at night."[2] In cases like these, some other form of visual aid will be necessary.

Models

Someone once defined a model as "a small imitation of the real thing," but thought better of it after he heard himself referred to as a model husband. A model is in a real sense an imitation, but its size is not a significant matter. It can be larger or smaller than what it represents, or it can be the same size. The important requirement is that it shows relationships. A model representing the solar system is possible, then, despite the enormous distances small spaces represent, provided only that the appropriate relative sizes and the spaces between them are in proper ratios. Globes that represent the earth are models of a sort, and although they aren't very accurate they do represent the earth in a way that might otherwise be difficult to visualize.

Besides being three-dimensional and representing objects in a comfortable viewing size, models have the added benefit that they can be simplified to omit unnecessary details without confusing, distorting, or misrepresenting. There are different kinds of models that show different aspects of an object. A *working model* shows how something operates, like how the moon revolves around the earth. A *cutaway model* shows the interior of the object. It can also be a working model and show how something like the interior parts of an automobile engine move. The model on page 206 in the photograph combines several of these features: It enlarges the object it represents to a convenient size; it eliminates structural elements not necessary for clarity; it is a cutaway model that shows the interior; and it is a working model as well.

Museums of science and industry all over the world have remarkable examples of models that are fascinating to watch. There is a major problem, however, in that models of this kind cost an enormous amount of money and are not easily available. If a model is not available and if it is not simple and inexpensive to make, other kinds of visual aids can be used.

Pictures

Petroglyphs, designs carved on rocks, and the prehistoric paintings found on cave walls show that human beings used pictures to communicate long before they learned how to use writing. No matter how much more sophisticated we may now be, pictures are still useful today.

A visual aid helps to clarify a point. (Forsyth, Monkmeyer)

Pictures help to clarify the fuzzy or erroneous notions people have about things and ideas. Moreover, abstractions are often easier to grasp when they can be visualized literally by the eye and not only figuratively by the mind.

Photographs   The kind of picture most often used is a photograph. Whether it is in black and white or in color is not important. It is more significant that the selection of photographs be made with a critical eye. Here are some criteria that will help you to choose:[3]

1. *Authenticity*. Photographs should be accurate.
2. *Simplicity*. Photographs should be uncluttered.
3. *Relative size of items*. Photographs should include a familiar object to give a correct perspective on the size of objects that are unfamiliar.
4. *Camera work*. Photographs should be technically good.

Drawings   You have probably said many times when you were trying to explain something, "Wait a minute. Give me a pencil and a piece of paper. Now, here's what I'm talking about." Then you drew a sketch of the golf hole you double-bogied, or a map showing the best way to get to your house.

Without a modest degree of skill in sketching, it is wiser to make drawings beforehand, as a part of speech preparation, rather than putting an impromptu and perhaps clumsy piece of work on the chalkboard. On the other hand, the claim has been made that drawing on the chalkboard during a speech often helps to visualize the idea better than presenting a finished drawing because the thought grows as the drawing develops.[4] In this case, however, the sketching must be done quickly so that it will not distract from the speech. One better solution is to make a series of drawings in advance and reveal them at appropriate times during the speech.

The accuracy of a drawing can range anywhere from the precise realism of a Norman Rockwell painting to the deliberate exaggeration and distortion of a cartoon. Although it does not pretend to portray reality with visual accuracy, the cartoon has the very useful advantages of clarity, emphasis, and humor.

Symbolic Representations

Among the most useful (and most frequently used) visual aids are those that explain relationships and operations symbolically rather than directly as models and pictures do. Among these are *maps, charts, graphs,* and *diagrams.*

Maps   The most obvious use for maps is to help explain geographic relationships. But this means a lot more than showing someone how to find the capital of West Virginia. The variety of maps and the kinds of information they can give is literally astonishing. Ordinarily a map is a representation on a flat page of all or some part of the earth's surface, usually showing such features as countries, bodies of water, cities, and mountains. *Physical maps,* for example, show not only the outlines of land masses and bodies of water but, depending on their size, scale, and purpose, can also show altitude, temperature, precipitation, vegetation, or any other significant physical data. *Political maps* show the boundaries of nations, states, and other political entities and usually include a number of physical properties as well: mountains, rivers, cities, deserts, and bodies of water. These examples are too familiar to need illustration here. Any good map will clearly identify the physical properties and political boundaries of an area.[5]

Other kinds of maps can be equally useful. An exchange student from Taiwan, who was recognized by other international students as well informed about Manchuria, spoke on the industrial development of that section of mainland China. She used an *economic* map to illustrate data important to the economy of the area, and to show the products and industries found there.

On another occasion, the same speaker used a *relief map* to compare the topography of Manchuria and the United States. Relief maps show the irregularities in the surface of the earth. They do this either by suggesting various altitudes with colors or other pictorial means, or by three-dimensional surfaces on the maps themselves.

Graphs   Complicated numerical data and the relationships among them are often the most difficult kinds of materials a speaker wants to make clear. It is quite easy to say clearly that there are 40,000 people living in a town. Nor would it cause confusion to say that there are several churches in the town, each representing a different denomination. But using oral language alone to show the number of members in each denomination and to compare that information with the number of people who do not attend any church very likely would cause unnecessary problems. One very helpful way of handling these materials and clarifying complex relationships among quantitative data is through the use of graphs. Not only are they useful in maintaining clarity, they also lend interest value to a speech.

There are many common types of graphs, each of which has its advantages and applications. We will discuss four kinds that are most likely to be useful. Any graph should meet the following criteria; failure to meet any one of them will simply defeat the purpose of the graph.

1. It should be *simple*. Too many data and too much detail will make the graph cluttered and difficult to comprehend at a glance.
2. It should be *legible*. The graph must not only be neat, it must also be large enough to be read easily by everyone in the audience. Lines, bars, and printing should be bold and clear.
3. It should be *accurate*. The data included on a graph should, of course, be correct, but it is equally important to construct the graph to correct proportions. Otherwise, it will distort and misrepresent the very relationships it is supposed to clarify.

One common graph is a simple type called variously a *sector, circle,* or (most often) a *pie* graph. It is nothing more than a circle with segments of appropriate sizes that show what proportion of the whole each of a number of elements contributes.

Another versatile and often-used way of representing relationships among numerical data is the *bar graph*. It can be used in several different forms. A "100 percent graph" is simply a single bar that shows what percentage each of several components in an entity contributes to the makeup of the whole. When it is used this way, it shows exactly what a pie graph shows. On February 1, 1984, President Ronald Reagan sent to Congress his proposed budget for the following fiscal year. A proportional breakdown of the sources of revenue and of expenditures could be visualized by using either pie graphs or bar graphs. Figure 16.1 shows how this might be done.

There are also *multiple bar graphs*. The number of elements and relationships that can be shown in one multiple bar graph is limited by how much the eyes of an audience can take in without confusion. Remember that an audience doesn't have time to study the graph at leisure; it must be clear at a glance. For an example, see Figure 16.2.

A visually interesting variation of the bar graph is a pictorial graph, or "pictograph." Instead of using bars to compare, for example, the number of submarine-launched ballistic missiles, bombers, and ICBMs maintained by the United States and the USSR, simplified drawings are used to represent them. This lends an eye appeal and suggests a three-dimensional quality that is lacking in a bar graph. Figure 16.3 illustrates the same material found in Figure 16.1 with a pictograph.

Perhaps the most precise graph of all, and the form most useful in showing not only relationships but trends, is the *line* or *curve graph*. Here, any kind of trend in any factor can be shown through any desired period of time. As Figure 16.4 shows, one of the values of this kind of graph is that it can also demonstrate the similarities and

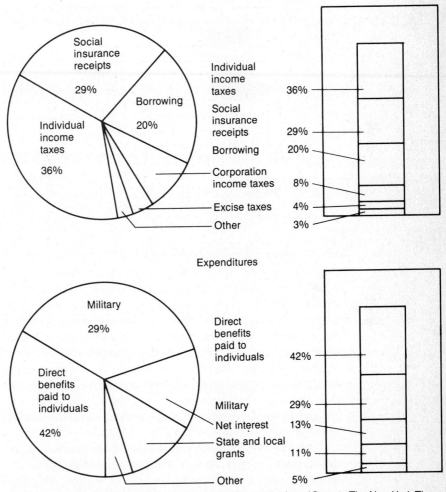

Figure 16.1   Pie graphs and bar graphs showing the same data. (*Source: The New York Times, Feb. 2, 1984, p.B, 7.*)

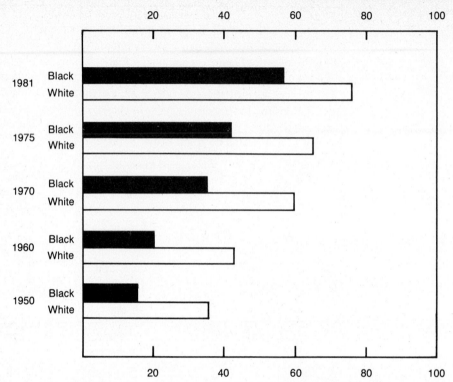

Figure 16.2   Percentage of black and white adults (25 years and over) who have completed four years of high school or more: 1950–1981. [*Source:* U.S. Bureau of the Census, *Statistical Abstract of the United States,* 103rd ed. (Washington, D.C.: U.S. Government Printing Office, 1982), p. 133]

differences among a number of factors on the same chart. Again, visual confusion and complication must be avoided.

Charts   There is almost no limit to the number and variety of charts. The term is used to refer to so many different kinds of visual representations that it can sometimes be confusing. A chart is a navigator's name for a specialized kind of map. It can be what a business man calls a graph of sales information. An engineer may call a technical diagram a chart.[6] The great majority of such visual aids, however, can be sorted into a relatively small number of groups. A chart of any sort must be simple and clear. It should concentrate on one central concept and summarize important points rather than trying to convey a large number of details. Let's take a look at some different kinds of charts.

    A wide variety of information can be outlined in tabular form for easy comprehension by the eye. Arrivals and departures of an airline schedule, or profit-and-loss figures of a business can be tabulated. These and other kinds of information are outlines on *data* or *tabular charts*. They are used for quick and easy reference, like

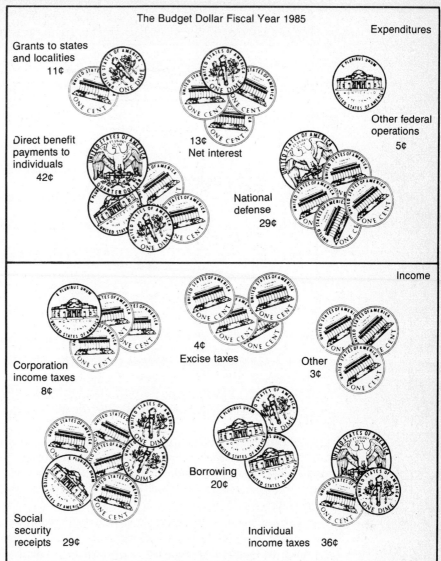

The Budget Dollar Fiscal Year 1985

Expenditures

Grants to states
and localities
11¢

Other federal
operations
5¢

Direct benefit
payments to
individuals
42¢

13¢
Net interest

National
defense
29¢

Income

Corporation
income taxes
8¢

4¢
Excise taxes

Other
3¢

Social
security
receipts   29¢

Borrowing
20¢

Individual
income taxes   36¢

Figure 16.3   Pictorial graph of 1985 proposed budget.

logarithmic tables. They are handy for such tasks as transposing Fahrenheit degrees of
temperature into Celsius, or the English system of measurement into metrics, or
fractions into their decimal equivalents. Figure 16.5 is a chart of this kind.

Many times a large number of chronological facts and the relationships among
them are quite difficult to visualize. Although it is generally agreed, for example, that
memorizing names and dates is not a good way of studying history, nonetheless,
knowing how the major figures in a significant era relate to one another chronologi-

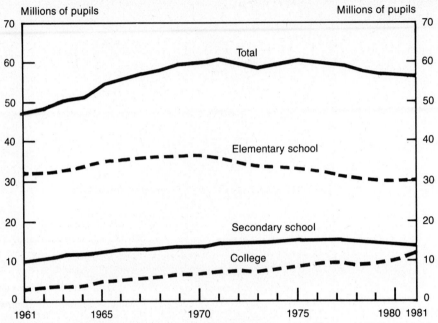

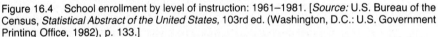

Figure 16.4   School enrollment by level of instruction: 1961–1981. [*Source:* U.S. Bureau of the Census, *Statistical Abstract of the United States,* 103rd ed. (Washington, D.C.: U.S. Government Printing Office, 1982), p. 133.]

cally can be important. A *time chart* such as Figure 16.6 will help to clarify the relationships.

When the relationship to be clarified is functional rather than quantitative or chronological, a *flow chart* helps to show how a process operates or how an organization is structured. In a classroom speech explaining how the editorial staff of a newspaper operates, the speaker used a flow chart like the one shown in Figure 16.7 to visualize the process.

Two variations of the organizational chart are useful. They are called the tree chart and the stream chart. They both look like an organizational chart, and they do very much the same thing except that they look at their materials from opposite points of view. That is, a *tree chart* visualizes a number of offspring arising from a central root source. A "family tree" is an obvious example, but this type of chart can be used to show any similar set of relationships: the multiple effects from a single cause, or the by-products derived from a single mineral, or the different industries that have been generated by a single invention.

A *stream chart,* on the other hand, does just the reverse. It is meant to show how a number of figurative tributaries flow together to form a common stream: how different elements contribute to a common goal—for example, the source of raw materials to produce steel or tires.

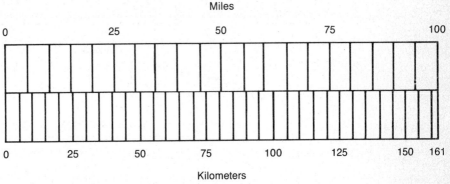

Figure 16.5   Chart for transposing miles and kilometers.

Diagrams   *Webster's New World Dictionary* defines a diagram as "a sketch, drawing, or plan that explains a thing by outlining its parts, workings, etc." In Chapter 17, the drawing of the principle organs of the speech mechanism (Figure 17.1) is a good example of a diagram.

Like charts and graphs, diagrams appear in a wide variety of forms and are put to a wide variety of uses. The purpose for which the diagram is intended will determine the amount of care given to producing it. That is, a set of plans for constructing a communication satellite to orbit the earth cannot be as casual as a rough guide for building a fence. In a talk about the basic operation of a spring motor or an internal combustion engine, for example, a schematic diagram will help to show the relationships among the various parts and functions of the object.

Of all the ways of representing an object or an idea, a diagram is the sketchiest. When you draw rough lines on a sheet of paper to represent the streets in your neighborhood, you don't intend to draw an aerial map. And even the most elaborate set of blueprints for a house is not a picture of the house itself, any more than a map is the actual territory it represents. The important thing to remember, therefore, is that diagrams are mere abstractions. As such, they have great power to confuse unless they are clear.

PRINCIPLES FOR THE USE OF VISUAL AIDS

For listeners a speech is nothing more nor less than what they understand it to be. Similarly, visual aids are useful tools of communication; when they are handled well they can be of great help in gaining a desired response from an audience. Happily, a little common sense is all it takes to use visual aids effectively. Here are some common-sense principles to keep in mind:

1. The visual aid must be large enough for the audience to see and read easily. If it is too small, it will be of no help. Either the audience will be dis-

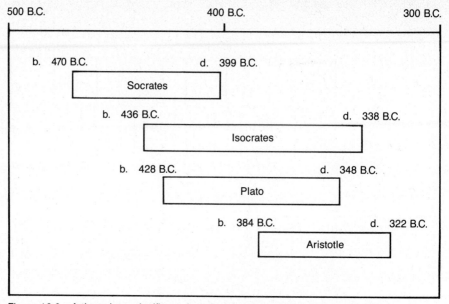

Figure 16.6   A time chart: significant rhetorical theorists of ancient Greece.

tracted from the substance of the speech by the effort to see the aid or, more likely, it won't bother to try. In either case, the utility of the aid is lost.

2. Talk to the audience and not to the aid. There is a tendency to turn away from the audience and give attention to the aid. This may help to focus the eyes of the audience on the aid, but it has the undesirable added effect of breaking the speaker's eye contact with the audience (see Chapter 17) and distracting the audience from the substance of the speech.

3. The language of the speech should be as vividly descriptive as if there were no model, map, or diagram. Visual aids are just that, aids. They are intended to add a visual dimension to the delivery of ideas and supporting materials. It defeats their purpose to use them as a substitute for the auditory element of oral language.

4. Avoid blocking the audience's view of the visual aid. The point here, of course, is obvious. We mention it only as a reminder not to be careless about where to stand or where to position the aid. Put it where you can see it without standing in front of it.

5. The visual aid should be as simple as the facts and ideas it explains permit. Necessary elaborations of detail must be supplied by the speaker. For example, trying to make a graph say everything will make the graph say nothing for the simple reason that it will be so complicated it won't make sense. Visual aids have to make sense very quickly or they might as well not be used at all.

6. The visual aid should be at the intellectual level of the audience. The number and type of labels that are used to clarify the elements of charts,

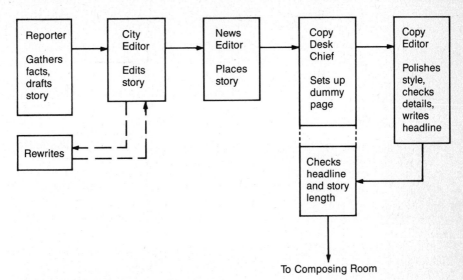

Figure 16.7   Editorial process of a newspaper.

graphs, diagrams, and the like are determined by the needs of an audience. If there are too many, the visual clarity of the aid will be lessened; and if there are too few, the intelligibility of the aid will be diminished. Ideally, the criteria of simplicity and clarity will both be met.

7. The relationships among the various items on the visual aid should be clearly indicated. What we have said in items 3 and 6 is relevant here. The factor to be stressed at this point, however, is that the criteria of simplicity and clarity should be applied to the speaker's language as well as to the visual aid. That is, the language of the speech and the visual aids that support it should work together to bring the speaker's ideas sharply into focus in the minds and imaginations of the audience.

8. The visual aid should be an integral part of the speech. Avoid using pictures, models, and the like unless they make a necessary contribution to clear communication of the central idea of the speech. No matter how attractive, a visual aid that does not support the central purpose of the speech draws attention away from it. It is in this regard no different from any other irrelevant bit of material.

9. To use a chalkboard for pictures, diagrams, and aids of this sort requires enough skill to make drawings that are both neat and accurate. And the sketching must be done quickly, because taking too much time is itself a distraction. It is usually better to prepare the needed drawings in advance. This saves time during the speech, assures higher quality in the drawings, and keeps them from interfering with direct contact between the speaker and the audience.

10. When the visual aid has served its purpose, put it somewhere out of sight of the audience. To leave it in view makes it a continuing distraction.

SUMMARY

Public speeches communicate through both hearing and sight. One way to increase the quality of the visual element of communication is with visual aids.

Visual aids are of four types. Actual objects are useful when they are available and can be safely and easily handled. Models are often better because they can be constructed to show precise relationships. Pictures, both photographs and drawings, are useful, provided that they are authentic, simple, of good quality, and show the relative size of the objects pictured. Symbolic representations include maps, charts, graphs, and diagrams.

Following a few simple rules will improve the effectiveness of visual aids. Make the aid large enough. Talk to the audience, not to the aid. Don't use the aid as a substitute for good oral explanation. Don't block the audience's view of the aid. Make the aid as simple as possible but detailed enough to make the desired point. Design the aid for the intellectual level of the audience. Use an aid only when it is an integral part of the speech. Don't spend too much time drawing on the blackboard. When an aid has served its purpose, put it out of view of the audience.

NOTES

1. Gilbert G. Weaver and Elroy W. Bollinger, *Visual Aids: Their Construction and Use* (New York: Van Nostrand, 1954), p. 4.
2. J. Romiszowski, *The Selection and Use of Instructional Media* (New York: Wiley, 1974), p. 89.
3. Adapted from James S. Kinder, *Using Instructional Media* (New York: Van Nostrand, 1973), pp. 58–59.
4. Kenneth B. Haas and Harry Q. Packer, *Preparation and Use of Audio Visual Aids,* 3rd ed. (New York: Prentice-Hall, 1955), p. 144.
5. For a brief and informative discussion of the variety and utility of maps, see Rhoads Murphey, *Patterns on the Earth: An Introduction to Geography,* 4th ed. (Chicago: Rand McNally, 1978), pp. 11–16.
6. Walter A. Wittich and Charles F. Schuller, *Instructional Technology: Its Nature and Use* (New York: Harper & Row, 1973), p. 118.

EXERCISES

1. Prepare a five-minute informative speech in which you use visual aids to clarify the main purpose of the speech. Be sure that the subject you choose needs visual aids and that the aids are essential to the whole speech, not to just a part of it.
2. Listen to three or four speeches by members of your class and note how they used visual aids or didn't use such aids. Write a short paper on one of the speeches

explaining how the speech might have been improved by more or less visual aids, or why it was well done in the use (or absence) of visual aids.

3. Get the official map to your college campus, or the diagram of the organization of the company you work for, or some similar official map or chart. Come to class prepared to discuss its possible usefulness and weakness as a visual aid for a speech.

chapter 17

Delivering the Speech

C. Involvement
D. Vitality
E. Intelligibility

All communication acts—spoken, written, recorded, filmed—are alike in many ways, the most obvious of which is that they all use some form of language. However, the uniqueness of *oral* communication cannot be denied. In some sense, every form of communication is adapted to its audience, but a speech must make an immediate and very direct adaptation. Its face-to-face oral quality gives it an immediacy that writing and other forms cannot have.

The physical and vocal aspects of delivery, therefore, are more than mechanical tools for converting a written page or an outline into sounds and actions. They are a vital part of the communication itself. Delivery is as much a part of a speech as subject matter, organization, or language. From the moment you select a subject and begin your preparation, you should think of the speech in terms of *oral* presentation.

Were it not for the two important senses of hearing and sight, all communication would be seriously impaired. In public speaking they are particularly important, because the only way you can get your message to your audience is through the use of voice and body. The greater your skill in this, the better your delivery. In this chapter, we will discuss the physical and vocal aspects of speaking, consider the different methods of delivery, and describe the characteristics of good delivery.

VOCAL ASPECTS OF DELIVERY

Any sound (and this, of course, includes your voice) has four elements: pitch, loudness, time, and quality. These are what your ear hears and transmits to your brain to be interpreted. Your ear is capable of distinguishing a wide range of variation in the pitch, loudness, time, and quality of the voices you hear. Because these are the only things the ear can hear, the better you use them, the better the vocal part of your delivery will be. To have a clear understanding of how these elements function in good delivery, remember how speech is produced.

Speech Production

A stream of air, forced from your lungs under pressure by the muscles of exhalation, vibrates your vocal folds, causing sound. The air pressure has to be greater than it is in quiet breathing, because otherwise the stream of air won't vibrate the vocal folds strongly enough to produce a sound with good quality and adequate loudness. The sound is resonated in the various chambers of your throat, mouth, and nose, giving it the characteristics that make your voice different from others. Once this has been done, you have, literally at the tip of your tongue, the raw material of speech. (See Figure 17.1.) But vocal sound does not become speech until you have modified it by articulation.

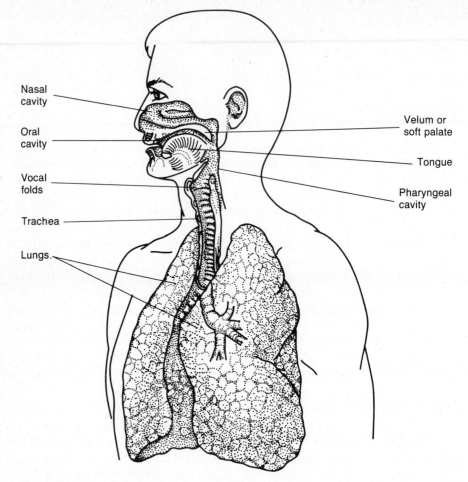

Figure 17.1   The principal organs of speech. The ribs, diaphragm, and thoracic muscles are not shown.

Articulation is the process by which the individual sounds are formed and connected into speech. The primary articulators of the human voice are the tongue, lips, teeth, upper gum ridge, palate, and the vocal folds themselves.

Think for a moment about the total physiological process of voice production. Muscles of the chest and abdomen must be tensed and relaxed to the right degree at the proper moment and for the right length of time to provide air at the proper pressure. The vocal folds must be lengthened and shortened, tensed and relaxed with great speed and precision to produce desired pitches. Those resonating cavities and articulators that can be changed in shape must be modified at a rapid rate and at precisely the right moment to form the different sounds of speech. The fact that anyone can talk at all seems almost miraculous.

Actually, this complex mechanism works so rapidly and each element is so thoroughly integrated with every other that an attempt to isolate and improve any single part of the process should be guided by a highly skilled professional. One seriously oversimplifies the process in looking for solutions to speech problems in "diaphragmatic breathing," "lower pitch," or "more careful articulation." In a public speaking class, only the most general problems can be solved.

Elements of Voice

The vocal mechanism is not only a means of producing sounds, it also controls variations in the pitch, loudness, time, and quality of those sounds. Let's examine the part each of these elements plays in effective communication.

Pitch   Sound is produced when an elastic system is set into vibration. The rate at which the vibrations occur (the number of vibrations per second) is called the *frequency*. It is the frequency of vibration that is interpreted by the ear as pitch. For example, to produce the pitch called A above middle C, the sound source must vibrate 440 times per second. As the frequency increases or decreases, the pitch rises and falls. *Pitch* can be defined as the relative highness or lowness of a sound in relation to a musical scale. By using the muscles in the larynx, a speaker controls the length and tension of the vocal folds in order to produce variations in pitch.

For a sound to be audible to the normal ear, the frequency must be within certain limits. If there are too many or too few vibrations per second, a human ear cannot hear the sound. This principle is used in "silent" whistles that are used to signal dogs. They are so high in pitch that a human ear cannot hear them, but a dog can.

Loudness   Perhaps the easiest element of voice to understand is loudness. When the stream of air from the lungs is not strong, the vocal folds move only a little and relatively slight disturbances are set up in the air. Consequently, the ear is not strongly stimulated and the sound is heard as a soft tone. When air is expelled more strongly from the lungs, the vocal folds are vibrated more vigorously and set up greater disturbances in the air. These strike the ear more forcibly, and the brain interprets the sound as being loud. There is no necessary connection between loudness and pitch— each can vary independently. There is a tendency, however, for pitch to rise as loudness increases.

Time   There are three ways the ear recognizes time in speech. The first is called *duration*. This is the length of time a sound lasts. For example, look at the two words *leap* and *gleam*. The letters *ea* are used to spell the same vowel sound in both words. The vowel is quite short in the word *leap*, but in *gleam* the vowel lasts noticeably longer.

The second factor of time is *rate*, or the number of words spoken per minute. There is no necessary connection between rate and duration, any more than there is between pitch and loudness. The two are independent. That is, the rate of speech can be slow, even though the individual sounds are of short duration. The result is a choppy, staccato delivery. On the other hand, when rate is slow and duration is long, a form of drawl results. By the same token, the duration of individual sounds can be long or short when the rate is fast.

The third factor of time is *pause,* the moment when sound ceases. Pauses are an essential part of speaking. You must breathe; you must think of what you want to say next, and you must allow the audience to grasp what you have said before you go on. The most efficient use of pause takes place when you make all three of these objectives coincide. That is, you should pause to breathe and to think at times when it will most benefit your listeners to have an interval for assimilating an idea.

Frequently nervousness will interfere with effective use of pauses. When you rush to get the speech over with in the shortest possible time, none of your pauses, for breathing, thought, or audience assimilation, will make much sense.

Often you may feel that if you aren't talking all the time, the audience will think you are stumbling. Many speakers are oppressed by this notion and fill what should be pauses with meaningless, nervous insertions of "er," and "yah know?" This not only distracts from what they are saying, it also makes them appear to be at a loss for ideas and words.

The length of a pause can indicate the importance of a point you have made and, at the same time, let the audience think the idea over. It also gives you time to think about what you are going to say next, and to draw in a good breath of air before continuing. When pauses are used properly, they do much to clarify the phrasing of a sentence and add emphasis to ideas. In a sense, they also function as a transition, and they contribute greatly to the audience's impression of you as someone worth listening to.

Quality   There is a wide variety in the sounds produced by different kinds of vibrating bodies. For example, it is easy to distinguish one kind of musical instrument from another because no two sound exactly alike. You don't have to know the name of a marimba or a glockenspiel to tell them apart even when they play the same music. The difference lies in the quality of the sounds they produce. Human voices differ in quality also. Even over the telephone, which is certainly not hi fi, you can usually recognize someone's voice. Characteristic articulations as well as pitch and time patterns help to identify it, but its unique quality is what most helps to single it out.

Using Your Voice to Communicate Meaning

Readers can pause to reexamine an obscure paragraph in an essay, but listeners can't stop to mull over what you say in a speech. When you speak, your ideas have to be instantly intelligible. Only the kind of delivery that brings your ideas sharply and immediately into focus will make your speeches meaningful and compelling. Here are some of the ways you can use your voice to give clarity to your ideas.

Use Standard Conventions of Pronunciation   Pronunciation is the sum of all the audible characteristics of a word: the individual sounds, the order in which they occur, their duration, the stress given to syllables, and so on. But you don't have good pronunciation until it is acceptable to your audience. In other words, it is quite possible for you to have very precise pronunciation and still have it be "wrong." A problem occurs when pronunciation is *inappropriate*—when it fails to meet the *expectations* of your audience. For example, if you pronounce the word "can't" as "cain't," even though your enunciation of each sound is quite precise, and even though all who hear you clearly understand, your pronunciation of this word would be wrong because it is not accepted by the vast majority of educated listeners. Acceptable pronunciation follows the standard usage of the educated members of a speaker's audience.

Dictionaries are the most obvious authority for the accepted pronunciation of words. But we say *accepted* rather than *correct* because as long as a language is spoken, it changes. Dictionaries report what is current usage at the time they are printed, and printing a word does not freeze its pronunciation for all time. But since language changes occur slowly, a dictionary's report of standard pronunciation can be safely accepted.

Emphasize the Important Words   Writers have an advantage that speakers lack: They can let their readers understand ideas at leisure. But when you speak, you have an advantage that writers don't: You can use your voice to say instantly what you mean. You do not have to depend on such relatively crude signs as commas, periods, exclamation points, and question marks to carry shades of meaning. With your voice, you can give a whole complex of different emphases to a single phrase.

In any sentence some words are more important than others. The less important ones can even be omitted without losing the basic meaning. To save both space and reader time, newspaper headlines are telescoped to the shortest form that will still make sense. Sometimes an obvious verb will be left out: "Midwest Flood Damage $100 Million." Such words as "a," "and," or "the" are seldom used: "Clouds, Fog Lift for Pleasant Day." To say more is unnecessary; to say less would be unintelligible.

But even after all the "unnecessary" words have been cut out of a newspaper headline, those that remain are not of equal importance. On Father's Day recently, the *Los Angeles Times* had a story with the headline, "Today's Fathers Not Afraid to Show a Caring Attitude." While all of the words may be needed, some carry a larger burden of the communication than others do. The headline is talking not just about fathers, but about *today's* fathers. The word "today's" would tend to get more stress. "Afraid," is significant, even more so than "Not," but the words "to" and "a" would get very little stress. The words "Caring Attitude" are central to the thought conveyed. Therefore they are very important and heavily stressed. No one can say, of course, what the "correct" reading of the headline is, but one way of using your voice to give an accurate sense of what the headline says would call for something like the following relative degrees of emphasis: '**Today's** *Fathers Not* **Afraid** to *Show* a **Caring Attitude.**"

You are the only one who knows exactly what you mean; you are the one who must decide which of your words carry the burden of your meaning. In every case, you select these important words and give them meaningful emphasis.

Emphasis is likely to be identified at first thought with loudness. One way to let people know what is important is to make it loud. When Mom and Dad say, "Come on in the house, right now," the kids often wait until the call gets loud enough to show that they mean business. However, sophisticated people soon learn that loudness is the simplest form of stress. Effective emphasis is created through *variety* in *all* the elements of vocal delivery: pitch, time, and quality as well as loudness.

Make Clear Distinctions Among Ideas   "Catholics make up approximately 5 percent of the population of West Virginia compared with 30 percent in Wisconsin." In this sentence there are at least two and possibly three opposing sets of ideas. Five percent is certainly not the same as 30 percent, and West Virginia is not to be confused with Wisconsin. There is also an implied distinction between Catholics and non-Catholics among the populations of the two states. The only way you can make your listeners *hear* these differences is with your voice, and the only way your voice can make the ideas distinct is through variations in pitch, loudness, time, and quality.

The same principle applies not only to words that communicate a contrast, but also to those that express ideas in a series. In a Midwestern area, the National Weather Service once chose the wrong person to read the midday forecast on a local radio station. He knew all the names of the different meteorological phenomena, but his voice patterns were so unvaried that they made *clouds, fog, rain, clear,* and *warm* sound the same. By all these words he might as well have meant the same. Some vocal variety would have made the words in this series distinguishable from one another.

Make Words Convey Feelings as Well as Ideas   Many words imitate the sound that they name. (This is called *onomatopoeia,* or "echoism.") For example, ducks quack, geese hiss, sparrows chirp, hens cluck. Insects buzz and hum. The word "boom" imitates the sound it names. The fact that words often imitate sounds can add color to speech.

Echoism, however, is only part of what we mean by making words sound like what you mean. A major function of words is to communicate not only the ideas you have in mind, but your feelings about those ideas as well. Through vocal quality you can make "war" sound heroic or outrageous, "peace" sound glorious or weak. Your voice can help you show the goodness or badness you impute to ideas, their rightness or wrongness, their ugliness or beauty, their merit or lack of it.

Speak in a Conversational Manner   Probably nothing in speaking contributes more to effective delivery than a conversational style. Even when you use in-appropriate pronunciation or grammar, if your delivery is spontaneous, direct, and conversational, you are likely to be more effective than if you had beautiful pro-nunciation and perfect grammar but lacked a conversational delivery.

Most Americans do not, as a rule, read aloud very often or at any great length. When they do, they often sound like children first learning to read. Even when they read fluently, the words of inexperienced and untrained readers sound crated for delivery, boxed in with stiff patterns, repetitions of pitch cadences, an unvaried tempo, an unchanging degree of loudness, and a dull quality of monotony that conceals much of what should be conveyed. Reading patterns almost always attach themselves to the recitation of memorized words as well. One mark of a poor actor is an inability to speak in a spontaneous, conversational mode.

Your speaking is an extension of your personality. Obviously, pronunciation, pitch, loudness, time, and quality have to be adapted to the size of an audience and the requirements of the subject matter but, at base, your delivery should be like the animated conversation that goes on among friends.

PHYSICAL ACTION IN DELIVERY

Everything you do in public speaking or in private conversation says something. "Everything" includes not only your words, but the way you use your voice and the "silent language" you transmit with your body. Each of these media, the linguistic, the vocal, and the physical, is a language and is interpreted by an audience as having some bearing on what you say. The more of these languages you put to use at the same time—that is, the more channels you use simultaneously to carry your message—the more likely your message will be to get through accurately. Of course, all of the languages must be saying the same thing: all of the channels must be carrying the same message. Otherwise, they will not only fail to make your message clear, they will actually obscure it by counteracting and contradicting each other. You want to make sure that there is *unity* in the messages carried by your words, your voice, and your physical actions. All of the audible and visible cues you give the audience should be saying the same thing at the same time.

Eye Contact

When you speak, *look directly at the audience*. This means something more than not looking at the floor, at the walls, out the window, or head down into your notes. It means more than sweeping the audience with an occasional glance. It means looking directly into the faces of individual members of the audience, making personal eye contact with everyone to whom you speak. Of course, when you talk to a large group, or speak in a large auditorium, you are too far from the audience to look directly into the eyes of each listener. But you can still give the impression that you are doing just that.

Your own experience will tell you that listeners do not respond well to a speaker in public or private who does not look at them. You have met people who avoided your glance. What was your reaction to them? There's no point in trying to make the case that someone who refuses to look you in the eye is shifty or untrustworthy; the important idea here is that you tend to react negatively to someone who does refuse.

There is another good reason for you to look directly at your listeners. The audience itself is an important source of information—and speakers need all the help they can get. As a rule, people respond overtly to what they see and hear, and those responses tell you what effect you are having on them. It would be wasteful not to take advantage of the feedback the audience gives you. Only by making direct visual contact with individual members of the group can you tell who is alert and friendly, who is bored, who is unconcerned, or who is just not listening.

Posture

It is futile to try to distinguish between you and your ideas. Therefore, the way an audience rates you as a person will influence how it will respond to your ideas. One of the things that affects an audience's reactions to you as a person is posture. Consequently, you should stand before your audience in a manner that indicates stability and assurance. Your posture should be poised but not stiff, relaxed but not sloppy.

Experienced speakers sometimes lean on a speaking stand, put their hands in their pockets, or even sit on the edge of a table. But when speakers are this casual, it usually means that they and the audience know each other pretty well. Whether such posture is acceptable depends more on the degree of formality in a given situation than it does on the "rules" of public speaking. Being overly casual is likely to work to the disadvantage of beginning speakers, because they usually don't know the audience

The speaker's posture can relay assurance or anxiety. (Carey, The Image Works)

well and audiences expect strangers to treat them with a kind of formal respect. A second and perhaps more important reason for not being too casual is that you are likely to dramatize your relaxation in an effort to dispel or disguise nervousness. Instead of covering up your anxiety, you emphasize it, and this detracts from your effectiveness.

Even so, you can communicate assurance by controlling your posture. Though you may not be able to control the trembling in your muscles, you can control what you do to cope with it. Stand straight, balance your weight on both feet, and look directly at your audience. The results will be far better than anything you can do by way of draping yourself over the lectern, crossing your ankles, slouching with your hands in your pockets, sitting on the edge of a desk, or pacing back and forth in front of your audience. Granted, this posture won't do much to keep your hands and legs from quivering, but it will help keep your nervousness from interfering with your communication. You may not think so, but your audience will. And that is the important point. Put the stress where the stress belongs. Conscious decisions about posture in any specific situation should always be determined by what is *appropriate* to the audience, the occasion, and the substance of your speech. Remember, you are there to *talk,* to talk about *ideas,* not to model clothes or make a pretty picture for the audience.

Movement

In general, avoid movement that is not necessary. Pacing back and forth on the platform is never necessary and is rarely useful. Many an anxious speaker has used this kind of wandering as a means of working off excess energy. But when there is nothing to justify it, stalking around during the speech detracts from the communication. A more useful way to relieve tension is through vocal intensity and firm gestures that are relevant to the speech.

An important detail of movement is the way you get from your seat to the place where you will speak and back to your seat again when you have finished. An audience will hold you responsible for everything you do from the moment you leave your seat until you sit down again. That is to say, your speech begins, not when you utter your first words, but when you first stand up. Similarly, your speech does not end with your conclusion; it goes on until the attention of the audience is no longer on you. In fact, the attention of your listeners will still be on you even after you sit down until something distracts them from you.

Under these conditions it is only reasonable to conduct yourself in a manner that will not detract from the general effectiveness of your speech. It will help to preserve your credibility if you neither race nor shuffle to the front of the room but walk to and from the platform with firmness and poise. Give the impression that you *want* to speak and are ready for the occasion. When you have finished speaking, maintain the atmosphere of dignity and competence you have built by returning to your seat quietly and deliberately.

Gesture

Another kind of bodily action is gesture. Gesture is distinguished from the kind of movement just discussed by the fact that it involves movement of the arms, hands, and head but does not carry the speaker from one part of the room to another. Gestures made with the hands and arms are of two kinds: those that emphasize words and those that are used for description. There is no set vocabulary of gestures. You can emphasize an idea by pointing with your finger, or you can pound a word home with your fist. You may spread your hands to show size, or extend your arm to show place.

To be effective, gestures must seem spontaneous and natural. When speakers are called "wooden" because they are so lacking in physical activity, they often say that gesturing is not "natural" for them. As often as not, the very remark will be accompanied by a completely natural gesture. The point is that gesturing is *natural* for everyone, but it is not usually *habitual* for a beginning speaker in a formal speaking situation. One solution to the problem is to carry over into public speech the same free movement of hands, arms, and head that you normally and habitually use in private speech and the same mobility of facial expression. Obviously, some speakers quite naturally gesture more than others. But those rare persons who do not gesture at all, even in private speech, should maintain the poise of private speech.

The more common experience has been, however, that although most speakers use some movement of their hands and arms, their gestures are unmotivated, choppy, and incomplete. They seem to feel the need for gestures but are inhibited from making them. One very good way of overcoming this kind of problem is role-playing. Deliberately and consciously *act the part* of a competent and effective speaker. You have a clear image of how that sort of person would behave, because you've seen a lot of examples in movies, television, and real life. Imitate speakers you like, including those in your own class. Given time and experience, you will develop your own habitual style. You will find that when you are enthusiastic about your idea and have a will to communicate it, your personal speaking habits will provide you with a spontaneous and varied group of gestures that are natural to you.

Facial expression in delivery is as significant as the gestures you make with your hands and arms. Listeners interpret your actions as clues to what you are saying, and audiences tend to read your face as closely as they listen to your words. Unfortunately, it's easy to give them the wrong clues. They may think you are bored or cynical, for instance, when you are not. How often have you had someone ask you what was the matter when nothing was wrong? It's up to you to give your listeners the right clues.

METHODS OF DELIVERY

The vocal and physical elements of speaking are, in a sense, the raw materials that you manufacture into an effective style of delivery. But then comes the question, what kind of delivery is best?

Four different methods of delivering a speech are commonly recognized. These differ from one another according to the kind of preparation the speaker makes for delivery. If the language of the speech is thoroughly prepared in advance, the speech can be delivered either from *manuscript* or from *memory*. On the other hand, if the language is not chosen before the moment of delivery, the speech will be either *impromptu* or *extemporaneous*.

Speaking from Manuscript

Since the audience judges what is required for an effective speech, it is impossible to know in advance precisely how a speech ought to be delivered. However, you have a much better chance of accomplishing your purpose when you speak in simple, direct, straightforward language to listeners with whom you are making close visual and psychological contact. With this kind of delivery, it is much easier to make any necessary adaptations to the occasion and to the idiosyncrasies of the audience.

A person in a position of great responsibility (such as the U.S. Ambassador to the United Nations) can't afford to make a mistake, no matter how small. That is a time for a manuscript speech. When very strict time limits are placed on a speech, as there are, for example, on radio and TV, or when a situation such as a commencement ceremony requires a polished speech, it might be delivered from manuscript. But unless an occasion of this kind should arise for you, your general rule should be, don't use a manuscript. If you ever have to, your delivery should have the qualities that characterize any good speaking. We will describe these characteristics later in this chapter.

Speaking from Memory

In preparing to deliver a speech from memory, you would ordinarily write out a manuscript and practice from it until you knew it by heart. This kind of delivery has few of the advantages and all of the disadvantages of the manuscript method. Unless you are a reasonably accomplished actor, you will find it difficult to deliver a talk from memory and maintain close contact with the audience at the same time. Even if you are a good actor, or recite well, you will meet with the same lack of flexibility that burdens the manuscript speaker. There is another disadvantage to speaking from memory: If you forget, you are lost. Categorically, we say *never* memorize a speech. If the occasion demands that kind of preparation, prepare a manuscript and use it instead.

Speaking Impromptu

An impromptu speech may be defined as one for which you have made no immediate preparation. You are unexpectedly called upon to speak and have to say things on the spur of the moment. You might imagine yourself swaying masses of people and crushing opposition, the epitome of impromptu eloquence. But you would know that was a daydream. Such skill is not impossible to attain, but it is very hard to come by.

Henry Ward Beecher, one of the most famous preachers of the nineteenth century, delivered a splendid talk that seemed to be completely impromptu. When he was asked how long he had worked on it, he said he had been preparing for the talk for 40 years.

Except when the occasion absolutely demands it, you should never speak impromptu. Take every opportunity to prepare as thoroughly as time will allow. If at all possible, take a few moments to think through what you will say and perhaps to jot down a few notes. Even if you must react at once, remember that the major functions of a speech are to introduce an idea, develop it, and conclude. If you do this, even the most hastily prepared talk will have the quality of order.

Speaking Extemporaneously

In speaking extemporaneously, the ideas, organization, and supporting material of a speech are still thoroughly prepared in advance. The only part of the speech that is *ex tempore* (grows "out of the time," comes at the actual moment of delivery) is the *language*. The delivery is practiced as well; the speech has been "talked through" several times. You do not write out the speech (although you should prepare an outline), nor do you make any effort to memorize the language you will use. Indeed, each time you practice the speech you will use different language and work toward a more precise and clearer statement of your ideas. When you deliver the speech, you will be so thoroughly familiar with the subject matter that you can in a very real sense "ad lib" the language.

We believe that extemporaneous delivery has the greatest number of advantages and the fewest disadvantages of the four methods. It can have all the spontaneity and immediacy of casual conversation without the disorganization that usually characterizes impromptu speaking. And it lends itself to direct visual and psychological contact with the audience. Unlike a manuscript or memorized speech, it affords flexibility in meeting the specific and yet shifting demands of an audience.

CHARACTERISTICS OF GOOD DELIVERY

People in general use very good delivery in their everyday conversational speech. Yet they do not carry it over in public speaking. This is unfortunate, because good delivery, even in the most formal situations, needs all the best qualities of good conversation.

Directness

Good conversational delivery is *direct*. Talk directly to your listeners. Look directly at them. Don't look over their heads, or out the window, or through them as if they weren't there. Recognize that they *are* there, and talk to them much the same as you would if they were guests in your home. Show that you *want* to communicate.

Spontaneity

Good conversational delivery seems *spontaneous*. This does not mean that you sound as if you were stumbling through the ideas of the speech for the first time. It contributes much more to your credibility to give the impression that you are delivering a well-thought-out, clearly developed, and carefully organized speech. Spontaneity gives the delivery freshness and immediacy. It puts you *in the presence of the audience*. Without spontaneity, delivery is dull and rote-like, much as if someone had turned on a tape recorder and left it unattended.

Involvement

Good conversational delivery clearly shows your personal *involvement* with your subject. Your own enthusiasm provides vivid clues to the audience about the significance of the subject and your desire to talk about it. If your listeners get the impression that you are not interested in what you are saying, there is certainly no reason they should be.

Vitality

Good conversational delivery has *vitality*. Liveliness in voice and bodily action provides clues to the audience about the relative importance of the materials in a speech. Vitality in delivery demands the kind of gesture and movement that you would naturally use to emphasize a point in ordinary conversation. As an experiment, pay some attention to what you and others do in everyday speaking situations. You may be surprised to see how much gesturing is done.

Intelligibility

Good conversational delivery is readily *intelligible*. Nothing you say will make any sense if your audience can't hear you. But to make the members of an audience "hear," you must make them *listen*. This requires that your voice be more than merely audible. Speak loudly enough not only to be heard but also to command attention in spite of the many normal distractions to be expected. To hold the attention of an audience, you must contend with such competitors as a noisy air conditioner in the back of the room or a group of children playing ball outside an open window.

Besides audibility, intelligible delivery has other qualities: Articulation (the forming and joining together of individual sounds) should be clear and precise without being stilted. Pronunciation should be acceptable; it should follow the standard usage of the educated members of your community.

SUMMARY

Speech is brought about when vocal sound is resonated by the cavities of the throat, mouth, and head to give each voice its characteristic quality. The indeterminate vocal sound is formed into language by the articulators: lips, teeth, tongue, palate, upper gum ridge, and vocal folds.

The ear hears speech in terms of four variable characteristics: pitch, loudness, time, and quality. By controlling these elements, you emphasize your ideas and bring clarity to your speech.

These five principles will help you to achieve good delivery:

1. Use standard conventions of pronunciation.
2. Emphasize the important words.
3. Make clear distinctions among the ideas.
4. Make words convey feelings as well as ideas.
5. Speak in a conversational manner.

Physical action is as much a part of a speech as ideas or voice. An audience judges you and your ideas by what it sees as much as by what it hears. Consequently, controlled physical action is an important part of effective delivery. Perhaps the most important visual aspect of communication is eye contact; look directly at your audience. Stand before the audience with a relaxed but not too casual posture. The way you move to and from the speaking position helps to show your enthusiasm, but you should not pace around the room during your speech. Gestures should be full and complete rather than choppy and undeveloped, defined rather than vague.

There are four methods of delivering a speech: from manuscript or from memory, impromptu or extemporaneously. Of these, extemporaneous delivery is by far the best choice except in extraordinary circumstances. In any case, good delivery has these characteristics: directness, spontaneity, involvement, vitality, and intelligibility.

EXERCISES

1. There are many opportunities to observe, analyze, and evaluate the part that vocal behavior plays in communication: The public platform, the pulpit, the theater, legislative assemblies, and the like. Observe one of these instances of communication and write a 500-word paper analyzing and evaluating the effectiveness of the part played by the use of voice in helping the speaker or performer communicate.
2. Analyze and evaluate the effectiveness of the part played by physical action in helping a speaker, actor, dancer, or pantomimist to communicate.
3. Make a recording of your own speech. Listen to the recording and evaluate your use of pitch, loudness, time, and quality.
4. Prepare and deliver a speech in which you consciously prepare some gestures to use at certain points in the speech. Does this help your speaking?

five

TYPES OF SPEAKING SITUATIONS

chapter *18*

Speaking to Inform

I. Determine the specific subject of the speech
   A. Limiting the Subject
      1. Narrowing the scope of a subject
         a. Limit the subject in time
         b. Limit the subject in space
         c. Narrow the subject to a subproblem
         d. Discuss a portion of a process
      2. Treating a series of narrowed aspects of a subject
   B. Formulating a statement of purpose
II. Organize the body of the speech
   A. Determining major points
   B. Determining the number of points in the body of the speech
   C. Patterns of arrangement
      1. Chronological pattern
      2. Spatial pattern
      3. Topical pattern
      4. Pattern of definition
      5. Pattern of comparison and contrast
      6. Pattern of cause and effect
   D. Using multiple patterns of arrangement
III. Add supporting materials
IV. Prepare the conclusion and the introduction
V. Practice the delivery

One fact of contemporary life is the startling rate at which knowledge is increasing. Bombs and populations are not the only things that explode. We are living in a period of "information explosion." But all the knowledge in the world is useless unless you can get it. Obviously, there is a need to transmit information. That is why such an enormous part of all the talking that goes on at home, at school, and at work, as well as on the public platform, is done to clarify ideas, transmit facts, or give instructions. Clearly, the ability to communicate information effectively is an important skill. This chapter is devoted to helping you develop it.

In every case, what an audience understands you to say, not what you intended to say, is, in fact, what you did say. In order for your intention and the audience's understanding to be as nearly the same as possible, your speaking has to be interesting and clear: interesting enough to listen to, clear enough to be understood accurately. To make this happen, follow these five steps:

1. Determine the specific subject of the speech.
2. Organize the body of the speech.
3. Add supporting materials.
4. Prepare the conclusion and the introduction.
5. Practice the delivery.

DETERMINE THE SPECIFIC SUBJECT OF THE SPEECH

Choosing a subject is the important first step in preparing a speech of any kind. Chapter 5 has some very useful advice to offer in this regard. The chances are good that the subject you first light on will be both broad and vague. Consequently, before you can make an outline, and even before you begin to gather materials, you need to establish what the specific subject will be. To do this, first limit the scope or breadth of your topic and, second, formulate a precise statement of your specific subject.

Limiting the Subject

There are two ways of limiting a speech subject. The more usual way is to narrow the scope or breadth of the topic. On some occasions, however, you might want to paint the subject with a broader brush. In that case, you can select a number of aspects of the broader subject and narrow each of those to suit your discussion. Let's see how these two limiting processes work.

Narrowing the Scope of a Subject   More often than not, determining the scope of a speech means limiting or narrowing the subject so that you can develop your ideas in sufficient detail within the time limit of your speech. What your listeners want or need to know determines in large measure the extent to which, and the methods by which, you fix the scope of your subject.

At first it may seem that you wouldn't have enough to say about a narrow topic. But if you go about your speech preparation in the right way, you will probably find that you have too much material.

Here are some ways to narrow a topic:

1. Limit the subject in time   Such a general subject as "American presidential elections" might be narrowed to a discussion of "The disputed election of 1876," or "The wartime elections of 1864 and 1944." The subject of music could be limited to the period of the baroque masters. A discussion on art could be limited to the period of "Dadaism."

2. Limit the subject in space   American foreign trade is far too broad a subject for a single speech. It can be the source of a successful speech subject, however, if you limit your discussion, for instance, to a consideration of Japanese trade restrictions, or the differences between sales of imported and exported wines.

3. Narrow the subject to a subproblem   Select as the specific topic of the speech a part of some larger problem. Instead of discussing energy conservation, for example, isolate the subproblem of the economics of solar energy.

4. Discuss a portion of a process   A prelaw student, who was also an Army veteran and wanted to talk about the administration of justice, selected a limited subject in this area relevant to both his military experience and his interest in the law. He made a very interesting talk on the differences between a court martial and a civilian trial.

It is not necessary to narrow a subject by all of these methods, but here is what might be done with a single topic, using all four methods of limitation:

General subject: International diplomacy

Narrowed in space: Central America

Narrowed to a subproblem: American–Nicaraguan Relations

Narrowed in time: Fall 1983

Narrowed to a portion of a process: The activities of the Central Intelligence Agency in supporting anti-Sandanista rebels

Treating a Series of Narrowed Aspects of a Subject   Sometimes, the speech situation is such that you cannot narrow your subject in one of the conventional ways just described. You might not want to restrict the scope. Nevertheless, the same demands for clear exposition must be met. Therefore, even though the scope may be broad, the number of points and the breadth of those points must be restricted.

When you must cover a broad subject, you can do it successfully by treating a series of *narrow aspects* of the broader subject. For example, a student who planned to study for the priesthood wanted to select a topic from the general subject of the Catholic Church. Using conventional methods of narrowing the scope of his subject, he might have arrived at this topic: "The Rite of ordination to the priesthood of the Catholic Church." Instead, this speaker chose the overall broad view of the general subject, but he selected three specific points. These, he believed, would be of interest to his non-Catholic listeners and would inform them of often misunderstood elements of Catholicism: the Mass as the central act of worship, the sacrament of reconciliation (confession), and the doctrine of papal infallibility.

Formulating a Statement of Purpose

A clear statement of precisely what response you want from your audience will be a great help in selecting the materials and organizing the ideas of your speech. The most common procedure for making such a statement is to formulate an infinitive phrase that identifies your purpose in speaking, specifies the subject of the speech, and sets its precise scope. The resulting expression of what you intend to accomplish in your speech is called a statement of purpose. It identifies for you exactly what idea you want to clarify for your audience. For instance:

> To inform the audience of the current economic limitations on the extensive use of solar energy
>
> To inform the audience about the differences between a military court martial and a civilian trial
>
> To inform the audience of the meaning that Roman Catholics place on three frequently misunderstood aspects of their church

The written statement of purpose is used as a guide for your speech preparation. It will help you to decide what material belongs in the speech and what does not. You can always find many interesting ideas and tempting pieces of material to put into a speech. The great problem is one of selection: including those items that are essential to the specific purpose and rejecting those that are not. Once it is formed, the statement of purpose should be used as a rigorous standard by which to identify necessary materials and to eliminate those that are not needed.

ORGANIZE THE BODY OF THE SPEECH

The earliest writers on public speaking recognized good order as an essential ingredient of effective communication. We say "good" order and "effective" communication because, no matter how badly you may jumble your ideas and materials, you will still communicate something. You have very little assurance, however, that what you mean will bear much resemblance to what your audience thinks you mean. If a speech is to make the impression you want, its parts should be so related that the speech as a whole is easy to understand and easy to remember.

An effective speech normally contains an introduction, a body, and a conclusion. We suggest that you organize the body of the speech first, because all the essential material implied in the statement of purpose is contained in the body of the speech. The introduction and the conclusion are important to the extent that they help the audience to perceive accurately what is in the body.

Organizing the body of a speech raises two questions: What are the reasonable parts of my subject? What is the order in which these parts should be arranged? The first question is answered through a process of *analysis* and the second through a process we can call *synthesis*.

Determining Major Points

Dividing the subject into parts is necessary because the whole idea of the subject cannot be communicated at once. The component ideas must be given to the audience one at a time. Analyzing your subject will tell you what these components are and will help you judge what kinds of information are needed to satisfy the demands of the occasion. Journalists long ago developed a rule of thumb to test the completeness of a news story. If the opening paragraph does not answer the questions, Who?, What?, When?, Where?, Why?, and How?, the writing is considered faulty. When you make an informative speech, you will profit from examining the content with a journalistic eye.

Determining the Number of Points in the Body of the Speech

Research on information processing has long shown that the number of individual pieces of information the mind will retain is quite limited. The popular formula says, "Seven, give or take two." Some researchers say less, others say more.[1] But whether you think five, nine, or twelve is a maximum, there is a real limit to human capability without special training. Given such a limit, it makes sense to keep the number of points in the body of a speech between two and five. More than this number gives the audience too much to remember. Keep in mind at all times that you are trying to give your audience ideas they can carry away with them. This is especially important in an informative speech. In a persuasive speech you might be satisfied if a listener is persuaded and remembers only one argument. But when your purpose is to give information, you want maximum retention.

The number of main points in the speech is also controlled to a large extent by the time you have available for speaking. Allow at least a minute to develop each of the major headings in the body. Thus, if your speech is to be five minutes long, considering the fact that you also need an introduction and a conclusion, four points in the body would be a maximum. Even in a seven-minute speech, three points are not too few. If you have more time, concentrate on extending the development of a few points rather than on increasing the number.

Patterns of Arrangement

The second aspect of organization, the process of synthesis, is deciding how to arrange the parts of the subject into a pattern that will maintain interest and impart a unified body of knowledge. Look for the organizational pattern that will best help your audience understand and remember what you say. There are several methods of arranging an informative speech to achieve clarity and retention. We shall comment on six of these: chronological, spatial, topical, definition, comparison and contrast, cause and effect.

Chronological Pattern   Many subjects will yield easily to a historical or chronological sequence of presentation. In the following example, the basic steps in the development of the table of atomic weights are clarified by using a chronological pattern as the means of ordering the main ideas.

STATEMENT OF PURPOSE: To inform the audience about the basic steps in the development of the Periodic Table
   I. Scientists observed certain similarities in the behavior of groups of elements.
  II. Mendeleyev found that the elements could be arranged in order of increasing atomic weight to bring the elements of these groups into columns.
 III. Ramsey completed the organization by assigning atomic numbers.
 IV. Later atomic chemists related the atomic numbers to the distribution of electrons in the shells of the various atoms.

Spatial Pattern   Another common pattern of arrangement is by location. Such an order shows the relationship of one point to another in space. The following example is appropriately organized in a spatial pattern. It explains the parallel between altitude and latitudinal life zones. This example is particularly interesting because two geographical principles actually are at work in one speech, and it helps a listener to understand why and how as well as where.

STATEMENT OF PURPOSE: To inform the audience of the parallel relationship between the plant life of a region and the region's altitude and distance from the equator
   I. Tropical forests flourish near sea level and near the equator.
     A. Climatic conditions
     B. Typical plants
  II. Deciduous forests occur in temperate zones at low altitudes.
     A. Climatic conditions
     B. Typical plants
 III. Coniferous forests grow far from the equator and at higher altitudes.
     A. Climatic conditions
     B. Typical plants
 IV. Mosses, lichens, and low herbaceous growths are characteristic of the far North and areas above timber line.
     A. Climatic conditions
     B. Typical plants
  V. Ice and snow cap both polar regions and the highest mountains.
     A. Climatic conditions
     B. Typical plants

Topical Pattern   Any method of partitioning that divides a subject into its component parts can be called a topical pattern. In this sense, both the chronological and the spatial patterns of organization are special forms of topical arrangement. The latter is considered a separate method of organization to accommodate natural or traditional classifications that are neither chronological nor geographical. Many such classifications are familiar to you: animal, vegetable, and mineral; political, social, and economic; strings, percussion, woodwinds, and brass. Any subject that can be analyzed into component parts can be organized by the method of topical arrangement. Here is an example of topical partition.

STATEMENT OF PURPOSE: To inform the audience of the available U.S. reserves of the sources of energy used for generating electrical power
  I. Fossil fuel
  II. Water power
  III. Atomic energy
  IV. Solar energy
  V. Geothermal energy

  Although it is not necessarily evident and the outline makes no point of it, the fact that the main headings come in generally accurate chronological order, relative to the sequence in which the various power sources have been widely exploited, will not harm the clarity of the speech and might even help. We shall have more to say about the use of multiple patterns of arrangement later in this chapter.

Pattern of Definition   A fourth method of division is by definition. Speeches intended to answer such questions as "What is radioactivity?" or "What is a recession?" or "What is a socialist?" can often use as main heads methods of definition selected from among those discussed in Chapter 8.

STATEMENT OF PURPOSE: To inform the audience of the essential nature of jazz
  I. Jazz is a form of popular music indigenous to the United States.
    A. Jazz originated in New Orleans.
    B. Jazz began just after World War I.
  II. Jazz differs from other popular music.
    A. It differs from spirituals.
    B. It differs from Western music.
    C. It differs from folk music of the hill country.
  III. Jazz takes several forms.
    A. Dixieland
    B. Blues
    C. Progressive jazz

The pattern follows the rules of formal definition. It first puts jazz into a general class: American popular music. Then it differentiates it from other American popular music. These are the only essential steps in organizing the topic by the pattern of definition. However, explaining some of its diverse forms helps further to clarify what jazz is.

Pattern of Comparison and Contrast   Speakers frequently make use of the similarities and differences of two items or concepts when an audience is familiar with one of them and not familiar with the other. Comparison and contrast are not only useful forms of definition and valuable forms of supporting material, they can also be used as an organizing principle for an informative speech. Both comparison and contrast can be used separately in defining, supporting, and organizing, but here is a speech organized by both comparison and contrast.

STATEMENT OF PURPOSE: To inform the audience of the nature of white-collar crime

  I. It is like many other forms of larceny.
      A. Theft is nonviolent and engenders no fear.
      B. Shoplifting is nonviolent and causes no fear.
      C. Like confidence games, it often depends on being trusted.
 II. It is different from many other crimes in two senses.
      A. It is defined in a different sense.
          1. The criminal is defined in terms of a class: "a person in business, government, or a profession."
          2. The definition emphasizes the method by which the crime is committed, not the fruit of the crime: "fraud . . . committed . . . in the course of one's occupation."
      B. It is different from crimes of violence such as murder and rape.
          1. It does not physically injure a person.
          2. It is not directed at individuals.
      C. It is different from robbery and burglary.
          1. It does not engender fear.
          2. There is no physical threat.

Pattern of Cause and Effect   When you want to explain what caused an event or when you want to explain the consequences of some event, you can use a cause-and-effect order. You would employ this pattern to explain either the *causes* for the stock market crash of 1929 or the *effects* of radioactivity on the human body. Although either can be used separately, in the following example, both cause and effect are combined in the same organizational pattern in order to clarify the subject more fully.

STATEMENT OF PURPOSE: To inform the audience of the problem of smog in the Los Angeles Basin

  I. Effects of smog
      A. Smog is harmful to the human body.
      B. Eleven billion dollars per year in property damage is incurred.
      C. Agricultural losses are sustained.
          1. Plants and crops
          2. Livestock

      D. Visibility is limited.
      E. The area loses tourist trade.
  II. Causes of smog
     A. Chemical
        1. Automobiles
        2. Industry
     B. Climatic
        1. Temperature inversion
        2. Weak winds

Using Multiple Patterns of Arrangement

In organizing an informative speech, you want a method of arrangement that unites the speech, most naturally expresses the sequence of ideas for your listeners, and makes it easier for them to understand.

You need not always use a single method of partitioning. It is quite possible that your ideas will become clearer if you combine two (or even more) of the methods. In some instances, the nature of the subject itself demands multiple levels of arrangement. When, for example, you explain the steps in building an automobile on an assembly line, you will necessarily combine chronological, spatial, and topical elements in the sequence of ideas. The following example is incomplete, but the outline illustrates the point at hand.

STATEMENT OF PURPOSE: To explain the legal process of extradition
  I. Extradition is the surrender of an alleged criminal by one governmental entity to another.
     A. In international practice, it can be likened to other treaty arrangements.
     B. It differs from other instances of forcible removal.
        1. Banishment
        2. Expulsion
        3. Deportation
  II. There are two kinds.
     A. International—between countries
     B. Interstate—within the United States
  III. It has a long history.
     A. Known in ancient and medieval times
     B. Developed chiefly after the eighteenth century
        1. Belgian law of 1833
        2. U.S. statute of 1848
        3. Netherlands act of 1849

The basic pattern of organization is clearly *topical*. But each of the subordinate headings is developed in its own way, not necessarily the same as the main pattern. The first main heading is a definition, but it is developed by comparison and contrast; the second main heading is given a topical development; and the third main heading is developed chronologically. Thus, not only does the speech have an overall pattern, each of the points is organized by a pattern. Taken together, the multiplicity of patterns, because each is appropriate, is valuable in strengthening the unity of the material.

In contrast, notice the lack of order in the following outline:

STATEMENT OF PURPOSE: To inform the audience of the essential nature of atheism
   I. Early Greeks
      A. Two meanings for atheism
         1. Believing in foreign or strange gods
         2. Believing that there are no gods
      B. The original Greek word was "atheos."
  II. Atheism and communism
      A. Associated with international socialist movement
      B. Part of the state philosophy of the Soviet Union
 III. Atheists and agnostics differ in their beliefs.
      A. Neither is convinced of the existence of God.
      B. Negative evidence is sufficient for atheists.
      C. Proof one way or other needed for agnostics.
 IV. Atheism today

The first main point appears to promise a chronological development. The second point shifts ground, however, and appears to be a topical heading of the central idea. The third point introduces yet another pattern in the form of comparison and contrast. The fourth point returns to the original chronological pattern. The result is a mishmash of tangled ideas. Even if each main point is made clear individually, the listeners will probably have only a confused notion of what atheism is. Imposing multiple patterns of organization on a speech is an advantage only as long as they are compatible and the variations fit into a consistent and unified framework.

ADD SUPPORTING MATERIALS

After you have established the organizational pattern of the body, you are ready to develop these main points by adding supporting materials. Listeners usually grasp an idea more readily when it is associated with some object, person, or event that they already know or can easily comprehend. The more vividly your examples, statistics, definitions, and quotations revitalize experiences that listeners have had, the better are your chances of making your speech interesting and clear. For this reason it is a good rule of thumb to use at least one supporting detail for every idea you bring into a speech.

Variety in supporting detail is a further help toward building interest. If you use statistics exclusively, or hypothetical examples only, or nothing but quotations, you may lose the attention of an audience because your materials lack variety. To be sure, having some supporting material, even if it does lack variety, is preferable to having no material at all, but get variety whenever you can.

PREPARE THE CONCLUSION AND THE INTRODUCTION

When you have organized your ideas and materials into the body of the speech, you have a unified and coherent view of what you want your audience to understand. Then you prepare the conclusion, which essentially summarizes the major ideas in the body. Finally, with a clear understanding of what the speech contains, you can prepare an introduction that will appeal to the interest of the listeners and let them know what the speech is about. The speech then follows the rules of the old preacher who said: "First I tell 'em what I'm gonna' tell 'em. Then I tell 'em. Then I tell 'em what I told 'em." Chapter 13 explains in some detail a variety of ways of developing the introduction and the conclusion.

PRACTICE THE DELIVERY

Until it is delivered, a speech is a growing thing, representing your increasing awareness of the subject and the audience. For this reason, your speech will continually change during the time you are working on it. You will be shifting points around, replacing one example with a better one, or considering new ways of partitioning the ideas.

Perhaps because so much emphasis in education is put on written communica-

A speech changes continually. It is not "an essay standing on its hind legs." (Ellen Shub, 1981)

tion, it is easy to think of a speech as something to write out and read. There is a temptation to prepare a careful outline, and then to stop revising it and begin practicing the delivery. But a speech is not "an essay standing on its hind legs." It will be judged by its impact on the audience. Consequently, it should be tried out *orally,* in parts and as a whole, from the early stages of preparation. When the first rough approximation of your speech has been drawn up, begin to "talk it through." As you hear things in the speech you don't like, change them, and improve them. The outline should be developed in the atmosphere of oral, not written, communication. With this kind of preparation, a speech will come to be part of you; more and more it will grow into a communication that reflects your ideas, your knowledge, and your individual personality.

SUMMARY

Of all the talking that goes on in the world each day, a large part is occupied with transmitting information. Informative speaking is an important process; therefore, skill in this kind of communication is both necessary and desirable. To ensure that the information you give will be interesting and clear, follow five steps in preparing an informative speech:

1. *Select and narrow the subject, and formulate a statement of purpose*   The conventional ways of narrowing a subject include limiting it to a specific segment of time, or of space, or to a subproblem in a larger controversy, or to a single portion of a process. One or more of these methods may be used. A speech topic may also be narrowed by discussing a series of limited treatments of selected aspects of the whole subject. Narrowing the whole gives a limited scope to the subject by developing in detail a very restricted view of it; narrowing the discussion to specific aspects of the subject gives a broader view without sacrificing concreteness and detail.

2. *Determine the main points and organize them into the body of the speech*   In determining the main points, consider how well those points answer the questions, Who?, What?, When?, Where?, Why?, and How? At the same time, the number of points needs to be kept to between two and five so that you will have time to develop them adequately and the audience will be able to remember them.

One or more of several patterns of organization may be used to impose a clear and reasonable sequence on the ideas of the speech, both in the main points and in their subheadings: (1) chronological, (2) spatial, (3) topical, (4) by definition, (5) by comparison and contrast, and (6) by cause and effect.

3. *Add the supporting details*   Use a variety of supporting materials to bring your ideas sharply into focus for your audience.

4. *Prepare the conclusion and the introduction*   For specific information on these points, see Chapter 13.

5. *Practice the delivery*   Familiarize yourself thoroughly with the ideas and materials of the speech by "talking it through" from the early stages of preparation. With the contents thus firmly in mind, you will be able to deliver the speech with fluency, vigor, and conversational spontaneity.

NOTES

1. George A. Miller, *The Psychology of Communication* (Baltimore: Penquin Books, 1969), pp. 14–44.

EXERCISES

1. Organize and deliver a five- to seven-minute informative speech on a topic selected from the subject matter of a course you are now taking (other than your public speaking course). Prepare the outline carefully, and give your instructor a copy of your speaking outline before you deliver the speech.

2. Select one item from the following list (or one supplied by your instructor) and prepare two statements of purpose for informative speeches on that subject. In the first instance, narrow the scope and limit the subject by using one of the methods explained in this chapter. In the second statement of purpose, do the same using another of the methods. Formulate a subject sentence for each statement of purpose.

Literature	Medical care
Biology	The national forests
World War II	College athletics
Summer jobs for students	Student government
Farming	Sports

3. Illustrate with a brief outline each of the six methods of partitioning the body of an informative speech.

4. With four of your classmates, select a subject for a symposium (each speaker delivers a speech on one specific phase of the general subject). Divide the subject into five subtopics. Have each speaker deliver a five- to seven-minute informative talk on a different one of the subtopics. The symposium topics might be

a. The basic beliefs (nature of man, God, and the relationship between the two) of the five largest non-Christian religions of the world
b. The main responsibilities of the five major executive officers of our state
c. The extent of the five most prevalent types of crime in our city
d. The main ideas about writing of five contemporary novelists

5. Write a paper of no more than three double-spaced typewritten pages explaining how a speech with the same general subject (such as getting a college education, owning a car, or exercise) might differ depending on whether the purpose was to inform, persuade, or entertain.

chapter *19*

Speaking to Persuade

The purpose of a persuasive speech is to give an audience grounds for thinking and acting as the speaker wants it to. In other chapters we have considered a number of the skills needed to do this successfully: Develop a claim, analyze an audience, find issues, seek out supporting materials, build arguments, and deliver the speech. This chapter will look primarily at a number of ways in which persuasive speeches can be *organized* in order to meet the needs of the audience and the demands of the occasion.

THE NATURE OF PERSUASION

Before we look directly at methods of structuring persuasive messages, we want to clear up two widely held misconceptions about the nature of persuasion. With these out of the way the role of organization in persuasion will be a lot easier to understand. First, it is incorrect to think that some persuasion is "logical" and some other is "emotional." Second, it is wrong to believe that a "good" speaker can persuade any audience on any subject. On the contrary, understanding that persuasion uses a variety of proofs and seeks limited objectives makes it easier to put the principles of organization (and all the other skills of speech) to a more realistic use.

Persuasion Uses a Variety of Proofs

Every sentence uttered expresses a belief and thus entails a claim. And every claim implies that there are arguments to support it. But a persistent misconception about the nature of persuasion is that messages and arguments can somehow be classified as either "logical" or "emotional." Such thinking confuses the nature of persuasion. Since proofs in persuasion are only *probable*, they cannot therefore be "logical." Since speakers and audiences are human beings, the arguments used in persuasion will always be given and received in some atmosphere of "emotion"—personal and social values and personal credibility.

Every argument involves three varieties of proof: (1) the contention that the claim is a *reasonable* conclusion from adequate evidence; (2) the intention that it is consistent with the *beliefs* and *values* of the audience; and (3) because explicitly or implicitly the phrase "I believe that . . ." is inherent in every claim, the suggestion that the speaker is a *credible source*.

The Limitation of Objectives

The dramatic picture of a speaker who meets a hostile audience and within the course of a half-hour address converts it into an audience of friendly partisans is a myth. It is much more realistic to recognize that under certain circumstances any attempt to persuade will be a waste of time. Frequently, the difference in beliefs and values between you and a potential audience makes persuasion impossible. In other instances, an audience *cannot* give the desired response. People who can't pay their rent won't give money to some project a speaker supports. In still other instances, "*De gustibus non disputandum est."* The old Latin adage gives the good advice that it's a foolish waste of time to debate a matter when the deciding factor is individual taste.

In such cases, remember the prayer of St. Francis of Assisi, in which he asked God to give him the courage to change what he could, the patience to live with what he could not, and the wisdom to know the difference between the two. The wisdom to know the difference is the important point here, because it would be a mistake to confuse a difficult rhetorical task with an impossible one. Nor is a speech successful only if it causes an audience to change its ways. The persuasive speakers most celebrated in history have often had to be satisfied with knowing that they moved the audience only a little way. With these ideas in mind, let's look at some of the methods of organizing persuasive speeches.

ORGANIZING PERSUASIVE SPEECHES

Since we have discussed introductions and conclusions at some length in Chapter 13, we will mention only briefly the general structure of a persuasive message. Our principal interest is in the organization of the *body* of the speech to persuade.

Persuasive Organization in General

The general structure of a speech to persuade is the same as that of any other speech. It has an introduction, a body, and a conclusion. The introduction catches the attention of the audience, arouses interest in the subject, and has a subject sentence that tells the audience what the speech is going to be about. In many instances, the subject sentence will state the claim clearly. In other instances, the nature of the subject or the attitudes of the audience may make it expedient to withhold for a time the specific thesis. The body of the speech advances the arguments and the evidence that support the claim. The conclusion brings the speech to a forceful and appropriate close. It may do this by summarizing the main arguments that support the claim, but more frequently the conclusion will characterize the subject in some way that emphasizes the speaker's appeals to the audience's beliefs and values.

Choosing the Best Pattern of Arrangement

As we said in Chapter 18, the patterns of arrangement used to organize *informative* speeches are designed solely to achieve understanding and clarification. But for that reason, they are unsatisfactory in *persuasion*. There the goal is to influence what an audience believes or does. This requires a different set of patterns.

A persuasive speech can be structured in a variety of ways, but we will describe three basic forms. What most clearly distinguishes any one of them from the others is whether and to what degree the speaker delays in stating the specific claim of the speech. The choice of persuasive order is based on several factors: the complexity of the claim, speaker credibility, the beliefs and values of the audience, and the presence or absence of opposition speakers, to name only a few.

In any case, the claim must be *explicit* at whatever point in the speech it does appear. An audience is rarely as interested in a proposal as the speaker is, and is probably not inclined to pay as much attention. Also, audiences tend to hear what they want or expect to hear. Consequently, the claim must be quite explicit. This is particularly important in the conclusion. A clear and precise statement of the claim leaves the audience with an accurate understanding of what the speaker wants it to think or do.

It is equally important to answer opposition arguments. Analysis of the issues provides the necessary rebuttals. When an audience is in agreement with a speaker, almost anything the speaker says will reinforce its beliefs.

The best evidence seems to suggest that if an audience agrees with a speaker, and knows little of the opposing position, showing only one side of the controversy has a stronger (but only temporary) effect. Showing both sides, however, produces better long-range effects, because doing this prepares the listeners to resist counterpersuasion.[1] A vendor selling a combination vegetable peeler and hair dryer shows only one side of the case, because the article has to be sold at that moment or not at all. But the undecidedness that characterizes most persuasive situations gives the audience an opportunity to see-saw. In general, therefore, it is best to answer the principal opposition arguments, because this will help to inoculate against counterpersuasion. Even audiences that favor a speaker's position need to be im- munized against later counterargument.

Suppose you believed that there ought to be students on the bookstore govern- ing board in order to give the student body some degree of influence over bookstore policies and profits. In looking over the arguments you find several good reasons to adopt the proposal:

1. Students, through their purchases, are the main source of revenue for the bookstore.
2. Profits from the bookstore could help meet shortages in other student body funds.
3. Student morale would be increased by their knowing they weren't being ripped off.

You also see an argument against the proposal in the claim that students wouldn't be qualified to evaluate the complex problems of bookstore finances. Your reply to this argument is that there are students in the School of Business who would understand the problems, including some who have run their own businesses.

Another argument against the proposal is that, because there is so much student apathy, few would be interested in giving service of this kind. The most qualified students would rather be working at jobs. Your response to this is that the student representatives would be paid like other members of the board.

You now have three arguments in favor of the idea and two against it, both of which you believe you can refute. Let's see how this speech would look in each of the three patterns of persuasive organization. They are called the *claim-to-proof pattern,*

Even the best speakers can't persuade everyone, every time. (Blanfort, Jeroboam)

the *problem-to-solution pattern,* and the *reflective pattern.* The following examples show the organization of the main points only; supporting details are not shown.

The Claim-to-Proof Pattern   In the claim-to-proof pattern, the claim is stated in the introduction of the speech and then developed in a series of supporting arguments in the body. The speech concludes with an appeal for acceptance of the claim.

INTRODUCTION

I. You're sure to be unhappy when you realize that the bookstore is a place where you are virtually forced to spend your money even though you have no say about it.

II. It's time students had some representation on the bookstore governing board and some say about how the profits are spent.

BODY

I. The $2 million a year the bookstore gets from us makes us the main source of its income.

II. The profits could be used to support underfunded student activities.

III. Membership on the bookstore governing board ought to be welcomed as a way of eliminating the student feeling of being ripped off.

IV. Despite what some say, there are qualified students who have the time and interest to participate.

CONCLUSION

I. Because student morale will go up, because students will have a say in how they spend their own money, and because it will mean better support for student activities, we should have student representatives on the board.

II. Let's take the issue to the University Senate next Monday.

Only rarely is an audience strongly opposed to a proposal. A lack of interest is a much greater danger than hostility. Consequently, most speeches can be organized in the claim-to-proof pattern. The audience needs to know what the proposal is as soon as possible, so that it can be reinforced throughout the speech. Stating the claim early also reduces any concern the audience may have about where the speech is going to lead.

Presenting a claim early makes it easier to be clear, because then it is constantly before the listener and its relationship to individual arguments can be continually reinforced. Moreover, if listeners know beforehand what the speaker's position is, there is nothing to gain from withholding the statement of the claim, even if the audience disagrees. In such a case, using the claim-to-proof pattern is a sign of candor. It builds credibility by showing that the speaker has nothing to hide, and it may tend to lessen somewhat the audience's objections to the plan.

The Problem-to-Solution Pattern   In the problem-to-solution format, the first task, as usual, is to get the attention of the audience, next to present a problem that needs to be solved, then to recommend a course of action and show how it will solve the problem. The audience is not told what solution will be proposed until after the problem has been explained.

INTRODUCTION

I. Most of us are happy with our education, but there are problems.

BODY

I. Several really worthwhile activities on this campus go unfunded.

II. There are not enough opportunities for students to get good business experience.

III. The students feel that they are being ripped off by the administration.

    A. The bookstore does a $2 million dollar business each year.

    B. There is no student input.

IV. There should be student representatives on the governing board of the bookstore.

    A. Qualified students are available.

    B. They will get business experience.

    C. They will protect the rights of the students.

CONCLUSION

I. Students today are mature enough to have a say in how they spend their own money.

II. Let's take the proposal to the University Senate on Monday.

The Reflective Pattern   Like the problem-to-solution pattern, the reflective pattern also withholds presentation of the specific claim until later in the speech. This pattern describes a problem situation and its causes. Then it suggests several possibilities for solution. Next, each of these is evaluated. Finally the best solution is proposed. This form looks like a thoroughly objective approach to a subject. Its purpose, however, is to persuade. Far from being objective, everything it says is intended to move the audience toward accepting the course of action it advocates.

INTRODUCTION

I. Most of us are happy with our education, but we have some problems.

BODY

I. One is the constant griping about the bookstore.
   - A. About the prices
   - B. About the service
   - C. About the lack of books when we need them
II. There are several causes for this griping.
   - A. Students spend $2 million dollars a year.
   - B. No one listens to their views.
III. We need a system that will give the students some say.
IV. We might have:
   - A. A suggestion box, but that would be a meaningless joke
   - B. A nonvoting student on the bookstore governing board, but that would be an empty token
   - C. Student representatives on the governing board
      1. Qualified students are available.
      2. They would be paid.
      3. It would end all the griping.

CONCLUSION

I. Students today are mature enough to have a say in how they spend their own money.
II. Let's take the proposal to the University Senate on Monday.

An audience may very well reject a claim once it is made known. Both the problem-to-solution and the reflective patterns help to prevent this by presenting the idea gradually, thereby letting the speaker develop and support a position before the audience has any reason to reject it. Therefore, when an audience is opposed to a position, and knows the arguments that support its own view, it is better for the speaker not to identify too early with something the listeners oppose.[2]

When an audience has no way of knowing where a speaker stands, the problem-to-solution and the reflective patterns give the analysis that underlies a case and the arguments that support it a chance to have some persuasive effect before the audience begins to think of counterarguments. Even if the primary purpose cannot be achieved, it is possible to mediate some of the opposition and make the audience more susceptible to later persuasion.

The reflective pattern is particularly useful when the audience has little knowledge of the subject. It is designed to create understanding first and get at the issues later. This pattern approaches the subject in such a way that the audience understands what kinds of decisions it must make before it makes them.

But the reflective pattern has another and perhaps more important advantage: It clarifies the analysis of the subject for the audience. The audience is thereby conditioned to that analysis, and later speakers will find it difficult to undo its persuasive effect; to do so, they must not only contradict the audience's earlier conclusions, they must counteract the prior analysis as well.

DETERMINING THE PLACEMENT OF ARGUMENTS

Once the problem of general arrangement has been solved, a more specific question arises: "In what order should individual arguments be put?" Some say that putting the strongest argument last will give the speech greater impact. Others, to the contrary, claim that it is better to put the best argument first to give the speech a strong start. The research that has been done on the question has produced mixed results. Here again, as in virtually every case, the decision depends on the state of the audience. However, some general, though tentative, principles are worth considering.

1. If the ideas in a speech are sufficiently unrelated, the speech will appear to lack a unifying theme. It becomes something like a grocery list. The available research shows that the listeners' comprehension and probably the speaker's credibility are damaged by a disorganized message.[3]

2. When one argument depends on another, it must obviously follow the one on which it depends. In supporting policy claims, the only order that makes sense is to present arguments associated with the need for a change first, and the arguments that show the desirability of a plan second. Only then can you argue for the feasibility of the proposal. It is useless, for instance, to argue that some federal medical plan will alleviate the shortage of physicians in rural areas before the audience believes that such a shortage exists. And it is equally futile to support the feasibility of such a plan before showing that it will, in fact, alleviate whatever shortage might exist.

3. Although there is substantial disagreement over the relative importance of the first and last positions, arguments presented early and late seem to be remembered better than those presented in the middle of the speech.

4. When a speaker has high status in the eyes of an audience, the arguments that appear early in the speech tend to have the greatest strength. Listeners have great expectations of high-credibility sources, and they grow less attentive only if a speaker fails to reinforce their expectations.

5. Generally, it is better to refute opposition arguments after presenting those that support a position.[4] When opposing arguments are heard first, they tend to build opposition in the listener's mind. Then not only must the opposition be overcome, but also whatever mechanisms the audience establishes to let it ignore or avoid the supporting arguments. There is an additional danger: Once an audience makes a decision in the course of a speech, it tends to pay less attention to what follows. Thus, even if the opposition arguments are refuted, the audience is less likely to "hear" the

arguments that support the speaker's position, and it will be poorly inoculated against future counterpersuasion.

There is an exception to this principle: When an audience has firm arguments against a proposal, it is probably best to refute those arguments as soon as possible after the claim has been stated. Otherwise, the audience may rehearse them throughout the speech and ignore the arguments that support the claim.

SUMMARY

A persuasive speech gives an audience grounds for thinking and acting the way the speaker wants it to. But the reasons given in persuasion can't always demonstrate the truth of a claim. Generally, the most they can do is create belief. The way a speech is organized helps to determine the level of its success.

An accurate and realistic view of persuasion recognizes two important concepts: (1) No persuasive speech is either wholly "logical" or totally "emotional." Instead, in every persuasive speech there is a variety of proofs that at one and the same time claim to be reasonable, appeal to the beliefs and values of the audience, and suggest that the speaker is a credible source. (2) There are often quite narrow limits on what a persuasive speech can achieve.

A persuasive speech, like any other, has an introduction, a body, and a conclusion, each of which plays its familiar role. Three organizational patterns are useful in persuasion: claim-to-proof, problem-to-solution, and reflective. They differ primarily in how early in the speech the specific claim appears. In the claim-to-proof pattern, the claim is in the introduction. In the other two, the problem-to-solution and the reflective patterns, the claim is withheld for a time. The complexity of the claim, the attitudes of the audience, speaker credibility with the audience, and the presence or absence of opposing speakers are all factors that help to determine your choice of persuasive order. No matter what order is used, the claim should be made explicit at some point in the speech and the speech should answer opposition arguments.

Most speeches can be safely organized by the claim-to-proof pattern, but the problem-to-solution and the reflective patterns are useful when an audience is opposed to the claim. The reflective pattern is most useful when the audience has little knowledge of the subject.

The placement of arguments in the speech can help to reinforce agreement and to diminish opposition. (1) The arguments that come first and last are remembered best. (2) Arguments that depend on one another should be placed together. (3) Avoid giving the impression that arguments are unrelated. (4) A speaker who has high credibility should put the strongest arguments first. (5) There is no need to refute opposition arguments first unless the audience has a strong case against the claim.

NOTES

1. Loren J. Anderson, "A Summary of Research on Order Effects in Communication," in *Concepts in Communication*, Jimmie D. Trent, Judith S. Trent, and Daniel J. O'Neill eds., (Boston: Allyn & Bacon, 1973), pp. 129–130; James C.

McCroskey, Thomas J. Young, and Michael D. Scott, "The Effects of Message Sidedness and Evidence on Inoculation Against Counter-Persuasion in Small Group Communication," *Speech Monographs,* **39** (Aug. 1972), pp. 205–212.
2. There is not much research on the relative advantage of stating your claim early in your speech or delaying it until later, but what there is supports the delaying tactic in a "threatening" situation. A. R. Cohen, *Attitude Change and Social Influence* (New York: Basic Books, 1964), pp. 11–12.
3. Anderson, op. cit., p. 128.
4. Ibid., p. 130.

EXERCISES

1. Organize and deliver a five- to seven-minute persuasive speech. Turn in to your instructor a copy of your outline, a brief analysis of your audience, and a brief statement of what values you will use and why you will use them. Include a brief statement of what organization you will use and why you will use it.

2. Write a brief analysis of one of your classmate's speeches evaluating the method of organization. Could you improve the speech by changing the order? How and why? How well was it adapted to the classroom audience? What persuasive order did the speaker use?

3. Formulate a policy claim from one of the general topics listed in Appendix A. Sketch the outline of a persuasive speech on this claim for each of the three methods of persuasive organization discussed in this chapter.

4. Examine one of the persuasive speeches in Appendix B and write a short paper evaluating its persuasiveness for a student audience.

5. Examine two of the persuasive speeches in Appendix B and compare and contrast them for organization, supporting materials, beliefs and values, credibility, and language.

chapter 20

Speaking on Special Occasions

4. Learn to laugh at yourself
5. Let the humor label itself
6. Stop when you're ahead

Instead of naming this chapter "Speaking on Special Occasions," we might almost as well have called it "Speaking on Ceremonial Occasions." Any occasion is "special" if it doesn't occur *regularly*. For the most part, however, the speeches discussed in this chapter are those that meet the *ceremonial* requirements of an occasion.

The oldest annals of humankind record the custom of celebrating important occasions with speechmaking. So important was the practice that Aristotle recognized it almost 2400 years ago as a separate form of oratory. In this chapter, however, we are talking about the special needs of the *occasion,* not any new principles or techniques of *speaking*. The speeches delivered on special occasions are like other speeches in all important respects: They have a subject and a purpose, they seek a specific response, they have structure and supporting details, and they require good delivery.

SPEECHES OF COURTESY

Speeches of courtesy are clear indications of the ceremonial nature of some occasions. Because they are ceremonial, it is easy for them to become ritualistic, patterned, and trite in both thought and expression. But if this happens to them, they will invariably fail in some part of their purpose. A significant need, then, is to avoid staleness and to find fresh ways of expressing the familiar notions the audience has learned to expect.

Introductions

It's quite possible that speeches of introduction are given more often than any other speech of courtesy. The task of an introduction is to present a specific speaker to a specific audience. The right person to make an introduction is usually someone who knows the speaker, if not personally, at least well enough by reputation to be able to relate the achievements of the speaker that warrant the respectful attention of an audience. The introduction must also make clear the significance, timeliness, and relevance of the subject. However, an introduction never discusses the subject itself. That is left to the speaker.

The formality of an introduction is determined by the degree of formality in the situation and the level of seriousness in the subject. Like any other speech, an introduction should fit the occasion.

The audience is there to hear the speaker, not the person making the introduction. Therefore, it should be brief. Anything that is required can be said in no more than a minute or a minute and a half. It is traditional, after all, to introduce one of the most important people in the world with the briefest of introductions, "Ladies and gentlemen, the President of the United States."

At the Republican National Convention in Dallas, in August 1984, Senator Howard Baker, acting in his role as temporary chairman, introduced Congressman Bob Michel, who had been appointed permanent chairman of the convention:

> Delegates and alternates, ladies and gentlemen.
>
> Fellow delegates, it's a great pleasure and honor for me to introduce to you now the permanent chairman of this 1984 National Convention.
>
> I know Bob Michel about as well as anybody in the Congress because I deal with him every day. He is my counterpart on the House side, but his job is tougher than mine because he doesn't have that fortunate majority of Republicans that we have on the Senate side.
>
> I know him to be a consummate, skillful and dedicated legislator. I've worked closely with Bob in his capacity as Republican leader of the House and he's been a great partner of our President and of our majority in the Senate over the last four years.
>
> Ladies and gentlemen, I have a special kinship with Bob because he represents the eighteenth Congressional district of Illinois, which my late father-in-law, Everett McKinley Dirksen, once represented in the House of Representatives.
>
> Bob Michel has great integrity, skill, and character. He's a worthy chairman of this convention and, ladies and gentlemen, it is my great pleasure to present to you now the Honorable Bob Michel, House Republican leader and permanent chairman of the Republican National Convention for 1984.

Nominations

A speech of nomination is, in very many respects, a speech of introduction. It tells whoever will do the voting what qualifications the nominee has for the office. The important point about a nomination is that the good qualities it ascribes to the nominee must be relevant to the position.

Speeches of Welcome

A not uncommon courtesy in a group is to welcome new members or visitors. Meetings of professional groups (sales meetings, academic or professional conventions, and the like) offer good examples of this custom. The purpose of a speech of welcome is to make the visitors, most of whom are usually from out of town, feel more comfortable and to perceive more clearly the significance of the business they have come to transact.

A welcome need not be long. For example, under International Olympic Committee rules, the statement that formally opens the games is precisely prescribed;

the name of the host city and the number of the Olympiad are the only changes made. In 1984: "I declare open the Games of Los Angeles, celebrating the XXIII Olympiad of the modern era." The rule limiting what the chief of state of the host country can say is intended to keep politics out of the games. Although President Ronald Reagan changed the word order a bit when he delivered the statement in 1984, he did not say more than the 16 words prescribed as a maximum.

In 1976, the Western Speech Communication Association held its annual convention in San Francisco and the host institution was the San Francisco State University. Lawrence A. Ianni, then Dean of Faculty Affairs and now Provost of the University, welcomed the members of the convention with these remarks:

> For several reasons, I am in a poor position to deliver a welcome. I can't really welcome you to the San Francisco State campus because we decidedly are not there. We don't get visitors much unless someone's running for the U.S. Senate. Secondly, I'm too late to welcome you to town, since you've already been here for several days. Finally, I'm really too lacking in knowledge to welcome you to the City and toss in all those good hints about where you ought to go while you're here. They have been working me so hard at State that I don't get around much. The first six months I was here I thought Carol Doda[1] was the type of bird that they have down at Seal Rocks.

> So, instead of a welcome, I want to offer a well-wishing. I believe in the importance of your discipline. I believe that it has an important contribution to make toward the rescue of contemporary life. I say that with some trepidation because I think that we should all be repelled by the cliche that our biggest contemporary problem is communication. The horrible naivete of those people who assert that "If we'd just sit down and talk to one another, we would work out our human differences" is a feeling that we have to outgrow. The fact is that if we got some people together, the best we could hope for is that they would limit their violence to the verbal kind. Chances are, they wouldn't.

> Our problem is not just to communicate, but to communicate constructively. To be a Dean of Faculty is to live continuously and intimately with the defeats of oneself and others at the hands of language. Faculty personnel actions are inevitably generators of differences of opinion, belief, and principle among faculty or between faculty and administration. Those differences must be resolved as they are generated, through language. We have got to confront the issues and not one another. We have got to bring issues to a conclusion while preserving mutual rights and mutual respect.

> The question that troubles most of us is not "How do we communicate with one another?" but "How do we resolve the conflicts that have been communicated to one another all too well?" It seems to me that the great burden of your discipline is to help us learn (provided we are willing learners) to use language for problem-solving. Sometimes that means accomplishing the difficult task of clarifying and exploring a conflict before we can resolve it. This is the difficult part. No one needs any instruction at pulling off a love feast. We never have any trouble talking to like-minded people. Shared delusions are so satisfying. It is contention that confounds us. It bewilders us so that we feel guilty to find

conflict has occurred. We feel that it was always somehow preventable. At times this is about as reasonable as blaming ourselves for the fog. I find it much more realistic to accept that there are circumstances in which the occurrence of conflict will defeat the sincerest efforts to prevent it. At these times, language is the only civilized tool to resolve that conflict. It is your job to help us sharpen that tool. I wish you well at that, and San Francisco State wishes you well at that.[2]

Presentations

According to a story in the *Los Angeles Times,* the Soviet encyclopedia identifies 37 orders and 47 medals with which Soviet citizens can be honored. And that's only a partial listing. There are even medals for motherhood: first class for having eight or more children, second class for six or seven. In the United States, awards in great variety and large numbers are given for many accomplishments. Honorary degrees are bestowed and Nobel laureates are honored. Oscars, Emmys, Tonys, Obies, and Grammys are among the awards given to outstanding entertainments and entertainers.

Awards, of course, are not the only occasion for making a speech of presentation. When someone donates money to a cause, books to a library, or a statue to a

A presentation speech gives an audience reasons to respect and admire the person who is being honored. (Treandly, Jeroboam)

public place, speeches are as inevitable as the photograph in the next day's news-paper. In any case, the speech outlines the reasons for making the presentation.

Thus, the speaker's task is to give an audience reason to respect and admire the person being honored. By implication, it suggests that others might emulate the bravery, generosity, pioneering spirit, or whatever the quality or conduct was that earned the award.

Soon after Lt. Col. John H. Glenn, Jr., later Senator Glenn of Ohio, made his historic flight as the first American astronaut to orbit the earth, President John F. Kennedy presented him with the NASA Distinguished Service Medal. The President said:

> Seventeen years ago today, a group of Marines put the American Flag on Mount Suribachi, so it's very appropriate that today we decorate Colonel Glenn of the United States Marine Corps, and also realize that in the not too distant future a Marine or a Naval man or an Air Force man will put the American Flag on the moon.
>
> I present this citation:
>
> "The President of the United States takes pleasure in awarding the National-al Aeronautics and Space Administration Distinguished Service Medal to Lieute-nant Colonel John H. Glenn, Jr., United States Marine Corps, for services set forth in the following: For exceptionally meritorious service to the government of the United States in a duty of great responsibility as the first American astronaut to perform orbital flight. Lieutenant Colonel Glenn's orbital flight on February 20, 1962, made an outstanding contribution to the advancement of human knowl-edge of space technology and in demonstration of man's capabilities in space flights.
>
> "His performance was marked by his great professional knowledge, his skill as a test pilot, his unflinching courage, and his extraordinary ability to perform most difficult tasks under conditions of great physical stress and per-sonal danger. His performance in fulfillment of this most dangerous assignment reflects the highest credit upon himself and the United States."
>
> Colonel, we appreciate what you have done![3]

Speeches of Response

Depending on the circumstances, any speech of courtesy can call for a response.

Although, depending again on the circumstances, any speech of response can be impromptu, the recipient is not likely to be surprised by the presentation of an award. No one, for example, ever received an Academy Award as a complete surprise. Acceptance speeches by recipients, breathless and startled as they may seem, are not naive. They are more artful than impromptu.

To feel considerably more at ease and at the same time improve credibility, it would be better for a recipient to have a better response than a bashful grin and a mumbled "thanks." If you are given an award for something you did solely on your own, accept it with openness. Don't gloat, but don't grovel in false modesty. If the award comes as the result of a team effort, or if others had any part in its success, give them a generous amount of credit.

After the President had pinned the medal on his lapel, John Glenn made a brief speech of response. The conversational quality of the speech and the lack of polish in the style suggest that it was impromptu. Nonetheless, he shared the credit with others who had played a vital role in his achievement and said what he wanted to say with forthrightness, propriety, and modesty.

> I can't express my appreciation adequately to be here in accepting this when I know how many thousand people all over the country were involved in helping accomplish what we did last Tuesday and knowing how particularly this group here at the Cape and many of the group here on the platform, our own group of astronauts who were scattered all around the world and who performed their functions here at the Cape also.
>
> We all acted literally and figuratively as a team and it was a real team effort all the way.
>
> We have stressed the team effort in Project Mercury. It goes across the board, I think. Sort of a cross-cut of Americana of industry and military and Civil Service, Government workers, contractors. The—almost a cross-cut of American effort in the technical field, I think. It wasn't specialized by any one particular group.
>
> It was headed up by NASA, of course, but thousands and thousands of people have contributed, certainly as much or more than I have to the Project.
>
> I would like to consider that I was sort of a figurehead for the whole big, tremendous effort and I am very proud of the medal I have on my lapel here, for all of us—you included—because I think it represents all of our efforts, not just mine. Thank you very much and thank you, Mr. President.[4]

Speeches of Farewell

Custom and courtesy often seem to require that exits as well as entrances be ceremonialized. An officer or member leaving an organization is frequently expected to make a speech of farewell. A long-time employee of a company, who is given the traditional "gold watch" upon retirement, may make a speech of farewell as an appropriate response. It is customary for such a speech to express sentiments of pleasure, gratitude, fondness, and the like.

Notable for its brevity and grace is the speech with which Abraham Lincoln said goodbye to his friends on February 11, 1861, when he left his home town of Springfield, Illinois, after he had been elected President:

> My friends: No one not in my situation can appreciate my feeling of sadness at this parting. To this place, and the kindness of these people, I owe everything. Here I have lived a quarter of a century, and have passed from a young to an old man. Here my children have been born, and one is buried. I now leave, not knowing when or whether ever I may return, with a task before me greater than

that which rested upon Washington. Without the assistance of that Divine Being who ever attended him, I cannot succeed. With that assistance, I cannot fail. Trusting in Him who can go with me, and remain with you, and be everywhere for good, let us confidently hope that all will yet be well. To His care commending you, as I hope in your prayers you will commend me, I bid you an affectionate farewell.

SPEECHES OF TRIBUTE

To a degree, all ceremonial speeches pay tribute to something or someone. But some of them make this their sole purpose. The speaker intends to arouse in the audience a high level of admiration and affection for the person to whom the tribute is paid.

Eulogies

In all of recorded history, there has not been a time when humanity has not, in some fashion or another, paid tribute to its dead. One common form of eulogy, therefore, is the funeral oration. In it, praise is given to someone's life, character, and deeds. Pericles delivered one of the most famous eulogies at Athens in 431 B.C. commemorating those Greek soldiers who had died early in the Peloponnesian War.

Adlai Stevenson, recognized as a master of style, was governor of Illinois when he delivered this brief "farewell to a friend," Lloyd Lewis. Although the speech was impromptu, it has been called "perhaps his most felicitous address."

I have been asked to share in these farewells to a friend.

I think it is a good day for this meeting. It is April now and all life is being renewed on the bank of this river that he loved so well. I think we will all be happy that it happened on this day, here by the river with the spring sky so clear, and the west wind so warm and fresh. I think we will all be the better for this day and this meeting together.

He was my neighbor. He was the neighbor of many of you. He was a very good neighbor; quick in time of misfortune, always present in times of mirth and happiness—and need.

I think Mr. Connelly was right when he said he was the most successful man he ever knew. I don't know much about the riches of life, and I suspect few of you have found the last definition. But I do know that friendship is the greatest enrichment that I have found.

Everyone loved this man. He enriched others and was enriched. Everyone was his friend—everyone who knew him or read him. Why was that? Why is he the most successful man that many of us will ever know? Our answers will differ. For me it was his humility, gentleness, wisdom and wit, all in one. And most of all a great compassionate friendliness.

I think it will always be April in our memory of him. It will always be a bright, fresh day, full of the infinite variety and the promise of new life. Perhaps nothing has gone at all—perhaps only the *embodiment* of the thing—tender, precious to all of us—a friendship that is immortal and doesn't pass along. It will be renewed for me, much as I know it will for all of you, each spring.[5]

Commendations

Eulogies are tributes paid to the dead. Commendations are given to those who are still alive. People earn commendations for a large number of activities of greater or lesser consequence. Mother Teresa is a Catholic nun who devotes her life to orphans and abandoned infants in Calcutta, India. The following tribute to her is not a speech. It was printed as an item of interest for readers of the magazine in which it appeared. Yet it could serve as the model for a speech of commendation.

This past week, Mother Teresa received one of the first Albert Schweitzer Prizes for her bold and beautiful commitment to the poorest of the poor in India and elsewhere in the world. In 1904, Dr. Schweitzer caught sight of the green-covered Paris Missionary Society magazine, read its article on "The Needs of the Congo Mission" and set out to found a hospital at Lambarene in Africa. On a train to Darjeeling in India some forty years later, Mother Teresa answered a "call to give up all" by going to serve the poor in the Calcutta slums. Her work since then has clearly shared Dr. Schweitzer's "reverence for life."

The focus of Mother Teresa's "reverence for life" is well known. For almost thirty years she has ministered to the dying poor, "Christ in his distressing disguise," and the unwanted—those suffering from "the worst disease a person can experience." As she herself has said, her motivation has been to "give the poor what the rich get for money."

When we look at the staggering scope of Mother Teresa's loving concern for the poor around the world, there is something incongruous and almost embarrassing about offering her a prize for a work that has been her happiness and our inspiration. Although the Schweitzer Prize has been presented to her, one is left believing that she will really receive it for the Christian community. The rest of us need to cherish a life that embodies so clearly what theologian Hans Urs von Balthasar means by his remark that the great lovers know God best and must be listened to. While theologians today may help the church better discover the inner unity of the love of God and neighbor, it is Mother Teresa's life that bears unmistakable witness to that unity—to her conviction that "faith to be true has to be a giving love."[6]

Commemorations

Virtually any holiday celebrated in America—Labor Day, Veterans' Day, the Fourth of July, to name only a few—calls forth speeches of commemoration.[7] Local politicians give speeches of commemoration when they plant a tree on Arbor Day. Unquestionably, the most famous commemorative speech in the literature of American oratory is Abraham Lincoln's deeply moving Gettysburg Address:

Fourscore and seven years ago, our fathers brought forth on this continent a new nation, conceived in liberty, and dedicated to the proposition that all men are created equal. Now we are engaged in a great civil war, testing whether that nation, or any nation so conceived and so dedicated, can long endure. We are met on a great battlefield of that war. We have come to dedicate a portion of that field as a final resting place for those who here gave their lives that that nation might live. It is altogether fitting and proper that we should do this. But in a larger sense we cannot dedicate, we cannot consecrate, we cannot hallow this ground. The brave men, living and dead, who struggled here, have consecrated it far above our poor power to add or detract. The world will little note, nor long remember, what we say here, but it can never forget what they did here. It is for us, the living, rather to be dedicated here to the unfinished work which they who fought here have thus far so nobly advanced. It is rather for us to be here dedicated to the great task remaining before us,—that from these honored dead we take increased devotion to that cause to which they gave the last full measure of devotion,—that we here highly resolve that these dead shall not have died in vain,—that this nation, under God, shall have a new birth of freedom,—and that government of the people, by the people, for the people, shall not perish from the earth.

SPEECHES OF GOOD WILL

Not all television advertising has the immediate purpose of selling a product or service. Instead, some is meant to win, hold, and build the prestige and friendly relations the sponsoring company has with its customers. Good will is so elusive, delicate, and important that corporations (insurance, oil, and communication, among others) spend literally millions of dollars a year to maintain it.

Business and industry are not alone, of course, in their desire to maintain a friendly image. The federal government has long used the office of "good will ambassador" to help maintain friendly relations with foreign nations. Indeed, this has been an important part of the duties of all ambassadors throughout history.

In essence, a good will speech is designed to show how the organization or service represented by the speaker is working in the interests of the audience. A speech of good will is basically organized to appear as an informative speech. As such, it does not deal directly with issues. That is, the speaker does not acknowledge opposing arguments, but rather acts as if there were no issues.

A telephone company representative comes to a local service club or PTA to tell the members about the new advances in technology that will provide better services and save the customer money. The president of a university addresses the chamber of commerce on recent achievements of the university. The secretary of a local union speaks at a high school about a scholarship the union provides to an outstanding graduating senior. All of these speeches are informative in content and strategy, but they have purposes that go beyond merely conveying information: They build good will for the organization the speaker represents.

The method of preparing and delivering speeches of good will is not significantly different from that of informative speeches. The principal concern in preparing a speech of good will is to keep it informative in tone. If it begins to argue a controversial point it will have a quite different purpose, and to be successful it will then have to meet quite different requirements.

SPEECHES TO ENTERTAIN

On occasion, the purpose of a speech will be to amuse an audience. But a speech to entertain need not be devoid of serious ideas. It can have a very real and useful point to it. For example, a talk about the "glories" of growing up that describes the dubious advantages of maturity—with its debts, taxes, responsibilities, and the like—would surely make something of a point. Nonetheless, it could amuse and divert an audience by approaching the subject from a deliberately offbeat, eccentric point of view.[8] What distinguishes a speech to entertain from a speech to inform or to persuade is the light touch with which the speaker takes up the subject.

However, a speech to entertain is not merely a collection of funny stories. As a speech it must have at least a semblance of unity and order. It has a central idea that the speaker develops. Some of the audience's pleasure may come from the zany way the idea is developed, but it must appear to start from a reasonable base. Digressions need only seem to be appropriate in order to be perfectly acceptable. But be aware of the digressions: They can be a conscious source of humor.

Good transitions are as useful for imposing a sense of order on a speech to entertain as on any other speech. The temptation to say, "That reminds me of a story," should be resisted because the speech must have not only sequence but unity as well. Instead, transitions that move from point to point, not joke to joke, will give the speech better organization. The stories and quips then fall into place with the force of properly used supporting material. In other words, the transitions emphasize the gist and not the jest.

A familiar occasion for speaking to entertain is the after-dinner speech. There is a good example of an after-dinner speech in Appendix B of this book. It was prepared for delivery at an intercollegiate forensics competition by Ian Fielding when he was an undergraduate student majoring in speech communication at California State University, Northridge.

The success of a speech to entertain springs from the ability to use humor well. But the value of humor in public speaking is by no means limited to speeches to entertain. It is a very important asset to any kind of speaking.

In a speech to entertain, humor is an end in itself. Amusement is the goal. But it plays a different role and works toward a different end in speeches to inform or persuade. Then, the humor is not an end in itself. Instead, it is merely another medium for communicating supporting detail. But no matter what the purpose of the humor or what it helps to achieve, it is useful to have some understanding of the types and uses of humor.

HUMOR AS SUPPORTING MATERIAL

Humor is as universal as language. It is found in the gentle teasing of a friend, in subtle quips understandable only to a few, in bitter satire that strikes at folly and vice. The things that cause amusement range widely, from the most highly intellectual delicacies of wit to the broadest form of slapstick, custard-pie-in-the-face comedy. In life's most serious moments, laughter breaks the tension. The grim jests of war are clear proof that individuals need release and frequently seek it in humor.

Types of Humor

The list of things that bring laughter is long and varied. We will mention here six types of humor that seem especially useful in speaking.

Overstatement   America as a nation has been credited with overstating situations as a characteristic form of humor. The tall tale, some say a product of the vastness of the continent that had to be conquered, is an important part of folk humor. Paul Bunyan and Babe, his blue ox, are only one example. To be most effective, overstatement must have some imagination to go with it. Here's an example:

> No old-time cowboy would expect to amuse you by saying that the outfit for which he worked owned a billion acres of land, as gross an overstatement as this would be. He would say that they used the state of Arizona for a calf pasture; that it took three days to ride from the yard gate to the front gallery; that the range reached so far that the sun set between headquarters and the west line camp. The folk humorist did not say of a hero that he had the strength of ten either because of his pure heart or because of his impure whiskey. He detailed concretely what the hero would do: he would fight a rattlesnake with his bare hands and give the snake three bites to start with. The roughneck of the oil fields did not say that Gib Morgan built a derrick five hundred miles high. He said that the derrick was so high that it took a man fourteen days to climb to the top of it. A crew of thirty men was required in order to have a man on duty at all times. There were at any given time fourteen men going up, fourteen men coming down, a man at the top, and a man off tower (that is, off shift). There were dog houses built a day's climb apart for the men to sleep in on their way up and down.[9]

Understatement   If one may believe them, the stories that are told about President Calvin Coolidge make him the champion understater of all time. "Silent Cal" wasn't much of a talker anyway, and what little he had to say didn't tend much toward elaboration. Mr. Coolidge returned from church one Sunday morning and was asked by Mrs. Coolidge what the minister had talked about. "Sin." "Well, what did he have to say?" "He's against it."

Irony   Ironic humor occurs when the meaning is the opposite of the literal sense of the words. According to Abraham Lincoln:

> A politician of less than ideal quality so aroused the citizenry of a small town that they decided to tar and feather him and ride him out of town on a rail. As they put him on the rail, he remarked, "If it weren't for the honor of the thing, I would just as soon walk."

Unexpected Turns   Two men were walking through the woods and saw a wildcat in a tree. They decided that it would make a great pet. So one climbed the tree to shake the cat down so the other could put it in a burlap sack. The first man climbed the tree and soon the wildcat came sliding down the trunk and the second man caught him by the back of the neck. There was considerable delay as the wildcat snarled and cried and thrashed about. The man from the tree called down, "Do you need any help to catch him?" "No," said his friend, "I need help to turn him loose."

Play on Words   One evening during a terrible storm in the English countryside, a knight rode up to an inn on a greyhound dog. He inquired of the innkeeper whether he could find a place to sleep. It looked as if the knight would have to go back out into the storm. But then the innkeeper noticed that the greyhound was sorely fatigued and in general quite the worse for wear. So he changed his mind, saying, "I wouldn't send a knight out on a dog like this."

Burlesque   Ambrose Bierce burlesqued Benjamin Franklin's sayings from *Poor Richard's Almanack:*

> A penny saved is a penny to squander.
>
> A man is known by the company he organizes.
>
> A bad workman quarrels with the man who calls him that.[10]

In more recent times, Lawrence J. Peter and Raymond Hull created a burlesque in the form of "The Peter Principle" in order to make a social comment: "In every hierarchy every employee tends to rise to his level of incompetence. A New Science!"[11]

Using Humor

The following suggestions will help to make the best use of humor in speaking.

Be Objective   Overriding all use of humor should be a sense of objectivity toward the situations and people the humor pokes fun at. Listeners must feel that the weaknesses a speaker sees in them and others are the normal weaknesses of human beings. Outlandish techniques may be used to point up these foibles, but listeners can laugh more freely if they are confronted with what is at base a true picture (though drawn in caricature), impartially presented.

Show Kindliness   Speakers are constantly tempted to be sarcastic, to ridicule some person, group, or idea. Sarcasm and ridicule are properly classed as forms of humor, and they are powerful weapons in the arsenal of an effective speaker. But they often strike an unintended sour note. Barbed attacks may seem to find favor with an audience, but the truth is that although they may please, they do so by inviting the audience toward smugness and the speaker toward insolence. Speakers also run the danger of offending their listeners or of having them realize that they have been cheapened by their part in the act. Pointing out incongruities is not in itself an act of unkindness. But to do so with bitterness is not likely to be perceived as humor. Raillery and banter lack the bitterness of sarcasm and ridicule. These may be used in a spirit of good will.

Use Good Taste   Good taste is difficult to define, and audiences differ in what they will accept. Therefore, arbitrary prescriptions to avoid jokes about nationality, race, religion, and sex do not always hold true. A good rule to follow is that if any bit of humor is at all likely to offend, avoid it. On the public platform, therefore, avoid any humor that even hints at vulgarity or obscenity. The stock-in-trade of nightclub comedians has no place in the kind of speaking that is of interest to us here. The world is full of fine humor that can be drawn upon without invading areas that might give offense. The cost of a laugh is too high if looking tawdry is the price.

Learn to Laugh at Yourself   One way you reveal both objectivity and kindliness in humor is to laugh at yourself. Before speakers can find effective humor in the weakness of others, they must first sense the foibles in themselves.

Let the Humor Label Itself   There is no joke that has to work as hard for a laugh as the one that is introduced with the suggestion that it is supposed to be funny. A speaker who seems to be working at being witty will never make it. Humor that is worth using needs no identification. Then, too, some audiences are strangely perverse. When they are told that something is going to be funny, either they expect too much or they set themselves (unconsciously or not) to resist. The most effective humor slides into the mind without announcement or fanfare.

Stop When You're Ahead   Developing a taste for applause is the easiest thing in the world. And the taste for applause is insatiable. It's hard to stop when you know you're doing a good job, the audience is responsive, and you feel that you could hold it indefinitely. There is always a tendency to exploit the audience just a little more. But one extra story or joke may be all it takes to push the humor past its peak of effectiveness.

SUMMARY

Many speaking occasions are ceremonial. They respond to the demands of social custom. The skills and techniques appropriate to informative and persuasive speaking will meet them successfully. Because these speeches are highly ritualistic, they are always in danger of being stale. Try to find fresh ways of saying what tradition demands. Sincerity and civility help greatly to balance the debits of dullness.

The most frequent occasions for ceremonial speaking are brought about by the social need to practice the simple courtesies that custom decrees for the situation.

An *introduction,* whether serious or humorous, prepares the audience for both the speaker and the subject.

A *nomination* presents a candidate for elective office and outlines the qualifications of the nominee for the position.

Speeches of *welcome* help visitors, either individuals or groups, feel that their presence is appreciated. They are often intended to give groups, such as political or professional conventions, a heightened sense of the importance of their meeting.

Awards are given to those who have earned them by meritorious behavior. Speeches of *presentation* describe the service or conduct that warrants recognition.

A *response* to a speech of courtesy expresses gratitude for the kindness, courtesy, or honor bestowed. The speaker is obligated in both courtesy and justice to credit any others who deserve it.

A *farewell* speech is a graceful departure from tenure in an office or membership in a group.

Speeches of *tribute* are designed to inspire an audience with such sentiments as admiration and affection for a person, zeal for a tradition, or rededication to an ideal. *Eulogies* praise the dead, *commendations* pay tribute to the living, and *commemorations* memorialize important events.

Speeches of *good will* are the means of building a favorable image for a group. Most commonly, they are used by commercial organizations to show how they are working for the benefit of the listener.

A speech to *entertain* has the purpose of amusing or diverting an audience. A familiar instance is the after-dinner speech.

No matter what the purpose of a speech, the ability to use humor is a valuable skill. If amusement is the goal, as it will be in a speech to entertain, humor will be the means of achieving it. In speeches to inform or persuade, even though laughter is not an end in itself, the interest of the audience can be heightened by using supporting details in humorous ways, through overstatement, understatement, unexpected turns, irony, play on words, and burlesque.

These suggestions will make humor more effective: (1) Be objective; (2) show kindliness; (3) exercise good taste; (4) learn to laugh at yourself; (5) let the humor label itself; and (6) stop when you're ahead.

NOTES

1. A nightclub owner and topless dancer well known in San Francisco.
2. Reprinted with the permission of Dean Ianni.
3. John F. Kennedy, *Public Papers of the Presidents of the United States: 1962,* (Washington, D.C.: U.S. Government Printing Office, 1963), pp. 159–160.
4. *The New York Times,* Feb. 24, 1962, p. 16. Copyright © 1962 by The New York Times Company. Reprinted by permission.
5. Adlai E. Stevenson, "Farewell to a Friend," *American Short Speeches,* Bower Aly and Lucile Aly, eds. (New York: Macmillan, 1968), pp. 122–123. Permission granted by Adlai Stevenson, III.

6. "Shared Reverence for Life," *America,* **133** (Oct. 25, 1975), p. 249.

7. The transcript of a speech by Ronald Reagan commemorating Memorial Day and delivered at Arlington National Cemetery, Arlington, Va., can be found in *The New York Times,* June 1, 1982, p. 14.

8. This is very much like what journalist Andy Rooney does. Watch him some Sunday evening on the television program, "Sixty Minutes."

9. Mody C. Boatright, *Folk Laughter on the American Frontier* (New York: Collier, 1961), pp. 97–98.

10. As quoted in R. P. Falk, *The Antic Muse* (New York: Grove Press, 1955), p. 27.

11. Laurence J. Peter and Raymond Hull, *The Peter Principle* (New York: Bantam Books, 1970), pp. 7–8.

EXERCISES

1. You are going to introduce a prominent attorney who is visiting your speech class. Prepare the introductory speech.

2. Prepare a nominating speech for a friend whom you think should be elected to the student senate.

3. The "Woman of the Year" from your state is visiting your campus. You are student body president. Prepare a speech of welcome for her.

4. A group of which you are a member (fraternity, sorority, Hillel, Newman Club, or the like) is making a substantial contribution to a medical research foundation. Prepare the speech of presentation.

5. You are being honored by the Rotary Club of your community for winning their annual student scholarship. Prepare a response to the presentation of the award.

6. Upon graduation, you, as valedictorian, will speak at the commencement exercises. On behalf of yourself and the other graduates, prepare a speech of farewell to the faculty and the campus.

7. Prepare a speech commemorating the anniversary of the death of someone such as John F. Kennedy, Martin Luther King, Jr., Woodrow Wilson, Franklin D. Roosevelt, or Susan B. Anthony.

8. Examine the speech in Appendix B by Ian Fielding, "The Wonderful World of College." That after-dinner speech was intended for a college audience. Do you think it is a good after-dinner speech for such an audience. Why? Why not?

chapter *21*

Speaking in Small Groups

Much of our oral communication takes place in small groups: in business conferences, around the family dinner table, on an outing with friends. Some of these groups are formally structured, others are informal, and many are even unplanned. In this chapter we are interested in the more formal situations wherein you may be called upon because of your work or your school to participate in a small group discussion. You can be a more effective participant if you understand the nature of small group speaking, the situations that arise, and the responsibilities of participants and leaders.

SMALL GROUP SPEAKING DEFINED

Small group speaking may be defined as *a process that involves a limited number of people interacting with one another about a problem of common interest in a situation wherein the group has the responsibility of making effective decisions*. To get a clear understanding of the definition, let's look at the important elements involved in it.

The group is *limited in size*. A group can be as small as two—for example, when two people are named as a committee to arrange a family gathering. A somewhat larger group would doubtless be needed to plan an alumni reunion. Depending on the given task, the size of the group will grow. But there is some maximum number beyond which a group can no longer be called small.

The group is *interactive*. A group can be small in size, perhaps no more than 10, and yet if it were the audience for a public speech, the members would not then be involved in any way in what we mean by small group speaking. In small group speaking, each participant must be actively involved as speaker, listener, and decision maker.

The group *makes decisions*. An intercollegiate debate team is a small group in that it usually has only two members, and these speakers interact with each other and with the members of the opposing team, but a judge who is a member of neither team makes the only significant decision. Debates, therefore, are not examples of small group speaking.

For other reasons, therapy groups are also of no interest to us in the present context. They have quite valid purposes, they are limited in size, and their members participate interactively, but any decisions made are personal and they are not applicable beyond the individual who makes them.

A final point: Our definition does not say so explicitly but, typically, a small group of the kind we are talking about operates under the guidance of a leader.

The decisions groups make are not limited to matters of policy. Juries make decisions on questions of fact: To what extent did the government's case depend on entrapment? Church groups make decisions on questions of value: What modes of conduct are the best in race relations? Sexual mores? The role of women? There are "learning groups" whose members pool information on a subject. You may have participated in such a group when you prepared for final exams last semester. And these are only a few examples from an unlimited number of groups and countless topics of discussion. Whatever the group and whatever the cause for meeting, small group speaking will have these characteristics:

1. The size of the group is limited.
2. Group members are independent but interactive.
3. The group has a decision-making responsibility.
4. The group typically has a leader.

Decisions made by small groups are not necessarily better than those made by a single person, but the process has certain advantages. It permits pooling of information and it provides for correction of individual error. Perhaps you've heard it said that a camel is a horse built by a committee. If you know how to plan a discussion, how to be a good participant, and how to lead on, you'll be able to profit from the advantages of the group activity and, above all, to avoid building a camel when you want a horse.

PLANNING FOR GROUP DECISION MAKING

Because different kinds of problems require different kinds of decisions, there are different ways of making decisions. Despite the different approaches, however, in the same sense that a speaker must first decide on a subject for a speech, the first need of a group is to understand the problem it must solve. Given this, the group can choose the plan of discussion best suited to the problem at hand. We are going to look at three such decision-making plans: division of labor, reflective thinking, and the argumentative plan.

Division-of-Labor Plan

The members of some groups are chosen because each has a special expertise or knowledge. For example, suppose that you are asked as a class exercise to lead a group discussion to determine what your university's Liberal Education program ought to be. To avoid undue bias, you want in your group a science major, a humanities major, an engineering major, a health major, and a social science major. If a division of labor were your plan of operation, you would ask each person to prepare an ideal program in his or her specialty and briefly present it to the group; then, based on whatever criteria you select (size of the program, purpose, emphasis, etc.), you and the group would negotiate among yourselves to determine the final program. The organization of the division-of-labor procedure looks like this:

  I. What contribution can each field make to the program?
     A. Humanities
     B. Sciences
     C. Engineering
     D. Etc.
  II. What criteria for a unified proposal can we negotiate?
     A. Size?
     B. Purpose?
     C. Emphasis on theoretical or applied?
     D. Etc.
  III. What single program based on our negotiated criteria can we agree upon?

In such a group every person has a role to fill as an expert in a particular area. Each one serves as a resource person and a decision maker. This is not the same as group meetings conducted for an outside audience—for example, an informative symposium wherein each person presents specific information, or a debate in which each speaker argues a position. Division-of-labor groups are not performing for an outside audience. They are truly interacting to find the best decision just as any other interactive small group would do.

Reflective Thinking Plan

About 75 years ago, philosopher John Dewey defined a systematic method of thought by which an individual might arrive at better decisions.[1] Others have adapted his system to the group situation. It has been interpreted in a number of ways with minor variations. The following is one of them. This plan develops the group decision-making process through the following five steps: (1) locating and defining the problem, (2) analyzing the problem, (3) establishing goals, (4) finding the best possible decision, and (5) putting the decision into operation.

Every person in a small group has a role to fill. (© Bodin, Stock, Boston)

Locating and Defining the Problem   You cannot be completely objective in looking for a solution to any problem. Your personal desires and knowledge will influence your ideas. But neither do you want this personal element to push you to a solution without giving the problem thorough analysis.

Imagine (and perhaps you don't need to imagine) a university parking lot that fills up early, and even though you have paid your parking fee, when you arrive for your 9 o'clock class at 8:45, either you can't get into the lot or you have to search so long for a place that you are late for class. You might respond with rage, demand that someone be fired, or kick the parking lot gate. You might also change your habits and come at 6:30 to be sure of finding a place. Both of these are decisions, but they are not reflective. Reflective decision making requires careful analysis to locate and define the problem.

Suppose that you are a member of a group formed to study the parking problem. First you must ask questions like these: What is the parking problem on the campus? Is it confined to certain lots? Certain hours? Certain people? Does it involve public transportation? Off-campus street parking?

In this first stage of the discussion the group must be sure that its members share a common understanding of the problem. When you talk with others about any set of circumstances, communication often suffers for lack of common ground. Failure to clear away at the outset as many of the obstacles to communication as possible will do much to destroy a potentially good discussion. Consequently, it is necessary to locate and define the problem.

Various methods of definition are discussed in Chapter 8. The method to use is the one that will best specify, through clarification of words and phrases, the nature of the problem under consideration. The participants in the group are searching for agreement; therefore, a series of dictionary definitions of the words that state the problem is not enough. Since the members of the group are the ones who discovered the problem, they are the only ones who can state it correctly. And at the conclusion of this step of the discussion process, they should be in agreement about the specific subject under discussion and should be prepared to analyze it with a minimum of confusion.

Analyzing the Problem   Analysis is the second step in the problem-solving process. Its function is to find the cause of the difficulty. The thoroughness with which this essential step is conducted determines as much as any other factor the success of the group in establishing a desirable new policy.

The first step in analysis is a review of existing conditions. A doctor who sees you for the first time needs to examine you thoroughly: taking your medical history, examining and questioning for symptoms. Symptoms are the clues to the cause of an illness. This determination of causes is a vital step in any problem-solving process. When a group discusses a policy question, it can be compared to doctors in consultation. Like doctors, those who act as physicians to the ills of society, or business, or education must make a thorough investigation of facts; they must be familiar with conditions past and present, in order that they may penetrate to the causes of the problem.

What are the symptoms of your campus parking problem: Lots fill up from 8:00 a.m. to 3:00 p.m.? All lots? How many spaces? How many cars? What are the fees? What are the fines? What are the causes for the problem? Inadequate space? Inadequate public transportation? Student refusal to walk from outlying lots? Inadequate fine system for violators? From the information the members of your group have gathered, they should be able to list the symptoms and the factors that helped to create those undesired conditions.

Establishing Goals   Before determining what solution will best meet a problem situation, a group must have some standard for judging or testing any proposal. What are the standards any acceptable solution to the parking problem must meet: Be fair to all? Not raise parking fees? Provide adequate parking within easy walking distance of classes? Clarify the parking regulations? Consider off-campus solutions? Once established, the goals serve as standards of judgment for evaluating potential solutions. Indeed, this is the reason the symptoms and the causes are explored in the first place—to know better what kind of solution to look for. Through analysis of the problem, the group distills the criteria that tell what a good solution must be.

Determining goals is frequently a difficult step in discussion. It is not a common practice for people to think through their goals when they make decisions. If you are asked why you bought a certain pair of socks, aren't you likely to say, "Because I liked them"? Likewise, you may support a certain political party, believe in stricter law enforcement, or want more government intervention to help our older citizens without clearly spelling out why. But there is a why—a goal or set of goals—and if someone insists, you can usually explain. However, if you are to be systematic in group decisions, you must identify goals *before* you propose solutions.

To determine goals, then, is to develop a yardstick to measure the many possible courses of action. If the analysis of the problem has been thorough, the goals will be more easily determined. The more thorough and realistic the goals of a group are, the better are the chances it will choose the most desirable solution to a problem.

Finding the Best Possible Decision   Determining the best policy requires an examination of the advantages and disadvantages of each possible course of action. Each is compared with the others to see which will come closest to achieving the goals that have been established. If these goals are realistic, the course of action that most closely fits their specifications will be the one that most effectively reduces the causes of the problem, and thus limits its undesirable symptoms.

All reasonable possibilities should be considered. That is, it is quite possible that the present policy (the status quo) might prove to be the most desirable. Your group investigating the parking problem on your campus might agree that arriving earlier or walking from a remote lot is better than a large increase in fees to build a parking garage at the center of the campus. It is possible, in other words, that any proposed change would be for the worse. At any rate, the status quo should always be evaluated in comparison with the alleged advantages of any proposed change.

Putting the Decision into Operation   The final step in the reflective thinking plan is implementation of the decision. In this part of the discussion, the group examines the decision to see what must be done and by whom. The problem-solving group must find the most practical way, in the light of its criteria, to put the solution to work. Your group may have decided that the solution involves better public transportation, so the city must be lobbied to change the bus schedule. It might also imply stricter enforcement of the parking rules (campus security) and a change in class scheduling (the university administration). How would your group approach these agencies, and what methods of implementation would you suggest?

In summary, then, the reflective thinking plan of group decision making develops through the following steps:

I. Locate and define the problem: Clarify the limits of the problem and define all vague, ambiguous, or unfamiliar terms to the satisfaction of all the members of the group.

II. Analyze the problem.
    A. Symptoms: Examine the status quo and its history to discover the nature and severity of the problem.
    B. Causes: Examine the symptoms and their history to determine what cause or causes produced the undesirable elements of the situation.

III. Establish goals: Develop standards of judgment for the group. That is, identify and state the criteria that constitute the requirements for a good solution.

IV. Appraise the possible solutions.
    A. List the reasonable courses of action.
    B. Evaluate each to see how well it attains the stated goals of the group.
    C. Select the course of action that most closely achieves the goals.

V. Determine procedures for putting the chosen solution into operation.

Argumentative Decision-Making Plan

Any reflective thinking plan is concerned with evaluating the nature of the situation *before* possible decisions are advanced. In contrast, there is some research and considerable experience to recommend using a pattern that we call argumentative decision making. In the argumentative plan, potential decisions are advanced tentatively and then tested by the group. Each testing permits the members of the group to understand one another better and so to advance new decisions that are additions to, or modifications of, the original proposal. In this way group decisions are built a piece at a time, but they begin with a proposal for decision, not with an analysis of the problem. This may not be the most desirable method for solving complex problems, but it is commonly used in everyday life.

This model has been described as a "spiral." When one person advances a decision, it is tested and altered until all have agreed upon it. It is then fixed and used as a basis for determining decisions about other questions.[2] Here's a sample of how it works: "Let's go to a movie tonight." "Okay, which one?" "How about 'Indiana Jones and The Temple of Doom'?" "No, I'm not into violence today." "Okay, how about

'The Natural'? You like Robert Redford." And so on. Although this plan is less tightly organized than the reflective thinking plan, it is still systematic. It involves "reach testing" a proposed step forward from an agreed-upon position. If the step is approved, an advance is made; if not, the group returns to the earlier position and "reach tests" another idea.[3]

A more general argumentative pattern is described by B. Aubrey Fisher. His research revealed that an untutored group will naturally use four steps in making a decision.

1. *Orientation*   Participants are tentative in advancing proposals and stating disagreement with others. They seem to be determining their positions in the group.
2. *Conflict*   There is strong ideational conflict among members of the group. They seem to have established their social positions and the most vigorous testing takes place.
3. *Emergence*   Argument tends to dissipate and movement toward consensus of opinion begins. There is some tendency to be more ambiguous, as in the orientation stage, because members who expressed strong opinions in the conflict stage are in the process of accepting the consensus.
4. *Reinforcement*   Although the group has actually made a decision, its members need to reinforce the views that reflect their unity of opinion.[4]

PARTICIPATION IN GROUP DECISION MAKING

No matter what pattern of group decision making is used, the members of a group must participate in its activities. In this section we will see how a participant can help to achieve the two objectives that are essential to effective group activity: cohesiveness and productivity.

Cohesiveness

Group members are individuals. They have their own reasons for being part of the group. They differ in how important a solution is to them. They differ in their relations to the other members of the group. Yet they must interact with one another. Their success as a group can be measured in part by the kind of cohesiveness the group develops. A group with considerable cohesiveness is one in which individuals are willing to work for the good of the group. You might call it "team spirit." It helps the group be more productive.

Productivity

Groups are judged by their productivity. If a committee that is supposed to come up with an idea for a homecoming float can't come up with a good theme, the committee will be judged negatively for it. Obviously, groups that provide new and imaginative solutions to problems get a lot of credit. But in some circumstances, even if a group doesn't come up with a good solution, it can be considered productive if it clarifies the issues that divide it.

Securing Cohesiveness and Productivity

To produce maximum cohesiveness and productivity in group discussion, each individual must participate efficiently and effectively. We will discuss four ways of securing this kind of participation: Identify with your group, be supportive of others, be prepared, and follow the plan.

Identify with Your Group   If the group product is going to be worthwhile, the members have to identify themselves with the group. This is a time to put aside personal reactions and any negative attitudes you may have toward others in the group. It is also a time to control any tendency you may have to take charge. Even if you have a good solution, it must be developed as a group consensus if it is to be accepted outside the group. The more quickly you can identify with the group, the easier it will be for you to influence the other members. When all the members can act their roles well as group members, cohesiveness will develop and productivity will increase.

Be Supportive of Others   Some members will be more shy than others. Some will have less knowledge than others. As a member of the group you will want to help those who are less talkative become more involved in the discussion. You will also avoid any personal put-downs even when someone is clearly wrong. Being supportive means that your comments should be related to the problem under discussion and the group's involvement in it. That means having respect for the others in the group. You may need to disagree, but do so without personal implications.

Be Prepared   The Boy Scout motto is as apropos here as it is in any other speech situation. Unfortunately, some people do not take group speaking situations as seriously as they do formal public speaking assignments. Somehow, they hope, others will have studied the question so they need not know as much. But pooled ignorance doesn't make for a good decision. The old adage, "junk in, junk out," applies here. The productivity of the group and its cohesiveness will be increased when all the members are well informed. And what all the members need starts with a single member, you.

Follow the Plan   The reason groups adopt a plan of analysis is to provide a more systematic examination of the problem. It is easy for a group discussion to drift off on interesting tangents. But nothing destroys cohesion more than for each member to go off on a personal tangent and ignore the analytical process. Of course, we are not advocating a slavish adherence to any plan. Indeed, the argumentative plan advocates reach testing, and to reach you need to try new ideas that may seem tangential. A certain amount of reach testing is necessary in any plan. But reach testing should always be done with a realization of its place in the analytical process.

If there is a division of labor, you as an individual need to accept whatever responsibilities are yours. You must also pay close attention to what others say, so that you can detect when the group may be losing track of the discussion plan.

These four guidelines for participating apply to everyone in the group, but they bind with even greater force for those participants who assume leadership responsibilities.

LEADERSHIP IN GROUP DISCUSSION

It is usual to think of the person in charge of procedure as *the* leader of the group. In fact, however, such a person may not be the leader at all. Assigned to control the group, some people become mere figureheads, not leading the group but following the procedural and substantive suggestions of some other member. This other member is the real leader. In short, the real leader is the one who guides either the procedure or the substance of the discussion, or both. That may or may not be the person appointed as chair.

The leadership role is a function of the group; that is, the members decide who will direct their thought. Leadership may change hands as the discussion changes. The members of a decision-making group may accept the leadership of one person on one topic, or on one phase of a problem, and at another time turn for leadership to someone else. The members of the group decide how much authority they will give, to whom they will give it and for how long.

Furthermore, groups do not always have an assigned leader. Your instructor may ask four or five of you to conduct a group discussion on some problem of your choosing but not designate a leader. Your employer may ask you and a few other employees to see if you can solve a merchandising problem. Even though it is usual for a committee, board, or panel to operate under the guidance of a presiding officer, you will work in many problem-solving groups that have no assigned leader.

Whether or not a leader is assigned, every member of the group must be prepared to assume the responsibilities of the chair. If you note, for example, that the group should move on to another phase of the discussion, don't wait more than briefly for someone else to make the suggestion; make it yourself. Perhaps someone else will emerge as leader, and you won't need to assume the procedural initiative. But every member of the group must be prepared to act if the need for leadership arises.

The Functions of Leadership

The functions of leadership are much the same as the four rules for securing cohesion and productivity. To be an effective leader, you will *identify with the group* and will show the others that you consider the group's goals important. You will *be supportive of others*. The most effective leaders are those who induce cooperative behavior in others by setting a good example themselves.[5] To be a leader you must *be prepared*, not only by studying the problem to be discussed but also by studying the other members of the group. A leader has to take a special interest in helping the group *follow the plan.* It is perhaps an oversimplified, but nonetheless useful generalization, that a good leader is one who does an outstanding job as a participant.

Specific Tasks of Leaders

An effective leader readily adapts to the requirements of the particular group speaking situation and to the expectations of the group. However, three specific tasks will generally be required of you.

Getting the Discussion Started   The first of your three responsibilities, getting the discussion off to a good start, is probably the most difficult. Once it has been started and the group is functioning, the discussion tends to move along.

Your introduction of the discussion topic should be clear, brief, and interesting. You may give a short resume of the history of the problem, or you may show briefly the nature and importance of the question. This sort of beginning, if you choose it, is only to permit the participants a moment to collect their thoughts. No one needs or wants a long speech from you. Under no circumstances should you take the responsibility of analyzing the problem. If necessary you should introduce the members of the group to one another by name.

This much is easy. It is a set of functions that must be performed but does not solve the vital problem in getting the discussion off to a good start. Most inexperienced groups have to be led into useful and worthwhile discussion. There are several ways of helping these less vocal groups to get under way.

One useful device for getting started is to ask a question designed to elicit an intelligent and relevant response. This opening question should ordinarily be directed to the group rather than to an individual. It would probably be unwise to put any one participant "on the spot" this early in the discussion. Moreover, the question should be general rather than specific. A specific question may require a specific piece of information that no one has immediately at hand.

Another useful maneuver is to quote a statement referring to the problem or cite some specific instance or illustration of the problem and ask for comment. If the topic is a broad one, you may want to ask for some specification or limitation. In each of these cases, any member of the panel, even one minimally prepared, should be able to make a reasonable comment.

Keeping the Discussion Going   Once started, a well-informed group will usually move along quite briskly with a minimum of prodding. Once you get the discussion started, your major functions are to encourage general participation, to keep the discussion on the track, and to guide the group away from hasty, unrealistic action. See that everyone participates, and that no one monopolizes the time of the group. If several speakers try to speak at the same time, the one who has spoken less frequently up to that point should be given the opportunity to speak first.

One of your most useful devices is frequent, brief summaries of what the group has accomplished up to that point. These summaries help to avoid needless repetition, keep the discussion on the track, and point out areas of agreement and disagreement.

Probably your most important function is to see to it that the group makes a thorough investigation of the problem at hand. Both evidence and argument must be submitted to rigorous test. This guarantee of testing can best be accomplished through the use of guiding questions. Differences of opinion are not to be stifled. Although you will want to point out and stress the areas of agreement that exist, it is also important that the differences be brought out; otherwise they can never be eliminated. Consensus is valuable only when it results from a realistic adjustment of honest differences.

Bringing the Discussion to a Close   Any meeting will eventually end, and the chairperson has the responsibility of bringing the discussion to a close. Usually, a summary is in order. When still-existing issues need further discussion, the concluding comments should be in the form of a progress report, summarizing the agreements and disagreements discovered in the group.

SUMMARY

Small group discussion is a common speaking situation. It usually involves a limited number of people interacting with one another on a problem of common interest where the group must make some kind of a decision. Participants have the advantages of being able to pool information and correct individual error. To realize these advantages it is necessary to plan carefully.

There are three major plans for group discussion. The "division-of-labor" plan provides for each person to approach the problem from a personal point of view and then participate in negotiating a group decision. The "reflective thinking" plan has five stages: (1) locating and defining the problem, (2) analyzing the problem, (3) establishing goals, (4) finding the best possible decision, and (5) putting the decision into operation. In the "argumentative" decision-making plan, the members advance ideas about solutions so that they can be tested and modified by the group. It naturally occurs in four steps: (1) orientation, (2) conflict, (3) emergence, and (4) reinforcement.

Although the members of a group are individuals, they need to develop cohesiveness as a group. They are also expected to provide the solution to a problem under discussion, or at least to clarify the disagreements that prevent consensus. To help secure cohesiveness and productivity for the group, you need to do four things: (1) Identify with your group, (2) be supportive of others, (3) be prepared, and (4) follow the plan.

Leadership cannot be assigned. A committee chair is not necessarily a leader. Leadership emerges from the group. It will sometimes change from person to person as the subject changes. In general, leadership comes to those who do a better job of meeting the four requirements of participation. In addition, the leader must be prepared to undertake the specific tasks of getting the discussion started, keeping it moving along, and bringing it to a close.

NOTES

1. John Dewey, *How We Think* (Lexington, Mass.: Heath, 1910).
2. Thomas M. Scheidel and Laura Crowell, "Idea Development in Small Groups," *Quarterly Journal of Speech,* **50** (Apr. 1964), pp. 140–145.
3. B. Aubrey Fisher, *Small Group Decision-Making,* (New York: McGraw-Hill, 1974), p. 138.
4. B. Aubrey Fisher, "Decision Emergence: Phases in Group Decision-Making," *Speech Monographs,* **37** (Mar. 1970), pp. 53–66.
5. H. Lloyd Goodall, Jr., "The Skills of Leading Small Groups in American Business and Industry," *Small Group Communication: A Reader,* Robert S. Cathcart and Larry A. Samovar, eds. (Dubuque, Iowa: Wm. C. Brown, 1984), p. 425.

EXERCISES

1. Make an analysis of some personal problem using reflective thinking: How worthwhile do you find this method? What alternate possibilities do you think would be as effective? More effective? Why?

2. Form a discussion group with four or five other members of your class. Select a problem to discuss. Word it. Come to some basic understanding about what the terms of the question mean. Let each member of the group gather material. Present the group discussion in class a week after you have chosen the topic.

3. Observe the chairperson of some group to which you belong. Write a paper of no more than three typewritten pages explaining what techniques the chairperson used and how successful they were.

4. Discuss in class how effective group discussion is in learning situations such as classrooms. Explain why they are as good, better, or worse than lectures, films, or textbook reading.

six

EVALUATING SPEECHES

chapter *22*

Speech Evaluation

In previous chapters, we have examined a number of ways to make speeches effective. Everything we have said is related in some fashion to increasing your skill in handling the substance, organization, style, and delivery of a message. In this chapter, however, we are going to look at speech making from another point of view—not that of the speaker, but that of the listener. In other words, we want to show you a method whereby you can make a sound *evaluation* of the speeches of others. We are still concerned with substance, organization, style, and delivery, of course, because those are the elements of every speech; they are what make it good or bad and, consequently, they are the only reasonable basis for evaluation.

When you evaluate something, you assess it; you determine what merit it has. Human beings have produced many different kinds of artifacts: paintings, statues, poems, plays and music, to name a few. All of these are subject to evaluation by many different methods. But in this chapter we will be concerned solely with the evaluation of speeches and how to judge them by the most usual standards.

WHY SPEECHES ARE EVALUATED

Perhaps the most obvious reason for evaluating a speech is to improve your own speaking. By examining the techniques used effectively by other speakers, you can better see what techniques to use. What may be effective at one time with one audience will not necessarily be effective in other circumstances; nonetheless, by seeing how an audience responds to various techniques, you gain insights into the kinds of situations wherein certain techniques are most useful.

Evaluating speeches will also improve your listening skills. Frequently, you hear a speech and judge it to be good or poor without testing your conclusion by asking what, specifically, makes it good or poor.

The evaluation of a speech also gives insight into the historical significance of the speaking situation. It helps you to see the interrelation of speaker, speech, and audience. When Franklin D. Roosevelt said in his first inaugural address, "We have nothing to fear but fear itself," his statement had great significance for the depression-ridden people of the 1930s. To read that speech and analyze it against the background of the times will bring more sharply into focus the problems of the era and the attitudes of the American people at that time.

The evaluation of speeches not only offers an understanding of some particular point in history, but more broadly, it gives insights into the nature of human beings in general. When you study speeches from a number of eras, you soon become aware that although issues change and techniques change, many attitudes remain constant. The arguments advanced during the late 1960s and early 1970s by opponents of the war in Vietnam are essentially the same as those advanced in the 1840s by opponents of the Mexican War. Effective public speakers, whether purposely or not, reflect the prevailing ideas of the times; they reflect, in addition, their own insights into all human existence.

THE STEPS IN SPEECH EVALUATION

There are three steps in speech evaluation: analysis, synthesis, and judgment. In an *analysis,* the speech is taken apart so that its various elements can be individually examined. These elements, as we have said, are the *subtance* of the speech (the arguments and their supporting materials, the value appeals, and the efforts to win credibility), the *organization* of the ideas, the *style* of the language, and the *delivery*. The individual facts you have gathered from your analysis are then *synthesized* around what seems to be the basic or central strategy the speaker uses. Finally, there must be a *judgment,* not merely a statement that a speech is good or bad, but an indication of strengths and weaknesses as you see them. If a judgment is based on intelligent analysis and synthesis, it will be worth the attention of others. No one expects that in a beginning speech class you will become an accomplished critic, but you can begin to develop evaluative skills.

Analysis

You analyze first the *substance* of the speech—the speaker's ideas and their support. From classical times three elements in proof have been recognized: argument *(logos),* value appeals *(pathos),* and credibility *(ethos).* Although all three are viewed as equally important and involve the interrelation of audience, speaker, speech, and occasion, the argumentative function is more directly related to the message than the others are; values bear most upon the audience, and credibility is attributed to the speaker.

Argument   Perhaps the most complex part of an analysis is in discovering what the central claim is and how this claim is argued and supported. The following is a section of an analysis of the argument in Elizabeth Stanton's address, "Lords of Creation," at the 1848 Woman's Rights Convention in Seneca Falls, New York:

> The content of Mrs. Stanton's speech suggests she did not assume her listeners readily agreed with her. Counter-refutation pervaded the entire address as she first attacked the assumption that man was intellectually, morally, and physically superior; then refuted traditional arguments against woman's rights; and, finally answered prevailing objections to woman suffrage—particularly objections that women themselves might raise.
>
> The graduate of Troy Female Seminary showed she was well versed in her subject. She referred to no less than seventeen women by name and deed to show it was "strange that man—with the pages of history spread out before him—is so slow to admit the intellectual power, the moral heroism of woman, and her identity with himself."
>
> Mrs. Stanton also revealed she was practiced in the art of argument. Eight times she turned to the Bible, a source of authority often used by her opponents, to support her contentions. In the story of Creation, for example, she found

evidence that man is not intellectually supreme, for did not the Evil One offer Eve the apple of temptation because he knew "man could be easily conquered through his affection for the woman, but the woman would require more management?"[1]

Here are some questions to consider in analyzing the argumentative dimension of the speech:

1. What appears to be the central claim the speaker wants to support?
2. Is the speaker aware of the issues that divide opinion?
3. What ways of looking at the issues does the speaker propose?
4. Does the speaker meet opposition arguments?
5. What form of reasoning does the speaker use in developing the arguments?
6. What kind of evidence does the speaker provide?

Value Appeals Your analysis also identifies the specific value system revealed in the speech. The value system the speaker appeals to is revealed by the words that carry value judgments, the positive and negative value terms in the speech. Your examination of these terms will help you determine the speaker's value system.

In his First Inaugural address, President Woodrow Wilson called for reform of the nation's economy in the interest of "New Freedom." In the following passage from that speech, terms labeling notions Wilson considers *good* are printed in italics and those he considers **bad** are printed in boldface.

> But the **evil** has come with the *good,* and much *fine gold* has been **corroded.** With *riches* has come **inexcusable waste.** We have **squandered** a great part of what we might have *used,* and have not stopped to *conserve* the exceeding *bounty of nature,* without which our *genius for enterprise* would have been **worthless** and **impotent, scorning** to be careful, **shamefully prodigal** as well as *admirably efficient.* We have been *proud* of our industrial *achievements,* but we have not hitherto stopped *thoughtfully,* enough to count **human cost,** the **cost** of *lives* **snuffed out,** of *energies* **overtaxed** and **broken,** the **fearful** *physical* and *spiritual* **cost** to the men and women and children upon whom the **dead weight** and **burden** of it all has fallen **pitilessly** the years through.

From an examination of the value words that carry Wilson's argument, you can see the value system underlying what he says. To paraphrase him: We must with candid and fearless eyes conserve our riches (the bounty of nature) through careful, efficient use of our genius for enterprise, with due pride in our industrial achievements. We must reject the corrosion of fine gold through waste, squandering, overtaxing, the snuffing out of lives, and the great spiritual and physical costs. Further, we must discontinue our attention to worthless things. We must stop being impotent, prodigal, and selfish.

Wilson appeals to the Puritan values so basic in American society: a respect for nature and enterprise; a rejection of selfishness, waste, and false pride. Further examination will show that the emphasis of this passage is negative; that is, President

Wilson uses the words of his value system to reject what he considers bad more strongly than to identify what he supports.

This illustration identifies the basis for some of the analytical questions you will ask:

1. To what value systems does the speaker appeal?
2. What general warrant does the speaker emphasize at the most important points in the speech?
3. Are the values justified by the subject?
4. Do the warrants remain consistent throughout the speech?

Credibility   Credibility is established when an audience judges a speaker to be trustworthy and competent. Speakers can establish credibility by projecting good images of themselves and bad images of their opponents. When you analyze credibility, ask yourself not only what qualities the speaker claims to possess, but also what qualities are ascribed to the opposition. In the 1982 congressional campaign, President Ronald Reagan argued that the American people should "stay the course." He characterized his opponents in the Democratic party as having a long history of errors in judgment. Supporting the Republicans ("staying the course") meant supporting the people who chose the rational solution to problems.[2]

Any political campaign speech will have a clearly identifiable opponent, but even when the opponent is not a specific person the antagonist may be an idea, a party, a way of life. The speech of Martin Luther King, Jr., "I Have a Dream," finds an opponent in the people who deny equality to blacks. King does not identify them directly, but who could deny that he knew his opponents?

> One hundred years later [after the end of slavery] the life of the Negro is still sadly crippled by the manacles of segregation and the chains of discrimination. One hundred years later, the Negro lives on a lonely island of poverty in the midst of a vast ocean of material prosperity.[3]

When an audience agrees with a speaker but does not act as vigorously as the speaker would like, we could say that the opponent is the apathy of the audience. Much patriotic ceremonial oratory is of this nature, and so is a substantial amount of preaching.

Credibility is further classified as either direct or indirect. In direct credibility the speaker's attributes and accomplishments and/or the defects of the opponent are referred to directly. When she accepted the vice presidential nomination of the Democratic party in 1984, Geraldine A. Ferraro spoke directly about herself:

> Tonight, the daughter of an immigrant from Italy has been chosen to run for Vice President in the new land my father came to love.
>
> Our faith that we can shape a better future is what the American dream is all about. The promise of our country is that the rules are fair. And if you work hard and play by the rules, you can earn your share of America's blessings.

Those are the beliefs I learned from my parents. And those are the values I taught my students as a teacher in the public schools of New York.

At night, I went to law school. I became an assistant district attorney, and I put my share of criminals behind bars. Because I believe: If you obey the law, you should be protected. But if you break the law, you should pay for your crime.

When I first ran for Congress, all the political experts said a woman could not win in my home district of Queens. But I put my faith in the people and the values that we shared. And together, we proved the political experts wrong.

Although speakers often seek to build credibility by showing the audience directly that they are competent to speak on the subject, indirect credibility is developed more subtly.

At that same convention, Governor Mario Cuomo of New York delivered the Keynote address. In the segment quoted below, although he says nothing directly about himself, Cuomo attributes the highest motives to his party and associates himself with what he calls the party credo. Therefore, what he says indirectly identifies his own image:

We Democrats still have a dream. We still believe in this nation's future.

And this is our answer—our credo:

We believe in only the government we need, but we insist on all the government we need.

We believe in a government characterized by fairness and reasonableness, a reasonableness that goes beyond labels, that doesn't distort or promise to do what it knows it can't do.

A government strong enough to use the words "love" and "compassion" and smart enough to convert our noblest aspirations into practical realities.

We believe in encouraging the talented, but we believe that while survival of the fittest may be a good working description of the process of evolution, a government of humans should elevate itself to a higher order, one which fills the gaps left by chance or a wisdom we don't understand.

We would rather have laws written by the patron of this great city, the man called the "world's most sincere Democrat," St. Francis of Assisi, than laws written by Darwin.

Organization The structure of the speech helps you to see how well the speaker gives the message *unity, order,* and *coherence.*

The primary constituent of unity is *singleness of theme.* Ask, are all the arguments and value appeals of the speech relevant to one main theme? If there are several themes, are they related to one another and developed in such a way as to give a sense of unity?

Similarly, *scope* is a function of unity, for the impression of unity is not only created by the singleness of the speaker's theme, it is influenced by the listener's perception as well. Is the speech limited to what the audience can attend to and yet broad enough to continually engage listener interests?

Order in a speech is the sequence of ideas. It is found in what can be called *thematic emergence*, the manner in which the central claim (the theme) of the speech is revealed. Does the main theme become clear somewhere around the middle of the speech? Is the cat let out of the bag one whisker at a time? Does the theme emerge at the beginning, stated unequivocally to the audience? In addition, ask by what pattern the speech is organized: Chronologically? Spatially? Claim to proof? Problem to solution?

Coherence is related directly to both unity and order. It can be checked by examining the transitions the speaker uses to link one thought with another. Ask yourself, to what extent do the transitions help a listener develop a clear and correct understanding of what the speaker says?

Thus, you analyze the structure of a speech to discover how its theme emerges, what order is used to organize the material, and what means are used to link one idea with another.

Language and Style   Language is the fundamental "hardware" of a speech; it is the vehicle that transmits the substance of the speech and manifests the organization. In a very real sense, therefore, whatever you learn about a speech must come through analysis of the speaker's language. In addition, however, you analyze the language of a speech to discover how the speaker achieves the primary goals of style: clarity and interest.

An important aspect of stylistic analysis is learning something about the level of the speaker's vocabulary in relation to the audience's understanding. That is, the vocabulary level of a speech helps to determine whether the language will be readily accepted and easily understood. No audience wants to hear a speech that is insulting because of its simplicity or confusing because of its complexity. Imagine addressing an adult audience in the language of a first-level reader: "See Puff. See Puff run. Run, Puff, run. Run, run, run." Or imagine the response of an audience addressed in the complex jargon of a field that it does not understand. Syntax is potentially as serious a problem as vocabulary. Given words it understands, an audience can often do a reasonably good job of straightening out unclear sentences; but when syntax is awkward and unsure, it will impair communication. However, just because there may be problems with syntax, we do not mean that simple sentences are always to be preferred. A well-developed complex sentence can be just as clear as a series of short ones, perhaps even more so. Indeed, subtle ideas or shades of meaning may be lost in simple sentences.

It is probable that among the characteristics of good oral style, the vividness in language that is achieved through the stylistic devices used to decorate and to embellish ideas does the most to add interest value to a speech.

First, consider the *level* of embellishment used. To a degree, you can determine how embellished the style of a speech is by comparing the language with that of other speakers in similar situations. Consider next what *kinds* of figures of style the speaker tends to use. President John F. Kennedy, for example, became well known for his use of antithesis. Some speakers make extensive use of metaphor, others do not.

In addition to humor (when it occurs) and vividness, any device that a speaker uses to heighten the interest of an audience can contribute to the success of the speech. For instance, *suspense* is created when speakers withhold for a time the information required to forecast the final outcome of what they are talking about. As long as listeners are guessing, they are interested. Curiosity, the desire for information, is not the exclusive property of monkeys, cats, and children.

An interest in *conflict* also seems to be natural. The popularity of sports, fights, and Western movies on television is a case in point. All sports involve competition in one form or another, and the essence of competition is conflict, hence the popularity of sports. Anything that suggests a fight draws interest, whether it is a schoolyard brawl, a chess game, professional boxing, or athletic teams in competition. Speakers create a similar interest when the language they use suggests conflict or struggle. And, since conflicts, like crime stories and jokes, have outcomes that listeners want to know, by timing the revelation of the outcome to create suspense, a speaker can heighten the interest further still.

Delivery   The facial expressions, gestures, vocal quality, and vocal emphasis of a speaker are all agents of communication that tell the listener what the speaker wants to say. The police officer holds up her hand to say "Stop." When the Indian of the Western movie holds up his hand, he means "Peace." Whether a speaker smiles or frowns, speaks loudly or softly, emphasizes one word or another, it says something to the audience.

In analyzing a speaker's delivery, you must judge whether gesture, facial expression, vocal quality, and loudness are coordinated with the ideas of the speech; whether they constitute emphasis or mere exhibition. Ask these questions:

1. Do the gestures, vocal quality, and other elements of delivery help to communicate the speaker's meaning?
2. Do they draw attention to themselves?
3. Is the delivery an aid or a hindrance in eliciting the meaning the speaker wants the listener to have?

Synthesis

When your analysis is complete, you know what the speaker has done with the various elements of the speech: the argument, value appeals, credibility, organization, style, and delivery. But you end up with a list of separate and independent items, each of which is a reaction to a different aspect of the speech, and some of which have greater significance than others. Just to go through your list, making isolated comments on argument or style or delivery, would give a reader or listener a jumbled notion of what your analysis had discovered. Some kind of synthesis is needed to form the series of isolated comments into a unified conception of the whole. The following four steps will help you to synthesize your analysis around a central idea that describes what the speaker's central strategy is, and how the strategy was aided (or perhaps hindered) by the way in which the speaker developed it.

1. Describe the central strategy of the speech—the plan by which the speaker tried to move the audience toward the goal of the speech.
2. Determine what specific elements of the speech are used to support this strategy.
3. Note any elements of the speech that detract from the strategy.

For one speaker, an argumentative development may be the central strategy: the basic appeal is to reason; the speaker generates credibility by building the image of a "reasonable" person. Another strategy will emphasize the trustworthiness of the speaker and other rhetorical elements will be subservient to credibility. Still another speaker may create a rhetorical strategy centered in the deeply felt values of the audience. This strategy reveals itself through the emphasis given to some particular value appeal throughout the speech and especially at critical junctures.

Jimmy Carter's presidential campaign in 1976 has been synthesized in this way:

> The dominant theme throughout Carter's rhetoric is his conception of the people as a repository of innate moral quality, competence, and potential for the future. Carter consistently characterizes the people in terms of their intrinsic goodness. . . . For Carter emphasis upon the innate goodness of the people clearly becomes the very foundation for politics. That is, the representation of the people is never simply an abstract or isolated concept since by its very nature it posits the aims of political action and evokes a vision of society restructured to reflect the humane aspects of its inhabitants. . . .
>
> In short, by portraying the people in terms of their intrinsic goodness Carter sets himself apart from other political leaders. The characterization of the people is thus used both to underscore the nature of the current political situation and, simultaneously, to identify grounds for the recovery of trust in government.
>
> Carter's view of the inherent character of the people and the moral qualities related to that character becomes the means by which particular audiences are united with a universal one.[4]

Judgment

Judgment follows naturally from your synthesis of the data you have gathered in making your analysis, and it is the natural culmination of the evaluative process. But every decision requires some standard of judgment. Several methods of evaluation have been advanced by writers on rhetorical criticism. You are the best judge of which one you want to use in any particular case. The important thing is to understand the requirements of the standard you elect to use and to apply it consistently. These four are the most common: effect, artistic merit, historical significance, and ethical worth.[5]

Effect   Some theorists maintain that a critic should only make judgments about the immediate and long-range *effects* of a speech on a listener and on society. Only the most naive evaluation of effects considers the merit of a speech to depend solely on whether it succeeded in getting the audience to do what the speaker wanted. One speech, standing alone, may have little discernible effect, but the results of a series of speeches may be cumulative. A speech, moreover, may produce results that the speaker did not even intend but that nonetheless introduce noticeable changes into society. It may be that in a particular case a speech has no significant effect because no adequate means of persuasion are available to the speaker. Nor does counting votes after an election necessarily determine the more effective speaker.

Judging by effect is based on an analysis of how well the speaker's strategy may have been appropriate to the situation and the audience. What characteristics of the speech situation might make the speaker's task more difficult? The reputation of the opponent? That was the case for Adlai E. Stevenson in 1952 when he (a little-known governor of Illinois) ran for President against Dwight D. Eisenhower, one of America's war heroes. The events of the recent past? Even though President Gerald Ford was better known than Jimmy Carter in 1976, he had been appointed Vice President by Richard Nixon, who resigned in disgrace. After Ford became President, he pardoned Nixon. Furthermore, Ford was challenged in a bruising Republican primary by Ronald Reagan. All these factors may have been as important in his defeat as anything he or Carter said. Thus, to judge by the standard of effect, you must assess the rhetorical situation at the time of the speech and consider how well the speech met that situation.

Despite its limitations, effects evaluation has strong support in the critical community. Here is an example from Marie Hochmuth Nichols' analysis of Abraham Lincoln's First Inaugural address:

> Any fair-minded critic, removed from the passions of the times, must find himself much more in agreement with those observers of the day who believed the inaugural met the "requirements of good rhetoric" by having "right words in their right places" and "right words at the right times," than with those who labeled it "feeble rhetorical stuff," and found it "inferior in point of elegance, perspicuity, vigor, talent, and all the graces of composition to any other paper of a like character from a President of the Republic." One who studies the revisions in phrase and word in the various drafts of the Inaugural must become aware that Lincoln was concerned not only with using the right argument, but with using words cautiously, and purposefully, to obtain a desired effect from his listeners and from his potential readers. To the rhetorician, style is not an aspect of language which can be viewed in isolation or judged merely by the well-attuned ear. Nor is it sufficient to apply such rubrics as clarity, vividness, elegance as absolute values, or as an adequate description of style. Words are an "available means of persuasion," and the only legitimate question is: Did Lincoln use words effectively to achieve his specific purpose?[6]

Artistic Merit   Some speech critics insist that the proper measure of quality is not how effective a speech may have been, but rather what level of artistic merit it achieved; in other words, how successfully it applied the principles of the art.

Every art form has recognized principles that govern the production of its artifacts. All of these rules, of course, are concerned with the way the substantive content of the art work is communicated. In painting, a visual art, the rules are related to line, form, color, and composition. In music, the rules have to do with tonality and harmony—all of the elements of sound: pitch, force, time, and quality.

For almost 2000 years, it was the practice to evaluate speeches by applying standards appropriate to *literary* criticism: the universality of the central idea, the unity of the structure, the level of the style. Students of Greek and Latin study the speeches of Demosthenes and Cicero primarily as exemplars of classical standards and only incidentally as masterpieces of influential public address. Thus, a speech may be judged by the established rules of the art of rhetoric embodied in the canons of invention, disposition, style, and delivery. If we look for examples of relatively modern speeches that have been judged by artistic standards, Abraham Lincoln's "Gettysburg Address" and Martin Luther King, Jr.'s "I Have a Dream" come quickly to mind.

Historical Significance   Sometimes a critic will ask whether the speaker's analysis of the past is accurate. For instance, Karlyn Khors Campbell made this critical evaluation of a speech by President Richard Nixon during the Vietnam War:

> Although this speech fails to meet the President's criteria of truth, credibility, unity, and responsibility, the most significant criticism is that this rhetorical act perpetuates the myths about America, which must be debunked and shattered if we are to find solutions to the problems that threaten imminently to destroy us. The "silent majority" may want to get out of Vietnam and to save face; it cannot have both—at least not quickly.
>
> To avoid Vietnams of the future we must make a concerted effort to discover and scrutinize *non*mythical America. If in that scrutiny we pay particular attention to the rhetorical discourses that thresh out and formulate ideas of ourselves and our society, we may begin to solve the problems of the *real* America and of this shrinking world. That President Nixon is unwilling or unable to face the *real* problems is precisely the reason why this address is doomed to be so disappointing. It is, as almost every commentator has recognized, just "more of the same."[7]

Such an evaluation might also ask whether later history supports what the speaker said. A critic making an evaluation on this basis determines the extent to which the ideas expressed in the speech reflect, lead, or trail behind the society.

Ethical Worth   Judgments are made by some critics as to the ethical worth of what the speaker says. An evaluation of this kind determines the merits of a speech by weighing the speaker's ideas in the balance of the critic's ethical norms.

The excerpt from Campbell's criticism of Nixon, quoted just above, carries much more than a hint of ethical judgment, and standards of historical significance and ethical worth frequently are found together. Kenneth Burke makes an overtly ethical judgment in his analysis of *Mein Kampf*, Adolf Hitler's blueprint for Nazi action:

> Our job, then, our anti-Hitler Battle, is to find all available ways of making the Hitlerite distortions of religion apparent, in order that politicians of his kind in America be unable to perform a similar swindle. The desire for unity is genuine and admirable. The desire for national unity, in the present state of the world, is genuine and admirable. But this unity, if attained on a deceptive basis, by emotional trickeries that shift our criticism from the accurate locus of our trouble, is no unity at all. For, even if we are among those who happen to be "Aryans," we solve no problems even for ourselves by such solutions, since the factors pressing towards calamity remain. Thus, in Germany, after all the upheaval, we see nothing beyond a drive for ever more and more upheaval, precisely because the "new way of life" was no new way, but the dismally oldest way of sheer deception—hence, after all the "change," the factors driving towards unrest are left intact, and even strengthened.[8]

PREPARING THE EVALUATION

Obviously, the form and depth of analysis will differ as situations differ. When you evaluate a classmate's speech, you will have far less time to consider, study, and prepare than when you have several weeks in which to pore over a text and check items in the library before you write a paper. However, the basic approach will be the same. A few general principles will be helpful as you begin to express your evaluative judgments.

Begin with Judgment

Evaluations are what your listeners or readers are most interested in. Avoid at all cost the "laundry list" analysis ("He said this, . . . then this, . . . then this. . . .") Center on two or three important evaluative statements about what you regard as good or poor in the speech.

Relate Judgment to Synthesis

Reveal in your evaluation that you see the strategy of the speech. Reconstruct, if necessary, the situation that led you to your judgment. Show how individual judgments join to provide an overall impression of the speech.

Support Synthesis and Judgment with Analysis

To say merely that something was good or bad, or that it was central to the persuasive effort, is not enough. Your evaluation must show how arguments, values, credibility, style, delivery, or structure illustrate the strategy of the speech. Of course, you won't use everything you have discovered through your analysis, but only what is necessary to support your judgment.

Analysis, synthesis, and judgment—the three elements of speech evaluation—are closely comparable to the elements of communication discussed in earlier chapters. Your judgments are like the specific purposes of a speech. They identify what you want the audience to know or to believe. Synthesis identifies major points and gives order to your evaluation. Your analysis provides the specific supporting materials necessary to understand your judgment. It is equally incumbent on speaker and critic to have something to say and to say it well.

SUMMARY

Evaluating the speeches of others helps you to improve your own speaking and listening skills. It also gives you insight into the significance of the speaking situation and a better understanding of human beings and their concerns.

There are three steps to speech criticism: analysis, synthesis, and judgment. In the analysis stage you look for the central claim of the speaker and the arguments, evidence, values, and credibility which support that claim. As a part of your analysis you will want to examine the structure of the speech to see if it has unity, order, and coherence. You will look at the language and style for clarity and interest. And, when possible, you will analyze the delivery.

When you synthesize this analysis you define the central strategy of the speech, and determine which specific elements of the speaker's technique are most important supports for the strategy and which detract from it.

Judgment is made on the basis of one, or a combination, of four standards: effect, artistic merit, historical significance, and ethical worth.

In preparing the evaluation you begin your statement with judgment. You point up the relationship of the synthesis to the judgment. The analysis supplies the evidence that supports both the synthesis and the judgment.

NOTES

1. Elizabeth Myette Coughlin and Charles Edward Coughlin, "Convention in Petticoats: The Seneca Falls Declaration of Women's Rights," *Today's Speech*, **21** (Fall 1973), p. 20.
2. Cathy A. Sandeen and Malcolm O. Sillars, "Stay the Course," *Exitasis*, **7** (Feb. 1983), pp. 13–37.
3. Martin Luther King, Jr., *Contemporary American Speeches*, Wil A. Linkugel, R. R. Allen, Richard L. Johannesen, eds. (Dubuque, Iowa: Kendall-Hunt, 1982), p. 367.
4. John H. Patton, "A Government as Good as Its People: Jimmy Carter and the Restoration of Transcendence to Politics," *Quarterly Journal of Speech*, **63** (Oct. 1977), pp. 250–254.
5. See Robert Cathcart, *Post Communication* (Indianapolis, Ind.: Bobbs-Merrill, 1981), pp. 26–30.
6. Marie Hochmuth Nichols, "Lincoln's First Inaugural," *American Speeches*,

Wayland Maxfield Parrish and Marie Hochmuth Nichols, eds. (New York: David McKay, 1954), pp. 65–66.

7. Karlyn Kohrs Campbell, *Critiques of Contemporary Rhetoric* (Belmont, Calif.: Wadsworth, 1972), pp. 56–57.

8. Kenneth Burke, *The Philosophy of Literary Form* (New York: Vintage Books, 1957), pp. 188–189.

EXERCISES

1. Act as a critic for one of your classmates' speeches. In your oral criticism explain what you believe to be the two greatest strengths and the two greatest weaknesses of the speech. Give specific examples to support your judgment.

2. Listen to a speech by some local person (your minister, for instance) and write an evaluation of the speech.

3. With a group of classmates, prepare and hold a group discussion evaluating a speech delivered on television by some nationally known person.

4. Write an evaluation of a speech of historical importance, such as Abraham Lincoln's "Second Inaugural Address," Booker T. Washington's "Atlanta Exposition Address," or Franklin D. Roosevelt's "Declaration of War." Emphasize the ways in which the same speech delivered today might be differently received.

5. Hear a speech by a person appearing on campus and write a paper on some phase of speech analysis assigned by your instructor.

APPENDIXES

APPENDIXES

appendix A

Speech Subject Areas

The following list is intended to stimulate your thinking about a speech subject. It is only suggestive. You will not find your specific purpose here, but one of the general topics may remind you of a topic of interest to you and your audience.

Education

Large universities
Private versus public education
Teaching a child to read
Federal aid to education
Vocational education
Education in another country
Grading systems
Vocational aptitude
Community colleges
Campus political parties
Small colleges

Progressive education
Revisions in the high schools
Foreign languages
Student government
Changes in education
Mathematics aptitude
Honors programs
Middle schools
Counseling
Drop-outs
Cheating

World Politics

Nuclear disarmament
United Nations
Israel and the Arabs
Japan's economy
Dictators
Alaska and Russia
Iran
International spies
Underdeveloped countries

Afghanistan
Africa
China
Cuba
Canada and the United States
India
Russia's army
Past wars
Propaganda

Soviet leaders
American tourists
Yugoslavia

Ambassadors
Satellite nations
Southeast Asia

National Politics

Deficit spending
Labor unions
Constitutional amendments
Antitrust laws
Electoral College
Lobbying
Social welfare
Wiretapping
Pump-priming
Balance of payments
Impeachment

Conservation
Revision of the Supreme Court
How different are the parties?
Ex-Presidents
Filibustering
State offices
Public power
Withholding tax
Civil disobedience
Military training
Political action committees

Science

Great scientists
Ants
Microscopes
Photosynthesis
Growth
Space travel
Psychiatry and psychology
Radiation
Organ transplants

Should nonscientists study science?
Solid state physics
Butterflies
Cell division
Perception
Dentistry
Fission
Disease
Computers

Humanities

Great writers
Recent novels
Understanding poetry
Sculpture
Does history repeat?
Civil war
Transcendentalism
Semantics
Popular fiction
Huck Finn
Sigmund Freud
The Trent affair
American humor

The study of history
Liberal versus technical education
Modern art
"Time spent in reading is time lost
from living"
Rationalism
Bertrand Russell
Modern music
Representational versus abstract art
Morality in art
Should a novel have a happy ending?
Movies made from novels

Society

Hopi Indians
"All men are created equal"
Police
Personal liberty
Distinctive features of American society

Child molestation
Censorship
Poverty
New roles for women
Double standard
Are Americans disliked?

Television give-away programs
Advertising
Popular music
Racial barriers
Human beings are unalike
Social Security
Marriage laws
Population explosion

High salaries for athletes
Polish wedding
"A woman's place is in the house"
Traffic accidents
Capital punishment
Juvenile criminals
Divorce
Abortion

Religion

Election of the Pope
What is a saint?
Varieties of Judaism
"The Great Awakening"
Islam
Hinduism
Psychology and religion
Education of the clergy
Symbolism of the Mass

Sermons in Protestantism
Puritanism in New England
Religious wars
Zoroastrianism
Confucianism
Science and religion
Buddhism
Evolution versus divine creation
Religion and politics

Definitions

Capitalism
Great Plains
Liberal education
Morality
Ethics
Rumor
Gossip

New Yorker
Loyalty
American
Individualism
Success
Socialism
Communism

Speeches for Study

INFORMATIVE SPEECHES

"The How and Why of Old Faithful"[1]

CHARLES F. PETERS
California State University: Northridge

When the American mountain men of the early eighteen hundreds, men like Jedediah Smith, Jim Bridger and Hugh Glass, came out of the West they brought with them incredible tales. "High in the Rockies," they said, "was a land where the earth boiled under your feet, where spouts of hot water as tall as a flagpole came roaring out of the trembling ground, and whole valleys streamed with sulphurous fumes as if the lid over Hell itself had been shot full of holes."

These early descriptions astounded the folks on the eastern seaboard and taxed their credulity but they cause us no surprise today. What our forebears had watched in awe we know were the geysers of Yellowstone. All of us have read about these. Many of us have actually seen, at least in travel films or pictures if not in person, the most famous, "Old Faithful."

But for many of us the working of this geological phenomenon is just as mysterious as it was to Jim Bridger. It interested me enough to try to find out the how and why of geysers and you may be interested in what I learned about these natural fountains which intermittently erupt, hurling steam, boiling water, and sometimes mud to great heights above the surface. The particular theory I'm going to discuss is not the only explanation of how a geyser works but it's the oldest and most widely accepted. It was proposed in 1847, interestingly enough, by Robert Bunsen, the German chemist who invented the Bunsen burner.

Beneath the geyser's mouth is the geyser well, which is made up of a network of underground channels. These channels may be from ten to one hundred feet deep. The geyser well usually goes down a short distance as a single channel and then branches into many offshoots. These offshoots may be contorted and twist about each other. They may be jagged and narrow in some places, and broad enough to form large subterranean cavities in others. Most passages are between one and five feet in diameter.

Molten igneous rock material beneath the geyser well furnishes the heat that keeps the well and its water at a high temperature.

All levels of the well have a delicate balance between the temperature of and the pressure on the water. The water temperature on the surface is nearly 100 degrees centigrade, while on the bottom it is above 270 degrees. The hotter water near the bottom of the well does not boil or vaporize because of the pressure caused by the water above it. This variation of temperatures within the well is possible only because there is no *convection* to transfer the temperatures around evenly. That is, there can be no mass movement or currents because of the contorted and restricted nature of the passages that form the well. If there were convection, we would have a boiling spring, where all the water boils evenly, instead of a geyser, where the variable pressure situation causes an eruption. The eruption itself occurs when the temperature of the water near the bottom of the well becomes great enough to vaporize the water, and the resulting bubbles of steam become trapped in the crooked passages near the bottom. Under these conditions one cubic inch of water will vaporize into fifty cubic inches of steam. Thus, some water wells up and runs over at the mouth of the geyser. This loss of water eases the pressure throughout the entire column and permits water at all levels of the well to flash into steam. The enormous pressure caused by the new steam forces the boiling water out of the channel network and into the air, sometimes as high as two hundred feet.

After the eruption the well immediately begins to refill. Some of the erupted water drops back into the well. Subsurface water seeps into the well through permeable rocks and fissures, or water may run into the well from a nearby hot spring. When this new water flows into the well, it does not immediately boil: If it did we would have nothing but a steaming vent. Rather, the water goes back into the pressure relationships I have already described and the cycle begins again.

The interval between eruptions varies from ten minutes to several weeks. Its length depends upon such things as the rate at which the channel network refills, the proximity of the well to its source of heat, the amount of constriction in the well passages, the size of the entire channel network, and the amount of steam that escapes through the rocks that form the geyser well.

It would seem that the eruption of a geyser, then, is neither a mysterious nor an unexplainable occurrence as the early mountain men thought, but is rather an ordered process of nature where the balance between temperature and pressure in a geyser well and the peculiar configurations of the channels of that well determine how frequent, how high, and how faithful Old Faithful's eruptions will be.

"Country Western Music"[2]

ARNOLD ROSENTHAL
California State University: Northridge

You've heard it said that the kind of music we call jazz originated in the United States, and it did. But there's another kind of music that was born and raised in America. It's country music, country western music to be more specific: music of the common man, truck driver music, cowboy music, hillbilly music and honky-tonk music.

In all its guises and forms, bluegrass, heart songs, western ballads, delta white soul, Memphis honky-tonk and, of course, the pop hybrid known as the Nashville sound, country music is growing astronomically in popularity and there's no sign that its popularity is going to stop. Today, for example, people like you and me spend $400 million a year to buy recordings of it. That's a fifth of the $2 billion spent in annual record sales.

It seems to me that anything in our culture that commands that much interest and is worth that much money is worth knowing a little something about. So let's look at the origin of country music, its popularity and present appeal, and the underlying significance of one of America's authentic art forms.

When people started to settle in our country, they brought with them, among other assets, their music. These settlers lived in separate communities many miles from each other and connected by poor roads. For the most part they had to entertain themselves. The most significant form of entertainment they had came from themselves. It was their music. The music they brought with them has changed very little since then and is referred to today as "folk music" or "rural music." This music told stories about their trials and tribulations and was handed down from generation to generation. It was either sung with no accompaniment or with instruments brought with them from where they had come.

[Slide of original instruments]

These instruments consisted of guitars, mandolins, violins, banjos, flutes, a washboard, spoons, or even two sticks of firewood. I mean anything they could get their hands on could be used as an instrument. Here's an example of one of these folk songs . . . "Down by the Riverside" as done by Peter Seeger:

[Taped recording]

Folk music remained pretty much the same until 1917 when America entered World War I. As a result of the war, cultural exchanges took place among the soldiers who had come from all over the country, bringing with them, of course, their own special brands of music. At the same time, radio was coming into its own, and beginning to experiment with recorded music. It is essentially these two events, the war and radio, which brought about a metamorphosis of folk music into country music.

Country music's first superstar came in 1927. He was Jimmie Rodgers, the Singing Brakeman from Meridian, Mississippi. He worked most of his life on the railroad. It's interesting to note that he was most influenced by work-gang blacks. In fact, his first hit song, "The Blue Yodel," reflects this influence. This is what it sounded like:

[Taped recording]

The early thirties witnessed not only the depression but a definite turning point in country music's history. It was now apparent that a country boy, singing about his kind of life, could fall into some big money if he merely learned a few tricks.

[Slide of cowboys]

The cowboy movies began bringing big money to former hillbilly singers such as Gene Autry, Roy Rogers, and Tex Ritter. They carried cowboy music into the nation's big cities. Western swing, heavy on the fiddle, and made for dancing, developed in Texas with a Mexican influence.

[Slide of newer instruments]

There were new instruments and new techniques for playing them: the steel guitar, drums, bass fiddle and the electric guitar, just to mention a few.

World War II brought country music not only to people of this country, but to people all over the world. For example, in Japan and in Europe today, country music ranks high as one of the most popular forms of entertainment. By the time the war ended, the Grand Ole Opry had become an institution and country music had branched out to the point that it had borrowed the ears of the nation and the world.

If Jimmie Rodgers was the first big solo singing star in country music, then Hank Williams was the second. He was more fortunate than Rodgers in that he came along when the nation was hungry for entertainment and had the money to pay for it. Williams was born in 1923 on a tenant farm in Mt. Olive, Alabama. Typical of so many country musicians, the strong early musical influences on him were the fundamental churches and the southern black street singers. And here's one of his most remembered songs, "Cheatin' Heart":

[Taped recording]

Country music was sailing right along, doing its own thing, having a ball, until Rock 'N' Roll changed everything. Rock snuck up and hit before anybody knew what was going on. It was the beginning of an era that is only now coming into full bloom. In the fifties, in other words, the kids took over and their leader was a snarling ex-hillbilly singer by the name of Elvis Presley:

[Slide of Elvis Presley]

Elvis had been raised on a farm near Tupelo, Mississippi, and was country, jazz, blues, and gospel, all rolled into one. He thumped bass fiddle on stage at the Opry at one point and wailed Assembly of God songs back home at another. After hacking out a living as a truck driver, he got to Memphis in 1954 and a recording contract with Sun Records. He recorded this song and the world was ready for him:

[Taped recording—"Mystery Train"]

The country boom, of course, has reverberated far beyond its historic home in Nashville, Tennessee—you hear it in Bakersfield, California, which is known for the scruffier, less-polished sound of Merle Haggard and such other stars as Buck Owens and Freddie Hart. There is another Nashville satellite—Austin, Texas, where Willie Nelson, Jerry Jeff Walker and Michael Murphy are exponents of what might be called progressive country, which has a strong hint of rock.

But, Nashville remains the capital. The Grand Ole Opry has now moved into a new $15 million auditorium at the Disneyesque Opryland, U.S.A., boasting such country artists as: Tammy Wynette, Dolly Parton, Charlie Rich, Charley Pride, Johnny Rodriquez, Waylon Jennings, Tom T. Hall, George Jones, and Johnny Cash.

Country music is a growing phenomenon. With durable syndicated programs like "Hee Haw" and "The Porter Wagoner Show," as well as several annual specials, network TV is hardly ignoring the trend. But the most dramatic illustration of all lies in pop radio. In 1961, the number of stations playing nothing but country stood at a mere 80; now there are over a thousand.

Country music has always been the cry of the common man. Today, however, country music is taking on a new sound and a new diversity of messages as well. This year we are celebrating our 200th anniversary, our Bicentennial, and I can't think of anything more American than America's musical art form: Country Western Music, U.S.A., music of the people, by the people, and for the people. In fact, I've gotten into the act myself by writing my own country song and this is how it goes:

> Well, I'm the world's first Jewish country singer,
> That's what I'm gonna be,
> From Hollywood to Nashville,
> We'll have a Jew . . . Balee,
> I can sing them country songs like all them stars do,
> Cause if Charley Pride can make it, Johnny Rodriquez, too,
> There ain't no reason on Heaven or Earth
> Why Arnold Rosenthal can't make it too.

"The Battle of the Bugs"[3]

STEVE E. CHAPMAN
Colorado State University

In the arena of insect pest control, we have in the far corner the chemical companies and in the near corner are the proponents of biocontrol which include environmentalists, entomologists, and health officials. Both groups have been strongly fighting over the controversy of whether chemical control of insects should be replaced by biocontrol. Biocontrol methods include the use of predators and microbes of the insect pests. Predators can include other insects, birds, fish, rodents, and the microbes can be viruses, bacteria, funguses, and protozoa that attack the insect pest.

In this speech I hope to present you with the issues at the heart of this controversy. These issues are: Is there a significant problem with using chemicals to control insects? Are the chemical companies to blame for these problems? Will the alternative of biocontrol eliminate such problems? And finally, will the benefits of using biocontrol justify the costs of their implementation?

Let us start with the first issue on whether there are significant problems associated with using chemicals to control insects. Both sides agree on the problem that chemicals can cause health problems. The persistent chemicals such as DDT, chlordane, and dieldrin have been documented by the EPA and many health organizations to cause nervous system disorders. The disorders have especially been found in people who apply and are in frequent contact with such chemicals. Both sides, however, are waiting on the results of possible long term health effects associated with chemical use.

The chemical companies and biocontrol proponents also agree on the problem that sustained use of a certain chemical can cause resistance in a population of insects. Resistance is the ability of an insect to detoxify a chemical rendering it harmless to the insect.

As you can see there are problems associated with chemical control, but are the chemical companies to blame for these problems? The biocontrol proponents say that they are while the chemical companies say they are not to blame. The biocontrol proponents back their claim that the chemical companies are at fault by research done by Stephanie Harris of the Public Citizen's Health Group. She stated that the estimated cost of research and development of a single pesticide can cost up to 15 million dollars, with only a fifteenth of that amount being used for studies on toxic effects on animals other than insects. Proponents say that this amount is grossly inadequate and that more money should be set aside for testing of new chemicals for possible health hazards. Their reason being that chemically related health problems can cost a person tens of thousands of dollars in medical treatment. Dr. Capinera, an entomologist at Colorado State University, also stated that chemical companies are not worried about resistance since they can just sell users stronger and more expensive chemicals to combat the insect pests.

On the other hand, chemical companies say they are not to blame. Dow Chemical Company says that all their chemicals are explicitly labeled with safe and proper ways of applying them along with any warnings of potential hazards to the user. They say that if the users follow the directions on the label the health hazards would be practically eliminated. On the question of resistance, Dow Chemical said that chemicals only cause resistance in insects if used more often and in higher dosage than stated on the instructions for their use. The chemicals are developed to be applied a certain way to eliminate this problem of resistance.

So now that we have both sides pointing fingers at each other, will the alternative of biocontrol eliminate the problems associated with chemicals? The biocontrol proponents say that it will solve the problems of health hazards and resistance and the chemical companies are forced to agree. Research and testing have shown that biocontrol agents act only on specific insects in which they kill. An example is the protozoa *Nosema locustae* which can only infect and kill grasshoppers and cannot live in any other animal. Biocontrol agents would also eliminate the problem of resistance. An analogy to this problem would be like a tiger killing a rabbit, if the tiger is hungry enough there isn't anything that rabbit can do. In other words, there is no way to defend against an attack.

Finally, this leads us into the issue of will the benefits of using biocontrol justify the cost of their implementation? This issue is a highly contested one with the biocontrol proponents saying it's effective and economically feasible while the chemical companies say that it will be neither. Biocontrol proponents back up their claim by saying that the benefits are long range control of the pests. The predators and microbes can remain in the system that they are applied to for a long period of time and produce successive generations. An example would be wingless ladybird beetles which remain in the area since they can't fly away and feed on aphids, a major pest of food crops. This would by far offset the initial high cost of implementing many biocontrol agents since it only has to be done once. Chemical companies, however, claim that biocontrol is not effective since most pests, especially aphids, can reproduce under cooler temperatures where biocontrol agents can sometimes not function. Hence, an outbreak of pests can easily happen in cool temperatures. The chemical companies also state that biocontrol agents can be wiped out by environmental conditions such as weather or seasonal changes. They would then have to be reestablished and if it has to be done seasonally could make the costs very prohibitive.

In summary, this controversy over whether biocontrol methods should be used to control insect pests instead of chemicals has both sides agreeing that chemicals can cause health problems and resistance. However, they wholeheartedly disagree on who's to blame. The biocontrol proponents are pointing their fingers at the chemical companies for the cause of these problems, but the chemical companies are blaming the chemical users for not carefully reading the labels. No matter who's to blame, biocontrol proponents say biocontrol would solve the problems of health hazards and resistance and the chemical companies are forced to agree. However, they disagree on the cost of using biocontrol. The proponents of it say that it is effective and cost efficient since it gives long term control. On the other side, the chemical companies argue that it won't work and is too expensive since the whole system depends on the weather which is too variable. In all, the controversy of whether biocontrol should replace chemicals can go into extra rounds with both sides bringing in new research and evidence every day to prove that their side is right.

PERSUASIVE SPEECHES

"Computer Crime but No Punishment"[4]

ANAMARIA LEWIS
Colorado State University

In 1980, a corporation employee sat at his computer terminal to finish some daily work. He was angry because in a few days he had to leave his job. When he sat at his terminal he thought, "I'll get back at them." And he did. He had programmed the computer to destroy all the accounts receivable files six months after he was fired.

This is just one example of what has become a fast growing problem in the United States—computer crime. There are many misconceptions concerning who the computer criminal is, and the nature of computer crime. Today, I would like to discuss these misconceptions and also explore some of the underlying reasons for the widespread nature of this form of crime.

One of the main misconceptions people have concerning the computer criminal is the view that he or she is a deranged person who cannot adjust. Actually this is not the case at all. Here are some characteristics discussed in an *Infosystems* article, "Catching the Computer Crook":

1. He or she is usually a well educated person between the ages of 18 and 30.
2. He or she is outwardly loyal to the company and has never been in trouble.
3. He or she is bright and is challenged by the prospects of beating the system.

In other words, a person just like you and me.

Another misconception that people have about computer crime concerns the nature of the crime. Computer crimes do not just involve the embezzlement of money. They also involve the theft of data (like programs and records), service thefts, the unauthorized use of another's computer time, physical damage to the computer, and sabotage. I gave you one example of sabotage earlier where one person destroyed a whole file. An example of embezzlement is the case where a federal employee stole $500,000 from the Social Security Administration in Washington, D.C. Computer crime is very costly, about $100 million dollars per year according to the Chamber of Commerce of the United States. This cost is paid by the firm and indirectly by you and me.

Why is there such a problem with this form of crime? For one thing, it is very difficult to catch the crook. Most computer crimes go undetected because employers lack the expertise required to catch such a criminal. Auditors have been assigned the task of finding discrepancies within a firm's records, but many times the crime is so well planned and executed that it is difficult for even them to detect. Still another problem is that most victims do not report the crime because they are afraid they will incur more losses from bad publicity. (Many people wonder what kind of company it is that cannot control its own employees or computer system.)

Even the criminal who is caught is usually just given a slight slap on the wrists and sent back out to the working world to be much sought after by firms who want to use the criminal's knowledge to reduce their own security problems. The main problem is that the criminal codes, as they are constructed today, are too narrow to include the computer crime. As a result, many criminals are simply set free since their crime is not considered punishable. For example, Title 18, known as the "Crimes and Criminal Procedures" makes it a crime to walk away with another's property, but the unauthorized use of computer programs or time does not fit this definition. "The Federal Omnibus Crime Control and Safe Streets Act" also excludes computer crimes by making it illegal to electronically intercept oral communication, not written.

Because of the problem with criminal codes, courts are very timid when it comes to prosecuting this type of case because they feel that they and the laws lack the expertise to do justice. An example of the courts' inability to prosecute these cases properly is the case where an engineering student, who stole one million dollars worth of supplies from Pacific Telephone and Telegraph Company, was sentenced to only 40 days imprisonment. Such weak punishments are not going to be a deterrent to many.

These factors compound to make computer crimes a major problem for most industries today. Millions of dollars are spent each year in undoing the damage done by the computer criminal through embezzlement, service crimes, physical damage and sabotage. The computer criminal is quite normal in most respects, and is, therefore, difficult to pick out as a criminal. Also, the perfection in the performance of most of these crimes and the narrowness of existing laws make it difficult to detect and punish these offenders. The main thing that people have to realize is that computer crimes are not committed by computers but by people. Something needs to be done to prevent this crime and reduce the ease of committing the computer crime.

"Effortless Exercise?"[5]

KIM PERRY
University of Northern Iowa

It matters not whether one is young or old, male or female, black or white. The victim is obsessed with single-minded purpose, and will do almost anything to reach their goal. I know I've suffered from this affliction, and I'm sure that you have or know of someone who has, also.

I'm talking about the new American obsession—becoming "fit and trim." Yes, it's great that we're more aware of the importance of exercise and fitness, but unfortunately, we're also seeking lazy alternatives for our overweight and out-of-shape bodies.

Passive exercise is one of the fastest growing gimmicks offering quick fixes to our body bulges. The main promotion involving passive exercise is EMS, electrical muscle stimulators. According to John Grossman, Editor of *Health* magazine, in January, 1983, "the promotion of EMS is reaching nationwide proportions." He claims that "hundreds of health spas, exercise centers, and beauty salons" are attracting "tens of thousands of Americans" to this latest fad. Jim Chandler, a consultant for the Food and Drug Administration, states the worst problem facing his area today is EMS. I'd like to explain what it is, the potential dangers associated with it, why little is currently being done, and what measures should be taken to forestall further problems.

To understand EMS, we must first consider how the device functions, and how it was intended to be used. Electrical muscle stimulators contract muscles involuntarily by delivering an electrical current through electrodes attached to the skin. EMS devices come in various shapes and sizes, and can be found in health centers, or purchased through mail-order firms for $20–$30.

The Food and Drug Administration admits that when EMS devices are used for purposes of physical therapy and medical practices and operated by licensed practitioners, they can be quite effective in relaxing muscle spasms, preventing blood clots, and retarding or preventing muscle atropy from disuse.

While you may not have even heard of the electrical muscle stimulator, many Americans have. Just last month the U.S. Olympic committee reported using EMS to strengthen muscle tone, under carefully guarded conditions.

And with the conflict between the fitness kick yet the increasing awareness of the dangers associated with overdoing such exercise as jogging, even more individuals may turn to EMS. As Ben Yagoda reported in a fitness article in *Esquire,* "The idea of passive exercise has a kind of logical necessity to it. Running is out."

So what are the complications associated with EMS? At least three can be identified; no significant muscle improvement, no cardiovascular benefits, and health hazards caused by improper use. The "muscle toning effects" from EMS devices are basically worthless. The tone only lasts through repeated application, just as exercise must take place at regular intervals. In a recent strength training study at the Human Physiology laboratory in Cupertino, California, Physical Therapists John Romero and Terry Sanford observed 18 female volunteers. They concluded that electrical stimulators had little effect in developing dynamic strength or performance, even in conjunction with weight training.

Not only does EMS fail to strengthen muscles, it may also indirectly contribute to reduced cardiovascular fitness. Dr. Steven Wolfe, editor of the book *Electrotherapy,* stressed that passive exercise would confer absolutely no cardiovascular benefits. People are being lulled into a false sense of fitness, which could stop them from performing the muscle strengthening types of exercise required in a balanced exercise routine.

And aside from the fact that EMS does not really improve muscle strength or promote cardiovascular fitness, many potential hazards are associated with its use.

Numerous problems are caused by the lack of licensing procedures. The AMA requires physical therapists to use electrical muscle stimulators only under certain conditions. But cosmetologists have no higher licensing authority to restrict their use of the devices.

The FDA and District Court Judge William Gray documented examples of hazards from improper use of EMS as including electrical shocks and burns, and health complications to pregnant women, people with heart problems or pacemakers, and those with cancer or epilepsy. Further, the EMS devices should not be placed where a strong current could pass through the heart, brain, or spinal column.

Dr. Steven Wolfe reported that electrical stimulation over the carotid sinuses should also be avoided, to prevent any sudden change in blood pressure. In addition, the gel and tape used to affix the electrodes have caused skin irritations.

In 1970, during a five-month court trial, 40 witnesses testified having suffered varying degrees of injury from a mail-order stimulator. The "Relaxacisor" produced electrical shocks throughout the body. While the FDA did take action, they merely seized the unsold devices—400,000 were already in use. And the FDA refused to place a ban upon further sales.

As of yet, there are no statistics summarizing exactly how many individuals have suffered pain or disfigurement from EMS. It seems to be such a relatively new problem that people fail to realize it is causing such ill effects, or victims either don't know where to report their difficulties, or feel too foolish to do so.

So in consideration of the intended uses and actual abuses of EMS, why isn't something being done to stop these multimillion-dollar industries from flourishing, at the expense of our pocketbooks and our health?

At the present time, FDA authority is limited for three reasons. First, as occurred in the Relaxacisor case, the FDA only has authority to seize not to ban. Second, any actions must be taken after the fact. With currently insufficient FDA funding, it will be some time before EMS will be thoroughly investigated. Third, the very basis upon which the FDA may order seizure is fraught with legal loopholes. As was exemplified with the "Figure Tron" device, the FDA attacked its false advertising claims, and not its risk to health. Clever promoters have merely become more careful with how they phrase their advertising claims.

Uninformed consumers are lulled into purchasing EMS devices in at least three ways. Advertising assurances are the first reason. Alice Shaefer, President of the mail-order firm Slendertone, admits that there is no proof of the effectiveness of her device. But as she states, "People are used to superlatives, if you simply say it's good, safe, and well designed." Second, consumers avoid the expense of lawsuits by resting on the promises of a "money back guarantee," and third, John Grossman described many examples of consumers who thought they saw some types of improvement. In reality, a sort of "placebo effect" was taking over.

So "tens of thousands" of untrained consumers are continually buying EMS devices. How can we stop this growing epidemic? First, I believe that the general public needs to be informed of the underlying facts behind EMS. In fact, we should forbid sales of EMS to untrained members of the general public. Its very availability is an invitation for further injuries to occur. The old expression, "Let the buyer beware" is callous in this instance, where human health is at risk. Second, stricter licensing procedures should restrict operation to licensed practitioners. Health spas and athletic programs could continue to use EMS only if their operators seek the necessary training and medical knowledge. Such regulations could be passed by either the FDA or state legislatures. And third, while you may assert, "I'll never be persuaded into using a gimmick like EMS," don't be so certain that friends or relatives might not be tempted to do so. You can find out whether health spas in your area are using EMS. While you may not be thrilled about writing another letter to your "Congressperson," you can certainly ask your local Health Department or city council to investigate the use of this device.

I hope you now have a clearer understanding of what EMS is, its definite hazards, and steps which the FDA, the state legislatures, and we can take to stop such hazards from arising. Most of you know the only way you can fit back into your size 9 dress or your favorite blue jeans is by proper diet and exercise. Yet it's clear that the problems we've seen to date are merely "early warning signals" and will multiply with the growth in the use of EMS. So if you're tempted to be an armchair jogger, maybe it's time to get out of your chair and into your jogging suit, or even your swimsuit. Who knows, you may find it "stimulating!"

"The Food and Drug Administration: A Barrier to Progress and Innovation?"[6]

DIANE MILLER
Vanderbilt University

Felice Abrams is a six-year-old child from Ohio who had suffered for years from epileptic seizures. Felice received no medical relief until 1978 when her father flew her to England to receive injections of Sodium Valporate, the only drug that could control her violent seizures. An astonishing illustration? Not really; you see, Felice is not alone. She is only one of the thousands of Americans referred to in the June, 1977 issue of *Newsweek* who have had to flee to other countries or import drugs illegally in order to seek medical relief.

Los Angeles cardiologist Dr. Myrvin Ellestad believes that "it's a national scandal that our patients are deprived of lifesaving drugs available elsewhere in the world."

My purpose is to suggest that the United States' drug development is lagging behind that of other countries at the cost of the medical well-being of all American patients. Nevertheless, the answers to three simple questions concerning the complex policies, procedures, and regulations of the Food and Drug Administration would foster the more rapid and efficient development of lifesaving and essential drugs. Is the excessive caution on the part of the Food and Drug Administration truly necessary? Is the Bureaucratic red tape which undermines the approval process justified? Can the inefficient administration personnel within the Food and Drug Administration be corrected?

According to the March, 1983 issue of *Health* magazine, excessive caution and its implicit restrictions has increased since the freak Thalidomide incident of the 1960's. *Science* magazine states that during that generation babies were born with phocomelia, the absence of one or more limbs, because their mothers had taken the sedative during pregnancy. Since this tragedy, the Food and Drug Administration has been locked into a mindset which absolutely mandates playing it safe prior to the distribution of any new drug. The implications of the current Food and Drug Administration's policy of extreme caution are explained by Dr. Franco Muggia in *The American Journal of Medicine,* September, 1981. He writes that escalating restrictions at all stages of drug development threaten to paralyze clinical investigation. The human cost is substantial in terms of morbidity and mortality. He maintains that the Food and Drug Administration's procedures are drastically restricting progress in cancer research. The Food and Drug Administration's restrictions have also undermined progress in cardiovascular medicine. According to *Newsweek,* in the last few years the Food and Drug Administration has unnecessarily blocked the introduction of at least twelve major heart drugs which are being successfully used abroad, while *Core Concepts in Health* states that over four million Americans have heart disease and at least 600,000 Americans will die of heart disease this year. Dr. Emil

J. Freirich commented in *The American Journal of Medicine* that "What is desperately needed is innovation and development, not regulation."

The Thalidomide incident and its subsequent policy of excessive caution has also prompted the Food and Drug Administration to distrust foreign drug studies. Gregory Ahart, Director of the Human Resources Division, testified before our Congress that the United States has rarely if ever used any foreign studies. The outcome of the questionable policy can easily be demonstrated. For example, French physicians successfully prescribed Sodium Valporate to treat epilepsy for eleven years before the United States approved the same drug; nevertheless, the United States ignored all of France's studies. Research performed by Dr. William Wardell, Director of Drug Studies at the University of Rochester Medical Center, has established that a wider variety of drugs are available in other countries because their drug development is more rapid. From 1962 to 1971, Dr. Wardell compared the drug development of the United States to that of the United Kingdom, two countries with analogous testing and safety standards. He reported that the United Kingdom developed nearly four times as many drugs than did the United States. During this same period, of the drugs marketed in both countries, 77% were available in Britain three years earlier than in the U.S.

At first glance, the Food and Drug Administration's precautions seem reasonable, given the potential adverse side effects of new drugs. But a review of the clinical investigation process, which is needed to test a drug's safety, reveals the damaging and time consuming process of the red tape jungle.

A drug must first be tested on animals in order to determine the drug's pharmacological properties and potential harmful effects. The Food and Drug Administration insists on knowing every detail of the drug, all the "hows" and "whys" of its performance—every chemical reaction. Do you know that no one really knows exactly how or why aspirin works? Fortunately, aspirin was in our system before the Food and Drug Administration matured into the bureaucratic machine that presently exists. Once the hows and whys are finally answered by the first level of testing, then and only then can a drug be tested on human patients. Dr. Muggia complains that there is simply too much delay before a drug is introduced into the rigorous arena of human experimentation. He points out that many adverse effects, including toxicities, have a disappointing predictive value in routine studies. Therefore, the time consuming process of complying with the red tape is seemingly counterproductive. There is little justification for test delays when the tests fail to provide reliable conclusive results. One must realize that all drugs have some risks. Dr. Ahart and many others have argued that the extremes of the Thalidomide incident could have been prevented, not by zealous testing, but by post-marketing surveillance, or more simply stated, studying the marketed drug. Then any uncommon adverse reactions can be detected immediately and corrective action can be taken.

The final deficiency in the Food and Drug Administration is the inefficiency and poor organization of the agency. Dr. Louis Lasagna, Professor of Pharmacology and Toxicology, states that the members more often than not "combine a lack of scientific sophistication with a paranoid hatred of the drug industry and an abiding distrust of clinical investigators." Most countries, including the United Kingdom, have medical experts who have the authority to make the final decision on a drug's approval, while the United States only has medical advisors who have very little input into the final decision. Donald Kennedy, the present commissioner, is not even a physician. Dr. Lasagna comments that because the Food and Drug Administration's members are unaware of medical terminology and chemical reactions, it takes them an unnecessarily long time to review drug studies.

The problems within the Food and Drug Administration are quite pronounced. Excessive caution, bureaucratic red tape and inefficient administrative personnel extend the lag time for the development of lifesaving and essential drugs. Because the Food and Drug Act allows the Food and Drug Administration to require evidence of both safety and efficiency, then the fault is not with the law, but with the way it is implemented. The most reasonable solution is a three-step proposal to change the structure and organization of the Food and Drug Administration without threatening the safety of our drugs. These changes are rather simplistic and could easily be authorized by Congressional legislation or administrative directives.

We must promote the use of data from proven drug studies of medically respected foreign countries. Dr. Ahart's Congressional testimony suggests that foreign studies and data can be used to complement, yet not substitute domestic studies. His research indicates that this minor alteration will save an abundance of time and clinical tests.

We must promote the implementation of post-marketing surveillance or rather monitor the patient's reaction to the marketed drug in order to prevent widespread catastrophe while allowing the drug to be marketed sooner. Dr. Lasagna points out that a lot that one wants to know about a drug is only discoverable after it has been marketed in the naturalistic setting of the real world. Dr. Ahart reported that post-marketing surveillance is an effective and positive technique used by other countries, including the United Kingdom, which have a more rapid drug development process. This solution also "gives the regulatory agency more confidence in being able to accept a lower number of clinical trials in the testing stages of new drug development."

We must promote the reorganization of the Food and Drug Administration with medical experts as the drug reviewers with the authority to make the final decision on a drug's approval. Dr. Lasagna points out that the "system would proceed more widely and smoothly if matters of drug development and regulation received the guidance and attention they deserve from the most knowledgeable members of our society"—the licensed physician. This way, more time will be spent in deciding and analyzing and less time spent in learning.

The impact of the drug lag affects the entire American population. Because of the time and money involved in drug development, the drug industry is becoming economically discouraged and clinical investigation is practically at a halt. Yet, our health problems seem to be worsening. We must weight the value of strict clinical testing in relation to victims of rare, incurable and painful diseases—victims who, like Felice Abrams, are desperately begging to try new medicines that their physicians have confidence in. To them, any hope is some hope.

SPEECH TO ENTERTAIN
"The Wonderful World of College"[7]

IAN FIELDING
California State University: Northridge

On September 15, 1952 my parents were married. On September 16, 1952 they began saving for my college education. By the time I was born nearly ten years later, and why it took ten years is another story entirely, my parents had accumulated $12,564.52. My fate had been sealed. I was going to college whether I wanted to or not. My only trouble was that I did not. By the time I was eighteen and ready to make my reluctant entrance into college, kicking and screaming all the way, my folks had amassed $189,214.87, all of it for my education. That may seem like an awful lot of money but several years earlier my parents had joined organized crime. Even so, Mom and Dad scrimped and saved and sacrificed and for twenty eight years cheated on their income tax just so I could go to college. That's why I knew in the summer of my eighteenth year that I would have one heck of a tough time telling my father I didn't want to go to college. I knew it would hurt him, even shock him, but I had to tell him. It was a lovely funeral. That fall, out of respect for my father's memory and under threat of severe bodily injury from my mother, I entered college. I was hysterical, but I entered college.

Yes, college. That grand and venerable institution of higher education. Today, I'd like to discuss three aspects of college life: the academic part of college, college professors (God love 'em), and social life in college. By doing this I hope we can all come to the understanding that there is life during college. It's bleak, but it's life nonetheless.

Before going any further, it's important to remember that there are reasons for going to college. The purpose, in fact, is threefold. First, you learn words like threefold; second, it gives you something for your resumé besides your name and address; and most important of all, it teaches you how to make important decisions in case you ever happen to become an adult. And there are reasons for becoming a college professor, as well: a love of knowledge, a desire to teach, . . . sadomasochistic tendencies.

When I first entered college I was not a happy person. I remember very clearly when my first tuition payment came due. I was peeved enough just having to be there and I thought I'd show them. I took a brown paper bag, filled it with tens and twenties, stormed into admissions and screamed, "Here you leeches, take my father's blood!" And they did. In fact, they wanted more.

After that rather humbling experience I thought it would be a good idea if I got clued in as to what was expected of me academically speaking so I went to see my advisor. She told me that I was going to have to work, I was going to have to study, I was going to have to apply myself. I hated that woman. I was shocked. I always thought that doing the work in college was optional, like P.E.

It also came as quite a surprise to me to learn that I had to select a major. After all, you can't get a B.A. in "undeclared." (God knows I've tried.) So being the smart alec that I once was, when my advisor asked me what I wanted to major in, I told her "Serbo-Croatian!" Little did I know they had it. See what happens when you don't read the catalogue?

I quickly decided a different approach was in order. I realized that as far as academics went, I was in college to seek out knowledge, to seek out understanding, to boldly go where no man has gone before—the women's locker room. But I also wanted to study something lucrative. In other words, I wanted to go for the cash. I did a little research of my own and I found out that the highest paying jobs in America today are computer engineer, chemical engineer, petroleum engineer and Michael Jackson's agent. Little did I know that Speech Communication majors, which I was to become, have the best chance of being found asleep on park benches.

Once you choose a major and select all your classes like Mickey Mouse this and bonehead that, your next big obstacles in college are the tests. College tests can sometimes be just a wee bit difficult. But then, circumnavigating the globe on a pogo stick is just a wee bit difficult. I, however, have a helpful hint for when you do take a test in college: cheat. It's so simple. If that fails, then chances are so do you.

The tests you're subjected to in college and in fact the classes you take will very often depend on the particular professor and this brings us to our second fact of college life. In college there are good professors and not-so-good professors; just like with cars, there are good cars and not-so-good cars. So why is it that as far as professors go I always get stuck with Edsels? I'll give you an example. For my social science class, "The History of Everything," I had a lulu of a professor. The man was a terror. His classes made "Friday the 13th" look like a Sunday picnic. Nothing can be said about this man that hasn't already been said about Stalin, Mussolini and toxic waste.

But don't let this one bad apple cloud your vision. For the most part professors in college do an excellent job, especially when you consider all the problems they face; namely, the students. Let's face it, as students we aren't perfect. (I come pretty close, however.) Professors have to put up with students who are complainers, whiners, smart alecs; students who are apathetic, indifferent, unconcerned—you know, your average business major. But professors do have one very effective weapon, it's called finals.

Up to now we've discussed some of the more "serious" aspects of higher education. Now its time to leave scholastic discipline and turn to the nonacademic side of college life. At many institutions it seems that this side involves nothing more than sex, drugs and rock and roll. If this is true, then I'm going to the wrong college.

Before I began college, my mother said to me, "You'll have fun. You'll make friends." She lied. I didn't. My first bright idea was to join a fraternity. What better place for an alcoholic pervert like myself? They turned me down—all seventeen of them. But I didn't despair, not much anyway. I figured I could always join a club. After all, there had to be something out there that would interest me. At just about any other university that would be true, but at my school—Hey U—the choices are rather narrow. The big organization on my campus is the Young Bedouin Society, which I couldn't join anyway because I don't have my own camel. I was getting desperate. Finally, I joined the Campus Crusade for Christ. I'm Jewish. They didn't care, those people will take anybody; not unlike the debate team.

I'm not disappointed, though, I've had a lot of fun in college even though my social calendar isn't filled to the brim. By the way, can anyone use 365 blank pages? I realized that whatever one's form of entertainment is in college, whether it's playing bridge at the dean's house or drinking a six pack and throwing up in the library (my personal favorite), college can indeed be fun, fun, fun. College should be fun, fun, fun. And when you consider the average cost of college is now sixty bucks a day, you better have some fun, fun, fun.

In the end, I'm glad I'm going to college. Soon I'll be graduating and ready to face that big world out there. I have no idea what I'll be doing, but I'll be ready to face that big world out there. I know that the money my parents set aside for my education has been put to good use: $15,000 for college and $179,000 for pizza and beer.

You know, I've often wondered why we're all here. Why are we all in college? It's not a difficult question to answer, really. Students are here because they wish to improve their lives. Professors are here because they enjoy teaching, they better, God knows it's not for the money. Finally, I'm here because if I wasn't, I'd lose my inheritance. Thanks Dad. Thanks Mom.

NOTES

1. Reprinted with the permission of Charles F. Peters.
2. Reprinted with the permission of Arnold Rosenthal.
3. Reprinted with the permission of Steve E. Chapman.
4. Reprinted with the permission of Anamaria Lewis.
5. Kim Perry "Effortless Exercise?" *Winning Orations* (Mankato, Minn.: Interstate Oratorical Association, 1984), pp. 27–30.
6. Diane Miller, "The Food and Drug Administration: A Barrier to Progress and Innovation?," *Winning Orations* (Mankato, Minn.: Interstate Oratorical Association, 1984), pp. 89–92.
7. Reprinted with the permission of Ian Fielding.

INDEX

327